Translating Caste

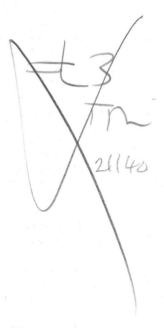

OUR RECENT RELEASES

Short Fiction

Katha Prize Stories 10
Ed Geeta Dharmarajan
& Nandita Aggarwal
Hauntings: Bangla Ghost Stories
Ed and Trans by
Suchitra Samanta
Forsaking Paradise: Stories from Ladakh,
Ed and Trans by
Ravina Aggarwal
Ayoni and Other Stories
Ed and Trans by
Alladi Uma & M Sridhar
Home and Away
By Ramachandra Sharma
Trans by Padma and
Ramachandra Sharma
Vyasa and Vighneshwara
By Anand
Trans by Saji Mathew
Joginder Paul: Sleepwalkers
Trans by Sunil Trivedi and
Sukrita Paul Kumar

ALT (Approaches to Literatures in Translation)

Ismat: Her Life, Her Times
Eds Sukrita Paul Kumar &
Sadique
Translating Partition: Stories, Essays,
Criticism
Eds Ravikant & Tarun K Saint
Vijay Tendulkar

Trailblazers

Paul Zacharia: Two Novellas
Trans by Gita Krishnankutty
Ashokamitran: Water
Trans by Lakshmi Holmström
Bhupen Khakhar: Selected Works
Trans by Ganesh Devy,
Naushil Mehta &
Bina Srinivasan

Indira Goswami: Pages Stained with Blood,
Trans by Pradip Acharya

Katha Classics

Padumaippittan Ed Lakshmi Holmström
Basheer Ed Vanajam Ravindran
Mauni Ed Lakshmi Holmström
Raja Rao Ed Makarand Paranjape
A Madhaviah Padmavati
Trans Meenakshi Tyagarajan

Katha Novels

Singarevva and the Palace
By Chandrasekhar Kambar
Trans by Laxmi Chandrasekhar
Listen Girl!
By Krishna Sobti
Trans by Shivanath

YuvaKatha

Lukose's Church
Night of the Third Crescent
Bhiku's Diary
The Verdict
The Dragonfly
The Bell

FORTHCOMING

Best of the Nineties:
Katha Prize Stories 11
Ed Geeta Dharmarajan
The End of Human History
By Hasan Manzar
Mountain of the Moon
By Bibhutibhushan
Bandopadhyay
Trans by Santanu Sinha Chaudhuri
Translating Desire
Ed Brinda Bose

Translating Caste

Stories by
Arupa Patangia Kalita,
Irathina Karikalan, K P Ramanunni,
Mahasweta Devi, Mogalli Ganesh,
M T Vasudevan Nair, Narain Singh,
Urmila Pawar

Essays • Criticism

Edited by
Tapan Basu

ȹ

KATHA

First published by Katha in 2002

The collection as a whole © 2002 Katha
The individual contributions
© 2002 the respective authors
"A Childhood Tale" © SPARROW

Copyright © for the English translations
rest with Katha

KATHA
A3 Sarvodaya Enclave
Sri Aurobindo Marg,
New Delhi 110 017
Phone: 652 4350, 652 4511
Fax: 651 4373

E-mail: academic@katha.org
Internet address: www.katha.org

KATHA is a registered nonprofit society
devoted to enhancing the pleasures of reading.
KATHA VILASAM is its story research and resource centre.

Studies in Culture and Translation
SCT Committee: Krishna Sobti, Malashri Lal, K Satchidanandan,
Sukrita Paul Kumar and Geeta Dharmarajan

Book and Cover Design: Geeta Dharmarajan & Moonis Ijlal
Line Drawings: Vikram Nayak

General Series Editor: Geeta Dharmarajan
In-house Editor: Mousumi Roy Chowdhury
Assistant Editor: Urmila Dasgupta

Typeset in 11.5 on 14.5pt Lapidary333 BT by Suresh Sharma at Katha
Printed at Usha Offset, New Delhi

ISBN 81-87649-66-6 (hardback)   ISBN 81-87649-05-4 (paperback)

1 3 5 7 9 10 8 6 4 2

CONTENTS

ACKNOWLEDGEMENTS

Translating Caste has been in the making for an inexcusably long period of time. Among the many that I must thank, now that the book is finally made are —

Geeta Dharmarajan, for encouraging me to take on the editorship of this book, and for retaining faith in my ability to deliver despite the delays that dogged work on the book almost all the way.

My contributors, who have been as patient a set of contributors that any editor might wish for.

Uma Chakravarti, for not only contributing two articles to the book, but also for readily taking on the role of friend, philosopher and guide at some of the most difficult stages of the book's formation.

Anand Chakravarti, Kumkum Roy, Sumit Sarkar and Tanika Sarkar, for generously loaning out to me valuable scholarly productions on caste studies from their personal libraries.

N S Harsha, the visual artist from Mysore, for the photograph used for the story "Married to Separateness." INIVA London for the photograph of NS Harsha's installation "Healing Space," from their project "Drawing Space" for the story "What is Your Caste." Sanskriti Kendra, New Delhi for the photographs used with the stories "Doiboki's Day" and "Sukritam." And UNICEF for the other photgraphs inside the book.

The Katha in house editors, especially Chandana and Swaati (in the initial stages) Mousumi, and Urmila, Moonis and Shayoni (in the final stages), and all else at Katha who participated in the process of production, for the pains they took to render the manuscript publication worthy.

My colleagues in the English Department, Hindu College, University of Delhi, for the emotional sustenance and intellectual stimulation which they always provide in ample substance no matter what academic adventure I am engaged in – Tarun Saint and Brinda Bose, each of them also an editor of a similar volume under the aegis of Katha, in particular, for a sense of solidarity.

Rajiv and Renu Agarwal, dearest of friends, for allowing me to weep on their shoulders whenever (all too frequently) the book appeared to have run into rough waters.

And finally, my mother and my family, notably Tonu and Bonny, for being there.

And, above all, Rekha, for so completely sharing my highs and lows through the tortuous making of this book. To Rekha, therefore, I dedicate my part of the labour that has gone into *Translating Caste.*

INTRODUCTION

TAPAN BASU

Translating Caste is, first and foremost, intended to fulfill a pedagogical function. It proposes to bring the issue of caste and its textual representation in contemporary Indian literature into the classrooms of universities in India and abroad. The textual representation of caste in contemporary Indian literature is, of course, to be made available and accessible to university students through their translations into English. But the issue of Translating Caste is not only an issue of communicating certain narratives about caste across languages or, even, across cultures. The narratives about caste which constitute the core of this collection, in themselves are engagements in an enterprise of translation – the translation of caste as a social institution into an assortment of cultural discourses.

The volume comprises an eclectic selection of eight short stories (six of them *Katha* publications) on the theme of caste in seven different modern Indian languages namely, Asomiya, Bangla, Hindi, Kannada, Malayalam, Marathi and Tamil, the aim being to erect a framework for the study of the treatment of the caste theme in an all India literary arena. The first four stories in the volume are elucidated by essays by experts who are fluent in the Indian language concerned and who are therefore able to comment on the nuances of translation in the stories as well as on matters of form and content. While acknowledging that the process of translation is important as much as it is imperative in the projection of local literatures outside of their parochial precincts and onto a global readership, each of the commentators alerts readers against the hegemonizing and the homogenizing tendencies involved in translating into a standardized English the specificities of the native idioms. The last four stories are submitted as self-expository illustrations of the theme of the book.

After this "literary" section of the book, and as a theoretical framework to it beyond the introduction by the editor, are four articles discussing some of the meta-"literary," socio-cultural aspects of caste in modern India, including two which try to outline the transformations in the treatment of caste in Indian literatures through the twentieth century. This section contains too an interview by an acclaimed author from Maharashtra belonging to one of the State's most subordinated (Dalit) castes in which she speaks about the life and literature of the subordinate castes of her region, and, by implication, from all over India.

The volume also includes a select annotated bibliography drawing upon published material from the territories of the sciences, the social sciences and the humanities, especially focussing on literature on caste and caste related issues.

All in all, therefore, *Translating Caste* contains a wide range of reference texts on the theme of caste, spanning disciplines, genres, perspectives, which might well extend its reach to readership constituencies outside of academia as well.

In recent decades there has been a plethora of publications on caste and caste related issues, specifically in the realm of literature. What then is the justification for a new critical anthology of writings about/around the same theme to burden the already overloaded student of the subject? Why and how is it necessary to introduce discourses on caste in the "secular" space of the classroom in universities today? These are the questions of relevance that require answers at the very outset of this project.

The 1990s have been in several respects the most decisive decade in modern Indian history. By the end of the 1980s, the country was poised to enter a phase of economic liberalization in tune with a new economic policy which sought to encourage economic "growth" by curbing economic "profligacy" by way of state expenditure in the public sector. The private sector, correspondingly, was induced to play a larger role than ever before in reconstructing the national economy which henceforth was slated to tread step by step on the path of economic globalization. For the urban middle classes in India, the single largest constituency for university level education, globalization betokened new aspirations as well as new anxieties. On the one hand, there were the promises of prosperity encoded in the razzle dazzle of a media-hyped marketplace and a marketplace-hyped media. On the other hand, there were the pitfalls of unfulfilled expectations engendered by employment uncertainties. The retreat of the social interventionist state implied poorer job prospects for a majority of the population, since most jobs sustained by the government would not be funded by commercial and corporate non-government organizations with a pure profit orientation.

This situation inevitably led to an exacerbation of existing contestations and contradictions in society and even social conflicts of a violent nature. A sense of social insecurity instigated individuals and groups among the urban middle classes, already enduring the alienations of an anonymous and atomized urban life, to seek refuge and relief in their age-old moorings of caste or community, whereby they might recover some traditional privileges in compensation for many modern deprivations.[1] Both the Ramjanambhoomi movement and the anti-Mandal Commission agitation, key events of the 1990s, may be read, in this context, as efforts on the part of the hegemonic clusters in society (i.e. upper caste Hindus) to resist perceived attempts at social assertion on the part of the subaltern orders (i.e. Hindu lower castes and non-Hindu minority communities) or social engineering on their behalf.

The ideological interlinkage between the anti-Mandal Commission agitation and the Ramjanambhoomi movement was acknowledged by observers and admitted even by eminent leaders of the Hindu right wing network called the Sangh Parivar, which implicitly or explicitly fuelled either conflagaration.[2] Thus L K Advani's infamous rath yatra of 1992, conceived and executed by the Bharatiya Janata Party, the political organ of the Sangh Parivar, was equally intended to instigate opinion for the handing over of the so-called birthplace of Ram to the Hindus and to heal the breaches among Hindus created by the "casteist" recommendations of the Mandal Commission. According to the Hindu right wing viewpoint which holds that Hindu cultural nationalism must be the basis of "Akhand Bharat" (United India),[3] both the movement and the agitation aimed at consolidating the Hindu national culture of India against divisive assaults from anti-Hindu and anti-national forces. Communal mobilization, was, therefore, regarded by the Sangh Parivar as an antidote to caste turmoils resulting from feared lower caste challenges to upper caste domination.

The anti-Mandal Commission agitation was spearheaded by upper caste students of universities all over the country, but it was especially potent in the cities of north India, which were to be, not so coincidentally, also the sites of the most virulent campaigns of the Ramjanambhoomi movement. Upper caste consciousness, among metropolitan youth, till now dormant, came to the surface, in most ugly manifestations, once confronted with the threat of lower caste "uprising." Through the 1990s, the discourses of caste engaged the hearts and minds of young, upper caste men and women who feared displacement by lower caste competitors in acquiring jobs for themselves. Caste had thus hit the classroom with a vengeance, and there was no use pretending that it was an obsolete factor which did not affect the day to day lives of educated city folk. In fact, the anti-Mandal Commission agitation opened up a Pandora's box as a consequence of which the principle of affirmative action for *all* backward classes of Indian society (enshrined in the Constitution of India under the name of "reservations") was interrogated and indicted by upper caste conservatives.

The catapulting of caste as a "concern" in the consciousness of upper caste metropolitan youth in response to the "challenge" of caste based reservations for lower castes in the arenas of education and employment conveniently obscured the chronicle of caste based prerogatives enjoyed by upper castes in almost every sphere of Indian society for centuries. The anti-reservationists who took to the streets of the north Indian cities in the 1990s appeared not to realize the irony in their projections of their "marginalization" from the public life in their country. Nor did they seem to be aware of a much, much older history of anti-caste movements away from the metropolitan centres which had long been struggling for redressal for the wrongs of the caste system, and of which the "reservation" policy of the Indian state was a compensating consequence.

How does one define caste as a system of social stratification? As to the "origin" of this system itself, this theme has been much discussed and disputed, but no end to the debate appears to be in sight. An early academic account of the advent of the caste system in the Indian subcontinent, articulated among others by Herbert Risley[4] and Arthur de Gobineau[5] attributes it to the arrival of the Aryan peoples, roughly in the period 1500 BC, into the territories in and around the Indo-Gangetic plains, and their subjugation of an indigenous non-Aryan population. This narrative of conquest and command of an "inferior" civilization by a "superior" civilization, frequently enabled upper caste Indians to assert a common Aryan essence with their English colonizers, English contempt for all Indians, upper caste and lower caste alike, notwithstanding. Conversely, lower caste Indians sometimes arraigned Aryanism and announced themselves the authentic inmates of India, and wrote of a pre-Aryan "golden age." The Aryan hypothesis, supported later, upto a point, by Max Weber,[6] more or less, doubled up caste distinctions with racial differences. The racial hypothesis poses a number of problems, not the least of these being the prevalence of the caste system among both the "fair skinned," purportedly "Aryan" progeny of North India and the "dark skinned," purportedly "non-Aryan" progeny of South India. Predictably, it was discarded, among others, by Bernard Cohn who has discounted the racial "superiority"/"inferiority" explanation itself.[7] Martin Klass has gone a step further in speculating upon a caste system emerging out of the beginnings of settled agriculture in the South Asian region, with some clans of previously egalitarian food gathering tribes asserting dominance over others in order to claim a greater proportion of the new surplus generated by the new mode of production.[8] This theory has the advantage of looking at caste in consonance with class, while conceding its discrete culturally determined existence.

The concern with caste as a core concern for a comprehension of Indian culture may be traced back to the work of well known nineteenth century Western Indologists such as Friedrich Max Muller[9] and J A Abbe Dubois[10] who, more often than not, sought to understand the "Indian reality" by consulting Hindu scriptures or Hindu pundits, either of which would have been heavily biased in favour of the Brahminical view of castes. The Brahminical view of caste also dominated the colonial administrators of India, who too got most of the information about caste matters from Hindu religious authorities. Not surprisingly, therefore, as Partha Chatterjee has observed, the colonials made inflated inferences about the importance of caste to Indians. "If there was one social institution that, to the colonial mind ... characterized Indian society as radically different from Western society, it was the institution of caste. All arguments about the rule of colonial difference ... tended to converge upon this unique Indian institution." Chatterjee contends that colonial discourse congealed into a general homogeneity the heterogeneous particularities of the caste system in India whose day to day operation was contingent upon the region as well as the period in which it was operating.[11]

The most eminent example of the school of scholarship that Chatterjee inquisitioned and interrogated is, no doubt, the influential investigation by Louis Dumont who imagined the caste system in India to be an ahistorical and an immutable and an unvariegated system of "homo hierarchus" – humans in hierarchy – that had the consensual acceptance of all its beings.[12] The idea of consensus around the caste system was not surprisingly and very stringently contested by other scholars, notably Joan Mencher[13] and Gerald Berreman[14] who denied that there could be consensus about the caste system among the different caste constituencies. Both these scholars rebutted what they felt was Dumont's Brahminical view of caste. Berreman castigated the caste system as a system of inhuman hierarchy, "guaranteed differential access to the valued things in life." Mencher critiqued the inhuman system of caste hierarchy as "a system of economic exploitation" because of which some people in society lived in plenty while most people lived in penury.

Mencher's and Berreman's views on the caste system, and especially on the issue of untouchables' complicity in the system, were in turn controverted by Michael Moffatt. Whereas Berreman and Mencher had argued that the "untouchables" could not but feel alienated from a system which denied them most of its material benefits, Moffatt averred that the "untouchables" internalize the logic of the system to the extent that they could think about it from within its parameters and not feel alienated from the system at all. In fact, according to Moffatt, the "untouchables" very often try to replicate within their own very varied ranks the hierarchies of the caste system of which they are at the receiving end.[15]

Given the glorious history of anti-caste resistance efforts across the span of Indian history from those of the Buddha through the Bhakti cult to those of Phule and Ambedkar,[16] it is evident that Moffatt, like Dumont, overstated the formulaic expectations of the caste system and underplayed its everyday functioning. Sekhar Bandyopadhyay's pioneering researches question the assumptions that lower caste communities are either absolutely appropriated by or absolutely autonomous of aspirations for upper caste status. According to Bandyopadhyay, who has studied the case of the Namasudra caste of Bengal between 1872 and 1947, such caste communities were very rarely monolithic in nature ... "The mentality of defiance and an urge for social revolution are thus accompanied by a preparedness to accept and accommodate. It is this tendency which indicates that all possibilities of conflict or disjunction, or in fact disintegration of the community cannot be eliminated, even though at a particular conjuncture the community may appear a real entity in a political sense."[17] The provisionality of caste communities has been highlighted also by Sumit Sarkar in a more recent essay on the Namasudras of Bengal in which he has warned against the search for immaculate caste identities. Sarkar holds that the solidarities formed on the basis of caste need to be always studied in their intermeshing interrelations with other sorts of solidarities which then help to put the character of caste solidarities into a proper perspective.[18]

The complex coordinates of caste in Indian society has been the focus of the work of Marxist scholars such as Claude Meillassox[19] and Maurice Godelier.[20] Godelier argued that in a society such as that of India, in which there is not yet a decisive differentiation between the ideational and the material levels of existence, the institutions of family and business, for instance, often intertwine and impinge upon either level, caste too belongs to both stratas. Meillassox contended that the constraints imposed by caste already ensured the siphoning of surplus wealth by a few sections of Indian society at the expense of very many sections. Hence, in the context of such a society, analysis of material power cannot be divorced from an analysis of the ideational power, each of which inextricably expresses itself through the caste system.

Gail Omvedt's "historical materialist analysis" of caste, in a book published in 1994,[21] followed the direction of Godelier's and Meillassox's conclusions. Omvedt observes that caste is analogous to class insofar as, like class, caste is a system of expropriation of surplus labour from actual producers by owners of the means of production. Nevertheless, unlike class, caste is a construct not of the methods of production in the material realm alone, but of the operations of reproduction in the ideational arena. The logic of the caste system is that of an inherited institution of division of labour within the community, sanctified by religion as well as by tradition, which frequently works in tandem with the class schisms of modern, capitalist society, though sometimes the rigidities of caste stratas are qualified and modified by the flexibilities within the class structure. It is the ubiquitousness of caste consciousness in Indian society, and its persistence in different guises through generations, defying and denying the logic of social transformation on the lines of class, that is the subject of K P Ramanunni's story "What Is Your Caste."

To come to the conception of the caste system, the caste system, as Uma Chakravarti explains in her article – "Through Another Lens: Men, Women and Caste" – "comprises a series of hereditary groups or jatis, characterized by hierarchy or gradations according to ritual status." The legitimization for the "ritual status" or "evaluative standards," as Chakravarti puts it, in placing particular jatis or hereditary groups in a descending or ascending order emanated, according to her, from the dharmashastras, the religio-legal texts of the Hindus. It has been suggested that these texts were compiled by Brahmins (priests) "who drew an ideal picture of what they thought the social organism should be."[22] In this "ideal picture" of the castes sketched out in Vedic literature, especially in the famous passage interpolated into the Rig Veda around 1000 BC in which the order of the castes was visualized in terms of the parts of the human body, the Brahmins occupied the topmost position, succeeded by the Kshatriyas (warriors) and the Vaishyas (traders and farmers). Together, these varnas or ceremonial ranks, each of which accommodated several hereditary groups or jatis in society, mostly with region specific or period specific variations, comprised the upper castes, who were categorized as dvija (twice born) because the males among them went through an initiation ritual (upanayana) at which they were ritualistically re-born. This was symbolized by their donning the sacred thread. The above scheme did not include the remaining varna, the Shudras (menials), who comprised the numerous lower castes of society.[23]

Gradually, as the system evolved, the upper and the lower came to be associated with opposed notions of "purity" and "impurity" respectively, ostensibly on the basis of the work performed by the castes. This value loaded characterization entailed the strict social segregation of the "pure" upper castes and the "impure" lower castes or the "outcastes" – sometimes called the Chandals – who had been rigidly demarcated from among the Shudras by the second century AD. The segregation requirements were the source of the untouchability fetish promoted by the caste system. By the era of the journey to India by the Chinese traveller Fa Hien, circa fifth century AD, the caste system had expanded and entrenched itself extensively across the Indian subcontinent and amalgamated untouchability as an integral portion of its practices.

The administration of the untouchability fetish of course varied widely from place to place and from time to time, frequently at odds with the facts and figures furnished in the official records published by the Government of India since the late nineteenth century. Even the Government of India Schedule of 1936, the earliest document earmarked to furnish a list of "untouchable" castes according to certain considered criteria, failed to fulfill its function adequately because of the innumerable different determinants for defining untouchability and enforcing it on the "untouchables" that were current in different parts of India.

But the Schedule was only one of many ways through which the colonial authorities in India sought to negotiate untouchability. The earliest European interest in the caste system in India expressed itself in the endeavours of the Christian missionaries from Europe towards amelioration of the lot of the Hindu "untouchables" of India. The Christian missionaries had been active in South Asia since the eighteenth century, and had been winning "native" adherents on an impressive scale through their proselytization. It was only in the last third of the nineteenth century however that the missionaries began to actually address the condition of the "untouchables" of India. The Christian missionaries' involvement was followed, inevitably, by the investigations of the bureaucrats of the British Raj into the intricacies of the Indian caste system. The instrument of their inquiries was usually the Census, which began on a India wide basis in 1871-72. Concerning caste, the key question that troubled Census officials was whether the "untouchables" ought to be considered as belonging inside or outside the Hindu fold. The nomenclature "Hindu" itself was more or less a modern invention employed by foreigners to broadly designate all the inhabitants of Hindustan. Among these masses of people, what exactly was the position of the "untouchables"? For the British bureaucrats, the problem of positioning assumed entirely unsurmoutable proportions by the Census of 1911. The Hindu "leadership," till then quite indifferent to the treatment of the "untouchables" within the Hindu denomination, registered their unhappiness at the listing of the "untouchables" as a category of the population by themselves in the Census, alleging Muslim League pressure on the British in this matter. Yet the category remained and was indeed formalized as the "Exterior Castes" in the Census of 1931 with the aim of providing state succour to the "untouchables." What this achieved, without any intention on the part of the Census Commissioners, was to slowly and surely give the "untouchables" a sense of collective identity which then enabled them to assert themselves as an integrated community.[24]

An overall survey of untouchability practices in the different states of India till the 1930s reveals that the notion that the upper castes could be "polluted" through contact with the lower castes was more pervasive and more powerful in Western as well as Southern India. In some areas of Maharashtra, in fact, the "untouchable" castes such as the Mahars and Mangs were forced to maintain prescribed distances – varying with the "lowliness" of the caste – from caste Hindus. There were unwritten and written edicts which forbade these castes from coming into the city of Pune, the capital city of Chitpavan Peshwas, between 3 pm and 9 am, because before 9 am and after 3 pm their bodies cast too long a shadow, and whenever their shadow fell upon a Brahmin, it "polluted" him so that he dared not take food or water until he had bathed away the "polluting" effect. Similarly, members of the "untouchable" castes were made to lie at a distance on their faces when caste Hindus came by lest their shadows fall upon the caste Hindus, and were forbidden to speak loudly in their (the caste Hindus') presence. A more or less similar edict applied against the "untouchables" in several areas of Kerala, Tamil Nadu and Karnataka. In certain districts of the south, a Brahmin would not cross even the shadow of an "untouchable" for fear of getting "defiled." Sometimes, "untouchables" had to ring a bell to announce their "polluting" arrival, and to wear spittoons around their necks (in the case, for example, of the Ande Koragas of Madras) so as to catch any polluting spittle that might drop from their lips. There was even a caste of "unseeables" (the Purada Vannans of Tinnevelly district) who washed the clothes of other "untouchables" by night and hid their "polluting" selves by day. "Pollution" norms such as these were prevalent well into the eve of Indian independence.

Distance pollution, the notion that the lower castes might "pollute" the upper castes unless a prescribed distance was maintained between them, however, never existed in the north to the extent that it existed in the south or the west. Certainly, there were no definite decrees in this regard. Nor did pollution by actual touch evoke the same consternation in the northern states as it did in the south. Only the castes of scavengers and sweepers – the Mehtars, Bhangis, Doms and so on (these are largely functional equivalents located in different provinces) – were comprehensively shunned in a physical sense. These are castes whose work is deemed "dirty," even if the consequences of their service is to make the surroundings clean for others. The Bhangis are even now especially despised almost all over north India, and debarred from sharing public facilities such as roads and wells and community services such as markets and temples with the upper castes. In the case of the other "untouchable" castes of many northern states, the taboos imposed on them are more to do with the strict structures against their interaction with the upper castes at a more close and personal level, such as the familial, the marital or the sexual.

The configuration of untouchability was different in Eastern India, where the pattern of land settlements, over the entire region which then constituted the Bengal province (including present day Bangladesh, West Bengal and parts of Orissa and Bihar), starting with the so-called Permanent Settlement of 1793, during the colonial period inevitably translated caste divisions into class disparities. These settlements bestowed upon the existing landlords, who very often were no more than caretakers of the land on behalf of some erstwhile princely rulers, or tax farmers at best, the status of stable landowners whose only due to the government of the colonizer was a permanent rent settlement. The amount of rent owed to the government, though substantial enough to begin with, gradually declined with the fall in the value of money. Frequently, the landowners further enhanced their earnings by raising their revenues from the peasantry. The three topmost castes – the Brahmins, the Kayasthas and the Vaidyas (the latter two belonging to the Vaishya varna) were benefited to the extent that they had absolute authority over all those in the activity of agriculture and over all agricultural activity itself. Gradually, these upper castes removed themselves from cultivation altogether. This they were able to do under the new land laws by installing a very long succession of complicated and calibrated order of rights and roles of tillage – from the landlord who paid government revenue to the tiller of the land himself. The upper caste, more or less all transferred themselves to white collar careers and transformed themselves thereby into the influential bhadrolok classes in Bengali society. The hegemony of the upper castes in social relations in Bengal, via the bhadrolok classes, remains largely intact even today. Despite quite a few land reforms implemented in the state by a strong communist movement and secure communist governments, the state's lower caste population, largely peasants, has remained relatively poor and outside the pale of genteel society. Upper caste disdain of the lower castes – the Doms, the Bhuyias, the Chamars, the Kaharas and the Kurmis – in several districts, reinforced by economic disadvantage of these castes, manifests itself in the form of social ostracization which is akin to untouchability. Despite some efforts to bring about systemic changes in the social organization or in social consciousness, and the improvement of the material conditions of living for the peasantry over the decades by their awareness of how to manipulate and manoeuvre the electoral politics of the state to their own advantage, a lot remains still to be done in the field of eradicating caste prejudices.

In Bihar, the Brahmins and the Vaishyas, along with the Thakurs and the Bhumihars, also entered the bureaucracy and the professions but did not absolutely give up their stakes as landlords. Here as well as in other states of the so-called Hindi belt, caste conflict is further riddled by the presence of the "backward castes," for example, the Yadavs, Kurmis, and Keoris, who are not "outcastes," but have for a long period been denied the social and economic privileges of the upper castes. These castes have always been quite organized and eloquent in claiming their dues, and in some regions have actually managed to upset upper caste domination. Nevertheless, their empowerment, through their own endeavours as much as through affirmative action programmes on their behalf initiated by the Indian state, in fits and starts since the 1970s through the 1990s, has not really had even a trickle down effect on the lower castes towards whom they have been notoriously hostile. The "backward castes" have persistently clashed with the lower castes, particularly in Bihar where lower caste assertiveness has been perceived by the "backward castes" as an attempt to neutralize the social and economic gains made by the "backward castes" during the decades after de-colonization.

Assam presents a distinctive picture altogether when pitted against all the other states. Casteism is confined only to the two third Hindu population, most of whom are Vaishnavites. Discrimination on the basis of caste against non-Vaishnavites as well as against the not insignificant populations of tribal origin assumed the form of taboos on them entering places of worship and devotion and against forming kinship bonds with caste Hindus.

The growing militancy among the lower castes in many parts of India and their advancing awareness of their prerogatives has paradoxically heightened the untouchability problem.[25] In a rearguard reaction, the upper castes have come down harshly on such "insolence" and insisted upon putting the "untouchables" back "where they belong." This has been the source of the increasing number of caste atrocities that have been reported from especially the Hindi belt over the last thirty to forty years. The refusal of the "untouchables" to perform their "designated" duties such as sweeping and scavenging and their demand for removal of segregation between themselves and the upper castes in all aspects of everyday life, at least in some districts, has invariably earned them the wrath of the upper castes.

The logic of caste segregation is that it prevents inter mingling of castes that must be kept apart from each other to avoid adulteration. While segregation has been rigorously imposed between the upper castes and the lower castes, it has also worked to distinguish the lower castes and the upper castes within themselves, once again in a hierarchical formation. Thus each caste, the Doms, for instance in Mahasweta Devi's story, "Bayen," therefore becomes a self-enclosed circle – eating, marrying and worshipping are ritually conceived and executed among the members of each caste.

If intra-caste dealings are informed by a spirit of self-sufficiency, the same cannot be said about inter-caste dealings. Exchanges between castes constitute the crucial dynamics of society, but these exchanges are never even or fair. The concentration of prerogatives at the top and obligations at the bottom (noted by Berreman and Mencher as the characteristic attribute of the caste system) makes for a social stratification that is not merely an arrangement of interdependence (that Dumont or Moffatt held it to be). As Uma Chakravarti argues, asymmetrical access to authority and affluence, in other words a class system, is an intrinsic condition of the caste system which therefore takes the caste system beyond the abstract high-low and "pure"-"impure" categorizations. The lower castes are inevitably dictated to by the upper castes regarding "purity"-"impurity" divisions and the penalties to be incurred by the lower castes for violating these divisions and "polluting" the upper castes. The "pollution" of sacred spaces, such as temples, for instance, constitutes the worst kind of "pollution" as the story "Doibokir Deen" by Arupa Patangia Kalita illustrates. Often there is no correlation between the threat of "pollution" apparently posed by a certain caste and the actuality of non-polluting occupations of its members. What remains constant, however, is the real power wielded on the basis of the "pollution" threat by the upper castes over the lower castes, as the story "Oorakali" by Irathina Karikalan illustrates.

Caste, then intersects with class, in a liaison which is more obvious in the villages than in the towns of India, to ensure control over material resources such as land and labour by the dominant interests in society. Class power usually replicates caste power, though it ultimately goes further. With its justification in Hindu religio-legal mandates, caste power is useful in concealing the concentration of class power in the possession of an elite, and in the perpetuation of that possession through compulsion and coercion. It is the coercive aspect of caste power, which can command even the administrative apparatus of a district, that is highlighted in the story "Battha" by Mogalli Ganesh.

The coercive aspect of caste power is apparent also in the denial of knowledge to those considered outside the pale of caste power. The monopoly overlay as much as theological knowledge enjoyed by Brahmin men and then, with the passage of centuries, by the upper castes as a whole, has been matched by lower caste marginalization in matters of education and learning, inevitably giving the so-called caste Hindus an advantage insofar as they utilized this to capture and continue to hold on to the instruments of cultural as well as economic production and emerge as the so-called class Hindus. Hence the strictures laid down by the Brahmins against theft of knowledge by the Shudras, and the severe retribution to Shudras such as Shambuka and Ekalavya in Hindu mythology for example, for transgressing these strictures. A modern version of the Shambuka and Ekalavya tales is Urmila Pawar's story "Gosh Seshvachi," in which the child protagonist (the alter ego of the author) and her mother have to combat the caste arrogance and caste bullying of the school teacher to establish that the subordinate castes too have a right to knowledge.

The subordinate caste mother's victory in her fight against casteism in "Gosh Seshvachi" is without doubt a memorable episode. Nevertheless, it is an incident which happens on an ideal rather than a real plane of events, because in the chronicle of India's caste society it is only with great difficulty that women, of upper or of lower castes, have been able to successfully assert themselves against the social system.

Mahasweta Devi's story "Bayen" as well as M T Vasudevan Nair's story "Sukritam," both testify to the truth of G Arunima's thesis in her article, "Some Issues in an Analysis of Caste and Gender in Modern India." Basing her conclusions on research into caste strife between the Nairs and Nambudiris against the backdrop of caste reform initiatives in early twentieth century Kerala, Arunima contends that both in the case of the upper and lower castes, the homogenizing tendency of caste politics, habitually glossed over gender difference "as caste politics has always been dominated by male leaders, the issue of gender is either subsumed within its general rhetoric, or simply set aside as trivial or frivolous."

Both Cheriyatti, the upper caste protagonist of "Sukritam" and Chandi, the lower caste protagonist of "Bayen," are victims of their caste leaders' concern for the untaintedness of their respective castes. Each is deemed to be tainted in her own way. So, while Cheriyatti has to safeguard the "purity" of her caste aggregate by drowning as a deity, Chandi has to safeguard the "purity" of her caste aggregate by accepting her ostracization as a witch.

A vital trope originating out of the "purity"-"impurity" problematic within the caste system is that of endogamy, that is, endorsement of marriages only when they are unions of persons belonging to the same caste. Endogamous marriages have been the primary means of preserving each caste as a discrete unit. It is thus that caste determines gender equations just as gender equations determine caste. Caste blood is always bilateral, that is, its hereditary traits are received from both parents, and as prescribed in the dharmashastras, it is desirable, if not imperative, that both parents must be of the same caste. Extra endogamous alliances contravene not merely the purity-impurity partitioning between castes, but also the principle of ownership of women and wealth. Such partnerships are a rebuff to caste power as nothing else is. The dharmashastras counselled chastisement for endogamy transgression. The sexuality of upper caste women was to be jealously protected from violation by lower caste men. Offenders from either end would be punished relentlessly.

The obverse did not hold good however. Upper caste men were allowed sexual approach to lower caste women, with or without their consent, as such "adventures" did not endanger the ideational and the material axes of caste society, but rather sometimes reinforced them. This is the social circumstance of "Oorakali" where the lower caste woman is abused sexually by the upper caste man and then abandoned to die. Likewise, in "Kulaghati," the story by Narain Singh, the protagonist, an upper caste man who is married to a lower caste woman, is hesitant when their daughter, associates herself with a lower caste man and the question of an exogamous marriage looms up before him. His desperation exposes upper caste double standards vis-a-vis endogamy – they can take a woman from the lower castes but they cannot give a woman to the lower castes.

One of the foremost objectives of the movement for social justice launched by the lower castes, the so-called Dalit movement, in modern India,[26] has been to expose the dualisms and the falsities of upper caste narratives on caste matters by authoring a narrative of their own. The emergence of the category of the Dalit itself as a frame of self-reference for the lower castes, from the category of the "untouchable," the frame of reference traditionally used by the uppermost castes for the lowermost castes, indicates a successful endeavour in the politics of narrative transformation.

In his essay, "The Politics of Naming," Gopal Guru examines the overtones of this politics for the Dalits by focussing precisely upon the point of their repeated renaming.[27] According to Guru, one of the earliest efforts at uplifting these castes was made through the attempted abrogation of their name – "untouchable" – with its undeniably pejorative connotations. The effort was made by S M Mate, the Maharashtra Brahmin social reformer of the nineteenth century, who used the label "asprustha" – untouched – to denote the "untouchables." A better known effort was made much later by Mohandas Gandhi when he introduced the term "harijan" – God's own people – in 1931. Though ostensibly informed by a reformist agenda and applauded for a while, the term has been now rejected by almost all radical constituencies of Indian society, including most of all by the "harijans" themselves, because of its undeniably patronizing and peripheralizing overtones.

It is interesting that the category Dalit – downtrodden – was first used by Bhimrao Ramji Ambedkar, the most outstanding of the Dalit leaders in Indian history. In his fortnightly, *Bahiskrit Bharat*, he defined it comprehensively, "Dalithood is a kind of life condition which characterizes the exploitation, suppression and marginalization of the lower castes by the social, economic, cultural and political domination of the upper caste Brahminical order." Ambedkar however did not use the category often. In his more formal statements on behalf of the victim of caste discrimination, he preferred to use the term "the depressed classes" or even more effectively, the term "the scheduled castes." This was evident when he used the term for establishing the political party, the Scheduled Caste Federation.

Finally, in an effort to radicalize his own social group, he used the term "pad dalit" – meaning those who are completely crushed under the Hindu caste order. In more recent years, the term Dalit was first comprehensively revived and reused by the Dalit Panthers of Maharashtra, who regarded themselves as Ambedkar's legatees. The Panthers' use of this term not only gave the oppressed, lower castes condition a concrete matrix which derived from their own perception of their position vis-a-vis the oppressive upper castes in Hindu society, but also a connectivity with other peoples suffering from other kinds of social oppressions.

There are of course several middle class intellectuals, including middle class Dalit intellectuals, who regard this term as an elite imposition which is derogatory as well as denigratory insofar as it reinforces upon the Dalit people the demeaning realities, past and present, of their condition, and constantly reminds them that they are underdogs. Such intellectuals often prefer to use the term "bahujan" – the majority – to designate the oppressed castes.

What these intellectuals, in my opinion, perhaps fail to recognize is that the term "bahujan," while apparently expanding the constituency of the oppressed, erases the vital history of caste oppression which has ever been the defining factor behind outcaste existence in India. No doubt, the term Dalit is an all encompassing nomenclature which homogenizes the otherwise heterogeneous identities of the various oppressed caste communities which inhabit almost every region of India. Yet it is equally true that the perception of a significant number of these castes, by the end of the twentieth century, that they are indeed Dalits, records a growing sense of shared commitments and conscious solidarity on their part on issues involving their subordination.

The Dalit movement, such as it is today, took off in the nineteenth century, to begin with in Maharashtra, where caste tyranny was intolerably oppressive under the domination of the Chitpavan Peshwas. Under their regime, the "untouchables" had no rights whatsoever either human or civil. Yet there is hardly any evidence of organized resistance on their part to the tyranny of the caste Hindus till the nineteenth century. Dissent of a sort was, of course, expressed through the devotional "bhakti" movement which manifested itself in several parts of the country during the pre-colonial period. Between the tenth and the thirteenth centuries, the "bhakti" movement spread all over the subcontinent to popularize a reformed Hinduism. Ramanand and Raidas in the north, Chaitanya and Chandidas in the east, Ramanuja and Basava in the south, and Chokhamela and Eknath in the west were some of the important bhakti movement figures. The bhakti movement emphasized the devotion of the individual believer rather than the location of the individual devotee in the caste hierarchy.[28] Protest was also expressed in the shape of legends and folklore which were constructed and circulated amongst the "untouchables" about their "authentic" caste origins, usually noble, now lost to them unfairly due to the intrigues of interlopers.

The anti-caste movements in modern Maharashtra starting with the Satyashodak Samaj movement led by Jotiba Phule, are of course well-known. Nonetheless, there were other movements against Brahminical Hinduism in other states of India which were contemporary to, if not antedating, the Maharashtra movement. There was, for instance, a movement of the "untouchables" in Madras Presidency, as also of the Ilavas of Malabar, the Chamars of Chattisgarh and the Namasudras of Bengal, but none of these movements were as sustained or as successful as the later movements in Maharashtra.[29]

The early Satyashodak Samaj movement was a movement against Brahminical hegemony. It was founded in Pune in 1873 by Phule who belonged to the Mali caste, along with four or five associates from castes which were not considered to be among the most elevated. The Samaj started out with the limited agenda of arresting the authority of the

Brahmins within an authoritative Hinduism, but gradually extended its scope to propagate and popularize the education of the masses.

Phule perceived mass education to be the panacea for oppression in the name of the caste order. He argued that even before destroying the economic power of the upper castes over the lower castes, which indeed was their fundamental power, it was necessary to deconstruct their cultural power derived primarily from religio-legal canons and customs. This deconstructive ability or "the third eye," as Phule labelled it, demanded not mere alphabetical competence but the capacity to see through knowledge/power equations in society and consequently to dismantle them.[30]

Phule was not unduly impressed by contemporary Hindu reform movements, such as the Brahmo Samaj (initiated by Raja Ram Mohan Roy) and the Arya Samaj (initiated by Swami Dayanand Saraswati), most of which arraigned the evil of casteism in no uncertain conditions and yet argued that caste was not an inherent component of Hindu dharma. Phule's view was that the Arya Samaj or the Brahmo Samaj merely aimed at modernizing Brahminical Hinduism rather than at neutralizing it. He was of the opinion that the notions of Brahma and Arya were essentially embedded in an anti-Shudra epistemology. According to Phule therefore, the caste Hindu forces established such organizations only to anglicize and aggrandize themselves. It was not accomodation within the Hindu community, but empowerment outside of Brahminical Hinduism that the lower castes required, felt Phule.

Phule was an unabashed admirer of the colonial government in India because he saw in the Indian colonial government an unstinted abettor of his goal of educating the masses. The goal of mass education, after all, had received a fillip ever since the colonial government had established schools in areas in which there had been no schools previously. Besides, he felt, the British methods of governance undercut the dominance of the "kulkarni," the village accountant of the pre-colonial period, a Brahmin who used to be the lynchpin of village affairs before colonial rule, although it must be stated that the government in Great Britain had neither the interest nor the intention of destabilizing native social structures.

The twentieth century Dalit movement in Maharashtra, which had its main constituency among the "untouchable" castes, followed the footsteps of the Satyashodak Samaj movement by espousing the western values of democracy, egalitarianism and fraternity as ideal social values. It was on the strength of these values that the "untouchable" leader, Shivram Jamba Kamble, demanded of the colonial government that it take steps to abrogate untouchability in India.

There was of course another strand of "untouchable" politics, which simultaneously, in Maharashtra and other parts of India, tried to instill self-regard and self-respect in the "untouchable" peoples by taking recourse to myths of origins. Among the "untouchable" movements which followed this trajectory were not only the movement led by Gopal Baba Walangkar in Maharashtra, which claimed for the "untouchables" an elevated caste status prior to their "degradation" by the Aryans, but also similar "adi" movements which sprang up at various points in the country – Adi-Dharam in Punjab, Adi-Hindu in the United Provinces, Adi-Dravida in Madras, Adi-Andhra and Adi-Karnataka in South India. The logic of these movements was explicated early in Maharashtra, where post-Phule, pre-Ambedkar, Dalit leader, Kisan Faguji Bansode(1870-1946), warned his caste Hindu friends in 1909 that :

> The Aryans – your ancestors – conquered us and gave us unbearable harrassment. At that time we were your conquest, you treated us even worse than slaves and subjected us to any torture you wanted. But now we are no longer your subjects, we have service relationship with you, we are not your slaves or serfs ... We have had enough of harrassment and torture of the Hindus.[31]

By the 1920's, "adi" movements, with their ideological claim to being heirs of a "non-Aryan," "original Indian," egalitarian tradition of society, had thrown up a host of new leaders – Bhagyareddy Varma in the South, Acchutananda in the United provinces and Mangooram in Punjab, not to mention Kisan Faguji Bansode himself in Maharashtra – all of whom abjured the Vedic Upanishadic heritage of Hinduism in favour of their "pristine," "pre-Hindu" identities.[32]

The repudiation of the Hindu heritage took an even more radical turn in the case of the Dravidian movement led by E V Ramasami Naicker,

"Periyar," in the Tamil heartland. Periyar's movement was rooted in a reassertion of Dravidian nationalism which strongly set itself up against what it perceived to be the Aryan cultural history of the Hindus. It advanced a blueprint for a Ravan Rajya as against the Ram Rajya model of the ideal social and economic order posited by a number of Hindu thinkers, including Gandhi. As against the celebrations of Ram Lila festivals in Northern India, held by him to be the bastion of Brahminical Hinduism, Periyar advocated that in Southern India there should be the celebration of Ravan Lila festivals, as a mark of regard and respect for the non-Brahmin, non-Hinduized legacy of the Dravidians. Finally, of course, Periyar was to reject religion itself because he felt that all religions reinforced systems of social repression.[33]

Periyar as well as the "adi" movement leaders provided inspiration to Ambedkar who entered the ongoing movement for Dalit liberation in Maharashtra in the late 1920's. The 1920's was a decade of unprecedented social ferment in colonial India with growing unrest among the peasantry, the proletariat and the patriots with the existing order of things in the country. Ambedkar(1891-1956), who had returned after acquiring his higher education at Columbia University in New York and the London School of Economics, and after training as a Barrister-at-Law from Gray's Inn, attended the first Depressed Classes Conference in Nagpur in association with his mentor, Shahu Maharaj of Kolhapur, who was notorious to Indian National Congress loyalists for his pro-British and his anti-Brahmin affiliations. Here Ambedkar spoke up not only against mainstream nationalism but also against upper caste programmes for lower caste progress. In 1926, he mobilized his supporters to struggle to break the ban on "untouchables" from drinking water from the town tank in Mahad in the Konkan. The Mahad Satyagraha, often called the "first untouchable liberation struggle," did not succeed in getting water for the "untouchables," but did conclude with the public burning of the *Manusmriti*, the most diehard text among the dharmashastras.

It was at this juncture that the Dalit movement found itself at a crossroad, torn between contending avenues of liberation offered by Gandhi's accomodationist "upper caste" approach on the one hand and Ambedkar's antagonistic "lower caste" approach towards the problem of how to deal with Hindu caste society. Though the former option seemed to appeal to a few moderates within the Dalit fold, the very many extremists within the Dalit fold clearly declared their preference for the latter option. For them, the "narratives of suffering," the title of the essay by Sisir Kumar Das, in terms of which upper caste liberals liked to look at lower caste misery, were just not adequate enough. What the Dalits needed, they felt, was primarily a strategy of their own.

By the year 1929 Ambedkar had emerged as the most articulate Dalit leader not only of Maharastra but of India as a whole, with small resistance efforts taking off in different parts of the country on the lines of the Mahad Satyagraha. An all India Dalit movement seemed finally to be in the making. It was natural that Ambedkar, the inspirational figure behind this development should be called to represent the "Depressed Classes of India" at the Round Table Conferences with Indian leaders called by the British Government between 1930-1933. The purpose of these conferences was to work out the modalities for self-rule for Indians. Here Ambedkar clashed with Gandhi and the representatives of the Indian National Congress over the issue of an award of separate electorates to "untouchables." For Gandhi, the integrity of Hindu society, with the "untouchables" as its indissoluble part, was a non-negotiable fact. In 1932, Gandhi went on fast against the award, ending his fast only when the award of separate electorates to "untouchables" was annulled, and combined electorates with some electoral constituencies reserved only for "untouchable" candidates was proposed. Ambedkar was averse to this compromise and interrogated Gandhi's sincerity on safeguarding the interests of the Dalits. However under pressure from the nationalists and from his own followers, he later relented and went along with the common consensus on this issue. But though Ambedkar agreed to this proposal in the so-called Poona Pact between different factions of Indian leadership, he felt disillusioned with the reformist tendencies of the mainstream Indian nationalists on social concerns.

His sense of disappointment inaugurated his revolutionary phase which led to an announcement in 1935 that he was "born a Hindu but would not die a Hindu" and the founding in 1936, of the Independent

Labour Party (ILP), a proletarian peasant party with a red flag. Along with the radical economic agenda of the ILP, a quasi Marxist agenda, Ambedkar advanced a cultural programme of demystification of the "superior" achievements of Hinduism. Culturally as much as economically, he felt, the Hindus had always subjugated the Dalits. Nevertheless, during the final run-up to the accomplishment of independence for India, Ambedkar was cajoled to co-operate with the more moderate streams within the Indian independence movement, and specifically with the Indian National Congress, and played a lead role in drafting a constitution for free India. He was persuaded also to join the first Union Cabinet of Ministers headed by Jawaharlal Nehru. But his disenchantment with Hindu society could never be diminished. A few years on, in the 1950s, before he led a mass exodus of 500,000 of his followers from the fold of Hinduism to the fold of Buddhism in a final repudiation of caste society, he was to make his celebrated, if purposely provocative, statement about the cultural accomplishments of the Dalits of India:

> The Hindus wanted the Vedas and they sent for Vyasa who was not a caste Hindu. The Hindus wanted an Epic and they sent for Valmiki who was an Untouchable. The Hindus wanted a Constitution, and they sent for me.[34]

This observation was to become the fountainhead for Dalit writings which started to emerge in a steady stream from the 1950s and the 1960s onwards, initially from Maharastra in the wake of the Ambedkar-inspired Dalit Panther movement, and then by the 1970s and the 1980s from Gujarat, Tamil Nadu, Karnataka, Andhra Pradesh, and Orissa. In its present phase, Dalit writings are coming out also from Uttar Pradesh, Delhi, Punjab and elsewhere across the country, and have earned literary recognition from literary reviewers at home and abroad. The trajectories of the writings of the Dalit authors are explored by me in my own paper in this volume.

Notes

1   An excellent insight into the operation of contemporary economic globalization in dividing societies on sometimes very traditional lines is provided by Jayati Ghosh in her essay "Perceptions of Difference: The Economic Underpinnings," *The Concerned Indian's Guide to Communalism*, ed. K N Pannikar, (New Delhi: Penguin Books India, 1999).

2   For a detailed discussion of the "Ideological interlinkage between the anti-Mandal Commission agitation and the Ramjanambhoomi movement," see Sukumar Muralidharan, "Mandal, Mandir aur Masjid: 'Hindu' Communalism and the Crisis of the State," *Social Scientist* Vol 18, no 10; Rajni Kothari, "Caste, Communalism and the Democratic Process" and Ghanshyam Shah, "The BJP and the Backward Castes in Gujarat," *Religion, Religiosity and Communalism*, eds. Praful Bidwai, Harbans Mukhia and Achin Vanaik,(New Delhi: Manohar Publications, 1996); and Achin Vanaik, *Communalism Contested: Religion, Modernity and Secularisation*, (New Delhi: Sage Publications, 1997).

3   For more elaboration on the Hindu right wing viewpoint on Hindu cultural nationalism, refer to Tapan Basu, Pradip Datta, Sumit Sarkar, Tanika Sarkar and Sambuddha Sen, *Khaki Shorts Saffron Flags: A Critique of the Hindu Right* (New Delhi: Orient Longman, 1993); Sukumar Muralidharan, "Patriotism Without People: Milestones in the Evolution of the Hindu Nationalist Ideology," *Social Scientist* Vol 22, no 5-6; and K N Pannikar, "Introduction: Defining the Nation as Hindu," *The Concerned Indian's Guide to Communalism*, ed. K N Pannikar, (New Delhi: Penguin Books India, 1999).

4   Herbert H Risley, *The People of India*, (Calcutta: Thacker, Spink & Co, 1908).

5   Arthur de Gobineau, *The Inequality of the Human Races*, trans. Adrian Collins, (New York: H Fortig, 1915).

6   Max Weber, *The Religion of India: The Sociology of Hinduism and Buddhism*, (Glencoe, Illinois: Free Press, 1958).

7   Bernard Cohn, *India: The Social Anthropolgy of a Civilization*, (Englewood Cliffs: N J Prentice Hall, 1971).

8   Martin Klass, *Caste: The Emergence of the South Asian Social System*, (Philadelphia: Institute for Study of Human Issues, 1980).

9   Friedrich Max Mueller, *Rig Veda Sanhita, the Sacred Hymns of the Brahmans*, trans. and explained (London: Trubner, 1869).

10   J A Abbe Dubois, *Hindu Manners, Customs and Ceremonies*, trans. H K Beauchamp (Oxford: Clarendon Press, 1906).

11   Partha Chatterjee, *The Nations and Its Fragments: Colonial and Post-colonial Histories*, (New Delhi: Oxford UP, 1995).

12   Louis Dumont, *Homo Hierarchus: The Caste System and Its Implications*, trans. Mark Sainsbury (Chicago: U of Chicago P, 1970).

13   Joan Mencher, "The Caste System Upside-Down or the Not-So Mysterious East" *Current Anthropolgy* 15 1974: 469-93.

14   Gerald Berreman, *Caste and Other Inequities: Essays on Inequality*, (Meerut: Folklore Institute, 1979).

15   Michael Moffat, *An Untouchable Community in South India Structure and Consensus*, (Princeton: Princeton UP, 1979).

16   For an account of resistance movements against caste and caste oppression across the span of Indian history see Eleanor Zelliot, *From Untouchable to Dalit: Essays on the Ambedkar Movement*, (New Delhi: Manohar Publications, 1992); Gail Omvedt, *Dalit Visions*, (Hyderabad: Orient Longman, 1995) and Ghanshyam Shah ed., *Dalit Identity and Politics*, (New Delhi: Sage Publications, 2001).

17   Sekhar Bandyopadhyay *Caste, Protest and Identity in Colonial India: The Namasudras of Bengal, 1872-1947*, (Richmond: Curzon Press, 1997).

18   Sumit Sarkar, *Beyond Nationalist Frames: Relocating Postmodernism, Hindutva, History*, (Delhi: Permanent Black, 2002) 38-80.

19   Claude Melliassox, "Are there Castes in India ?" in *Economy and Society*, Vol 2, no 1, 89-111.

20   Maurice Godelier, "Infrastructures, Societies and History," in *Current Anthropology* 19 763-71.

21   Gail Omvedt, *Dalits and the Democratic Revolution: Dr Ambedkar and the Dalit* Movement *in Colonial India*, (New Delhi: Sage Publications, 1994) 21-58.

22   L S S O'Malley, *Indian Caste Customs* (Cambridge: Cambridge UP, 1932), n 10, 13.

23   For an introduction to the basics of the caste system in India, in its original as well as in its operational schemes, see Anand Chakravarti, "Some Aspects of Inequality in Rural India: A Social Perspective," *Equality and Inequality: Theory and Practice*, ed. Andre Beteille, (New Delhi: Oxford UP, 1998).

24   See Oliver Mendelsohn and Marika Viziany, *The Untouchables: Subordination, Poverty and the State in Modern India*, (Cambridge: Cambridge UP, 1998).

25   Oliver Mendelsohn and Marika Viziany, *The Untouchables: Subordination, Poverty and the State in Modern India*.

26   For more information on the Dalit liberation enterprise and its leadership at different stages, and especially on B R Ambedkar, read Barbara R Joshi ed., *Untouchable! Voices of the Dalit Liberation Movement*, (London: Zed Books, 1986); Gail Omvedt, *Dalits and the Democratic Revolution Dr Ambedkar and the Dalit Movement in Colonial India*, (New Delhi: Sage Publications, 1994) and Valerian Rodrigues ed., *The Essential Writings of B R Ambedkar*, (New Delhi: Oxford UP, 2002).

27   Gopal Guru, " The Politics of Naming" in *Seminar* 471, Special Issue on " Dalit." See also Guru's essay "The Language of Dalit-Bahujan Political Discourse" in Ghanshyam Shah ed., *Dalit Identity and Politics*, (New Delhi: Sage Publications, 2001).

28   For more information about Chokhamela and Eknath, see Eleanor Zelliot, *From Untouchable to Dalit: Essays on the Ambedkar Movement*, (New Delhi: Manohar Publications, 1992) 3-32.

29   Many of these movements unfortunately are not very well documented. The Madras movement is the focus of Eugene F Irschic's *Politics and Social Conflict in South India: The Non-Brahman Movement and Tamil Seperatism 1916-29* (Berkeley: U of California P, 1969). The Ilava movement has been extensively studied in at least a dozen recent publications. The other movements, however, deserve more research than has been done on them.

30   Two recent books on Phule which provide useful information about him and his movement are Rosalind O' Hanlon, *Caste, Conflict and Ideology: Mahatma Jotirao Phule and Low Caste Protest in Nineteenth Century Western India*, (Cambridge: Cambridge UP, 1985), and G P Deshpande ed., *Selected Writings of Jotirao Phule*, (New Delhi: Leftword Books, 2002).

31   Quoted by Gail Omvedt in *Dalit Visions*, (Hyderabad: Orient Longman, 1995) 35.

32   For more information on "adi" movements see Gail Omvedt, *Dalit Visions*, (Hyderabad: Orient Longman, 1995) chap 5.

33   For more information on the Dravidian movement led by E V Ramasami "Periyar," see Gail Omvedt *Dalit Visions*, (Hyderabad: Orient Longman, 1995) chap 7.

34   For more information on the Ambedkar movement see *Dr Balasaheb Ambedkar: Writings and Speeches*, (Mumbai: Govt. of Maharashtra, 1987) and Barbara R Joshi ed. *Untouchable! Voices of the Dalit Liberation Movement*, (London: Zed Books, 1986); Gail Omvedt, *Dalits and the Democratic Revolution: Dr Ambedkar and the Dalit Movement in Colonial India* (New Delhi: Sage Publications, 1994) and Gail Omvedt, *Dalit Visions*, (Hyderabad: Orient Longman, 1995).

Irathina Karikalan

OORAKALI

TRANSLATED BY HEPHZIBAH ISRAEL

Sami, I bow before you. There's no reason why you should know anything about me. I'm telling you about myself only because you asked. Not that I think I will benefit in any way by telling you this. Only, do try to understand the plight of the low born, sami. But then, having understood, what is it that you can do about it?

My father was called Mandayan. I don't think my grandfather had given him any other name. The man was jet black, and shone like the bark of a palm tree rubbed down with castor oil. He grazed the cattle of the entire village. Pavunamma, my younger sister, and I would accompany him every day. It was not an easy task to graze the cattle of the five streets of the padaiaatchi.

"I, Oorakali, am coming. Untie the cattle, sami-yo," Appa would shout as he approached the houses. Hearing his call, the women of these households would free the cattle. To control the unruly ones, he would take the rope around their necks and tie this to their forelegs, forcing them to limp.

On sunny days, paddy, black gram and coriander seeds of various households would be spread out on the streets to dry. Appa would call out, "The oorakali cattle are coming. Stand by your grains. Guard your grains!" He would ask me to give the call on days when he was not able to. If, by any chance, the cattle put their mouths to the grain, the curses that the masters let out were quite unbearable. "Dog ... drunkard," were the abuses that rose to their lips immediately.

And what could we do? We are outcastes, sami. Could we have dared to talk back? They would have said, "What? Has that oorakali's tongue swollen? That dog lives on food begged from the whole village. His tongue should be pulled out and cut to pieces!" Why did God create our tongues? Are our tongues and stomachs only for drinking the

---

Oorakali: a person, from among the lowest castes, whose job is to collect the cattle of the entire village, take them out to graze, and bring them back safely. In return, the oorakali gets food and clothes from the village. Literally, this word would mean "cowherd."

Sami, Ayyah: both are respectful ways of addressing men of the upper castes, the masters.

The five streets of the padaiaatchi: Or "the village" or "the village streets" refers to that part of the village where the upper castes live and which is generally far from that inhabited by the lower castes.

watery kevaru koozhu of the masters' houses?

I don't recall my father ever having worn a shirt. On occasions such as Deevali or Pongal, weddings and funerals in the masters' houses, those who took pity on him would tear out four mozhams of coarse cotton cloth for the oorakali. This alone served as his veshti, his underwear, a towel to protect his head from rain, and as a covering against the cold. Appa always carried a stout bamboo stick, about a mozham long, to drive the cattle. While walking through the village streets, he would take his slippers off and hook them to the thicker end of the stick and hold it against his shoulder. We had never seen him hitting the cattle with that stick though. The cattle were that dear to him.

It would be ten, eleven in the morning by the time we managed to gather the padaiaatchi cattle under the banyan tree by the road. From the streets of the outcastes would come Hamsa, the vettiyan's daughter Rasaya, Kanangam, Kodipavunam, the woman from Paloor's daughter, and many others. And what fierce competition would arise between them to collect the dung! Eyes fixed on the dark, shrunken anus of the cows and bulls, the girls would start screaming the moment they saw the skin expand and dung being pushed out. "The myla cow's dropping are mine" ... "The black bull's are mine" ... "I'm taking the pregnant cow's droppings" ... "The dung of the maniyar's heifer is mine" ... they would shout. No one but the first person who had claimed it could take the dung of a particular animal. They would collect it, pat it into cakes, and sell these in the houses of the padaiaatchi. With the money they made from selling dung cakes, they bought bangles to wear on Deevali, Pongal and Padunettamperu. If the amount was more than usual they could even buy blouse pieces from the bundle-men, the travelling hawkers.

Kevaru koozhu: a kind of cooked paste made of ground ragi. The oorakali were not thought to deserve rice or any food that would make them feel they could "talk back." The practice still continues in some parts of Tamil Nadu.

Deevali: Deepawali.

Pongal: the harvest festival, usually January 13. Dedicated to Surya, the sun god.

Mozham: a handmeasure, from the tip of the middle finger to the elbow.

Vettiyan: one who works in cremation grounds, burning corpses.

Padunettamperu: the festival associated with the coming of spring waters in the river Kaveri. An occasion for community celebration.

3

From the banyan tree, we would take the animals to the lake by the Korrayathai Temple to drink water. Then we would drive them to the forest by the big lake and let them graze there.

My sister, Pavunamma, was not dark like Appa or me. Fair in complexion, Thangatchi was like the lotus that bloomed in the lake. For my father and me, she was our very life. I used to dig the roots of the water lily out of the lake for her. Because she liked millet, I would slip by the watchman who guarded the fields near the forest, to pluck millet cobs there, which I would later roast for her. I would dig up the clay on the bank of the lake and pat out radio sets and trucks for her. When her play tired her out, Pavunamma would doze off. In the heat, Appa too would lie down to rest. Then, it was I who had to watch the cattle.

The animals would trouble us no end, sami. The uncastrated bulls were never still. They would chase the virgin heifers the moment they caught their smell. Sometimes they even pursued the heifers of neighbouring villages that came to graze there. The abuses that the masters heaped on us when they found their bulls missing are too foul to be repeated.

Sami ... was it blood that ran in my father's body? The abuses had hardened us. Of what use were feelings of self-respect to our bodies? If ever the fire of resentment raged in my father, he would douse it with liquor. So, why did he live, why did he keep himself imprisoned in that body of his? Wasn't it to raise me to manhood and give my sister's hand in marriage to someone? Our mother had died three days after my sister's birth. It was he who was mother, father, everything to us. And, next to us, if he loved anything, it was his cattle.

What could these poor, dumb animals do about the atrocities of their masters, sami? Their condition was as miserable as ours. Sometimes, a pregnant cow's water sac would burst in the forest. It was my father who would carefully pull the calf out by its head, and pinch out the tender parts of its hooves. He would heat water with karuva leaves in the pot kept for this purpose, on a stove built of loose stones. He would rub the cow down with hot water and hay to soothe it and clean the blood splattered on the ground. Appa would then express the cow's first milk.

Yet, sami, what did we gain by grazing cattle with such care? My father would run about ignoring the cold and the summer heat. And all he managed to get were corns on his feet since he never found time to pull out the thick karuva thorns that pierced them. His legs would always be covered with wounds made by the kicking and stamping of unruly cows. But, for all the cows we grazed, did any of the masters ever pour us a tumbler of coffee or a little buttermilk for our parched throats?

At sunset, Appa would drive the cattle back, leave them, each in its master's cowshed, and bring us home. He would go to the village street once again, with a brass vessel this time, and at every house call out, "Oorakali has come. Give some food, thai." Unwilling to serve the first helping from the rice pot to the Oorakali of all people, they would say. "The food has been delayed a little today. Come tomorrow, Mandayan," When Appa did get food, the rice, the lumpy kevaru kazhi and the thicker kamba koozhu would fall into the same vessel. He always carried a smaller vessel for the vegetables, the kari, and he'd invariably come back with kari and rasam all mixed together in it. If it was an auspicious day, the women of the masters' houses would offer vadai and sweets, small sized ones that were specially made to give to the sarker vettiyan, the village vettiyan, farm labourers, domestic servants, the village guard, the barber and the washerman.

Appa would always separate the rice portions for Thangatchi and me, and drink the remaining kevaru-kambu kazhi mix himself. Then he would fall asleep, to get up only when the village guard's cock crowed at dawn. On waking, he would go to the teashop in the village street and get some tea for us. We would have put the rice, left over from the previous night's begging, to soak. This we would drink after our morning ablutions, and leave to graze the cattle.

On rainy days, our existence was absolutely miserable. We were allowed to enter the village only through the byways, and these would be all slushy with mud when it rained. The outcastes and the village people would squat on either side of the path, defecating. Rain water, mixed with faeces, stagnated in puddles on the path through which outcastes, field labourers and rice planters had to pass. Our legs would itch, infected with scabies. Later, at night, red ants would discover the wounds and feed on them. Oozing pus, the discoloured skin of our legs would resemble a leper's.

And, in this manner, we grew up. My sister was healthy and fair. But I, at eighteen, was like an old worn-out broom, thin and emaciated. The eyes of the whole village fell on Thangatchi. They said that Oorakali's daughter looked like a brahmin girl. The village boys would gossip within our hearing. "She wasn't born to Mandayan. Chellathai has lain with our Nattar." What could I do but walk away, embarrassed and humiliated. We, who had no right to walk the streets of the village with our slippers on, could not afford to be assertive.

Appa lamented that he could die peacefully only after Thangatchi had been safely handed over to some man. With the passage of time, he found it difficult to graze the village cattle. The palm tree like body stooped, wrinkled and shrunk to half its size. There had been a gradual decrease in the number of cattle, too. Tractors had been bought to plough the fields. The masters now maintained only a cow or two for milking. And, to graze these, each house had found a small boy. That was the end of the oorakali's livelihood. Appa could no longer move about. But we had to survive, after all. So, I was sent to the Nattar's house as a bonded labourer for a thousand rupee advance and ten sacks of rice a year.

I worked all day, repairing bunds, digging the sides of the canal, removing weeds from the fields. At night, I had to run the motor pump. People said that on rainy days poisonous gases filled the open wells which were fitted with motor pumps. It was often necessary to go down such wells when a valve had to be rethreaded, or to change small motor parts when the bearing broke. In some households, they would first lower a hen into the well. Or, an open flame. In my master's house, they lowered me into the well, telling me to shake the rope if I felt breathless. Sami, are our lives even more despised than those of hens?

The womenfolk of the bonded labourer's family were supposed to look after the threshing floor. My sister began coming to my master's house as well. She had to clean the mud floor of the house and the huge threshing floor every day, and swab or sprinkle them with cowdung. Then she had to separate the chaff and stones from the threshed grain.

Lightning struck our lives then. It rained heavily in the first week of Deevali. The rains just would not stop. Our huts overflowed with water.

It was not possible to go to the village street. One night, Thangatchi, who was pouring out the kanji for us to drink, began to retch suddenly. The spasms seemed to rise from the very bottom of her stomach and she ran to the door to vomit.

She had not been well for some days. Though I could not understand anything then, Appa moaned and lamented as if he was on fire. Going up to her, he asked, "Pavunamma, Pavunamma, my child ... what is ailing you, kannu?" Thangatchi only stared at him, blinking in confusion. What had happened to the little one Appa and I had brought up with such care? But my father seemed to understand what was happening. "Get the washerwoman," he said.

So I did. The vannathi, who doubled as midwife, came and checked Thangatchi's pulse. She whispered a few words in my father's ear and he burst out, saying, "You were the one who tried to abort her mother. Whether she had desired to lie down with one of the men of the village or had been forced to do so, she came to you not wanting to carry the child. Both of you hid the matter from me. This girl was born. I have brought her up as if she were mine, dearer than my eye. My son loves her dearly, too. Today, she has been cheated and I don't know by whom. If he were of our caste, she would have told us who he is. Like her mother, she must have gone to the village boys. These men will come to lie. But will they marry? She must have thought that the whole village will be against us if she tells her brother. Let that be. But another child given by a village man should not be born in this house. How you will do it, I don't know. Abort the child."

What had come over my loving father? I had never seen him in such a state before. He seemed to be speaking as if possessed by Karuppu, the dark spirit of the canal.

The vannathi asked me to go and buy some liquor. I bought some. "Young boys, who have come of age, should not see such things. Raja, go outside," she pleaded.

It was still raining heavily outside. My father, not wishing to see the gruesome scene, left for the liquor shop. I stayed. Who had sat my sister on his legs and helped her relieve herself when she was young? Who had washed her without a feeling of disgust? Wasn't it me, her

7

brother? What secrets about her were unknown to me? Why should I have gone out?

The vannathi finally let me stay, bolting the door from inside. She drank half of the liquor that I had brought and told Thangatchi to drink some as well. Thangatchi resisted, retching. Asking me to hold Thangatchi's hands and legs, the vannathi poured some into her mouth. Half of it fell out. Thangatchi's body was bathed in sweat, despite the chill of the heavy rain. She began to mutter incoherently.

The vannathi tied a thin cotton cloth around a coconut reed, and dipped it in the poisonous milk of the yerrakkam plant kept in a coconut shell. Thangatchi was still restless. I was asked to hold her legs apart. But she trembled and kicked. "It'll be over in a minute, little one," I said as I held her legs apart. The vannathi lifted her skirt. Sami, do you know how my heart trembled when I saw her tender, green-veined thighs? The vannathi pushed the wetted stick in deep enough to touch the walls of her uterus. Thangatchi shuddered. Finally, the vannathi drew the stick out, gave my sister some green leaves to chew and, saying that she would come back the next day, went away.

My sister lay bruised and limp, like a torn leaf. Later that night, her body began to heave and convulse. Her skirt was covered with clots of blood and she was screaming. Blood from her body soaked into the sack she lay on, and a foul smell began to rise. Ants and flies were about. Sami, my sister was in the grip of a fit. "Leave me alone, Ayyah ... I'm scared, Ayyah," she mumbled.

As time passed, her screams sounded beyond the streets of the outcastes which were in the northern part of the village. Feeling utterly helpless, I watched the sister I had carried on my hips and shoulders, the sister I had raised, die a tortured death before my eyes. I was shaken, as one turned into stone, sami.

I understood that day what people mean when they talk of a person dying along with someone they love. My father died with my sister. Why sami, would I want to live when the two people I loved and lived with were snatched away from me?

We had grazed the village cattle. When the animals refused food, Appa had sucked out the thorns from their tongues with his own mouth. When they were sick, he had pounded the medicinal peranda and fed them. Sami, is it fair for the village to graze on the very family that had grazed all its cattle?

Witness to these atrocities, the spirit of the canal remains mute. The spear that stands in front of its sanctum, is it there merely for piercing lemons and impaling sacrificial hens?

What did the masters, who wail in self-pity at even the thought of someone casting an evil spirit on them, do when my Pavunamma and my father died? Weren't they happy as long as their own cattle and fields were safe, Sami?

"Oorakali" was originally written in Tamil and first published in *Kavithaasaran*, July 1995, Chennai. It was translated by Hephzibah Israel and published in *Katha Prize Stories 6* in January 1997 by Katha.

Mogalli Ganesh

PADDY HARVEST

TRANSLATED BY K RAGHAVENDRA RAO

Muttanna's forge blazed like a small factory as the scythes fell in a heap around him. The rhythmic clinking of the hammer on the anvil, the hissing of hot metal suddenly dipped in cold water, the murmur of people, their breathing, coughs and laughter, and the snake hiss of the furnace, all together created an incredible sense of life in the night black colony. As the flames from the furnace rose, the shapes of those gathered there expanded and shrank by turn, as if they were waiting eternally, devoutly, for some joyous event. As Muttanna's sweaty body swayed, the crowd carefully gauged the sharpness of the scythes emerging from the furnace. Never before had Muttanna put the furnace to such use. He was sharpening every customer's scythe to a fine point, as he wove dreams of the vast quantities of grain all this work would fill his house with. The people of the colony usually paid him paddy, not cash, for tending their scythes.

The next morning, they arrived at a collective decision to harvest the crop in the paddy fields of the Olagere plain.

There had never been so much bustle and hope before in the history of the colony. Their dreams of gold hued paddy, transformed into an illusory, alluring enchantress who filled their homes with wonder, grew moment by moment. The front yards of those who did not need to hone their scythes afresh filled with the metallic sounds of tools being sharpened on stone slabs. The small children, eager to take part in the elders' activities, were trying hard to drive away their sleepiness. The women fondly ran their hands over dust covered pots lying helter-skelter in corners. They boasted of their "high class" vessels that would be used to store tomorrow's paddy.

Some old scold muttered, "I told the wretched fellows a thousand times – don't do it. Don't ruin these vessels, don't sell them. But who listens? They sold the mud pots to feed their bellies. "And who should I go to now and beg for a vessel to collect tomorrow's paddy?"

Her anger had a history. Years ago, her ancestors used to steal cattle, slaughter them and eat them, not leaving a trace behind. They filled the storing vessels with the remaining bones. Then they dug pits in the backyard and buried them. This was how they escaped detection by the cattle owners. This was how they hid the hunger of their bellies while saving their honour. Then the backyard was dug up for some reason, the vessels were removed and sold. The old woman was inconsolable, she saw this as the public sale of her family's honour. She felt not only sorrow but also rage. Now, remembering this bit of the past when it was time for the paddy harvest, she ranted against the members of her household.

That night, the stars in the sky's garden looked like paddy grain, hung for drying or scattered for sowing. This encouraged them, and made them more determined about their plans for the next day.

The noises from the forge melted and merged into the old woman's loud cursing. People came out of every house and collected at one place, as the nymph called paddy danced in a myriad ways. One said, "The last time we ate rice was during the last harvest."

Another interrupted, "No, no. Didn't we eat a sumptuous meal at the death anniversary of the headman's wife?"

A third cut in with enthusiasm, as if he had to blurt it out before it fled his memory forever, "Good Lord, what are you talking about? It was the feast you ate in the house of Dase Gowda. How can I describe the glory of that meal, recount its magnificent story? There was rice palav ... served on plantain leaves ... and what a beautiful smell ... The lovely aroma of spiced rice filled the room, so that the entire house seemed to be something made out of sandalwood. Well, I have enjoyed such rice. In all your lives you may never eat anything like it." He looked as if he was drowning in an unearthly bliss.

Yet another, disgusted with this story, said angrily, "Let me assure you that you are not the only one to have feasted on such rice. I too ate rice like this four years ago in Channapatna." Then the others began to pull his leg, wondering aloud whether he was really remembering a true past, and managed to silence him with their laughter. Their merriment attracted more and more people.

Back at home, the women were getting ready, finding all sorts of containers to collect tomorrow's harvest, seeing all the while the dishes they could cook with the harvested paddy. The little children collapsed with sleep on the shoulders of the elders. The men smoked their bidis, cursing the fact that their women never cooked tasty dishes.

Meanwhile Thopamma, the bazaar harlot, thought of the ragi hittu she had borrowed from every house in the colony. She began to calculate – out of the paddy gathered tomorrow, I can pay back one seer of paddy for every quarter seer of ragi hittu I have borrowed, then I will have cleared all my debts.

The champion toddy drinker of the town, Chilre, was making his own calculations. "Somehow I must grab some five bags of paddy during the harvest tomorrow, then sell them, put the money in the coconut business, and ensnare the widow Janakavva into my net!"

The entire colony warmed with dreams, with a hundred plans. Then they all went to bed, hoping and believing that at last their empty, wasted lives would be filled with riches. Their bodies felt the cool breeze from the plain, a breeze that travelled across the wide fields and wafted in with the aroma of paddy.

The town's pond, which had turned into a plain, had been transformed into a fertile field thanks to the yearly sedimentation of earth over it. The landlords who owned land adjacent to Olagere plain began to encroach into the fertile Olagere fields. Some of their own caste fumed. They owned land further away, they did not have the benefit of water and they harvested nothing. Then someone sent an anonymous petition to the government about the illegal encroachment.

The tehsildar, who always responded promptly to such developments, used all his official powers and acted immediately. This efficient officer welcomed such challenges. He thought tackling them was historically necessary to bring about justice in the country. An official proclamation was issued to say that this time the government was confiscating the crop of the fields in the dried-up pond, because it had been illegally cultivated. Though the officer's predecessor had issued a notice against this illegal act, it had been ignored, this time the government meant business and would itself harvest the crop. At the same time, the government went ahead with its programme of reviving the public pond.

An official statement was also issued to say that the government would employ people of that colony as labour to harvest the crop, this was the tehsildar's own decision. The tehsildar announced that people would be allowed to take home as much of the crop as they could harvest. All this

---

Ragi hittu: millet flour.
Chilre: the name is a pun as chilre also means small change.

was announced to the village through the official drummer, rousing the colony to feverish activity. Everyone was waiting for dawn to break!

It seemed that even the cocks responded to their anxious anticipation, and crowed the coming of day sooner than they should have. Some got up even earlier, with lit bidis between their lips. They had never had a day like this to wake up to. Their lifelong dreams – of sumptuous heaps of rice – seemed to have finally come true.

The illegal owners of the fields, taken by surprise by the sudden announcements, seemed helpless for the time being. The other landlords didn't care, they had nothing to lose.

As the morning light wrapped itself round the colony like a warm cloth, they sprang to action. Their scythes stirred with metallic sounds. Muttanna was dreaming of the huge heaps of paddy that would be his reward for his labour. Almost everything, objects both likely and unlikely, were grabbed to collect the paddy – baskets, bags, blankets, rugs, even old saris.

Thopamma was running around with a piece of cloth, urging the womenfolk, "Come on, you whores. What are you waiting for? Are you going to sit there dumb, waiting for fortune to knock on your doors?" Even the little boys were getting ready to collect the paddy. Many of them had forgotten to eat last night's leftovers, and were content with the jaggery sweetened tea from the shop. The very old felt disappointed that God had cheated them of being part of the harvest.

The pond area now bustled with activity and noise as if a fair or festival was on. Everybody marched towards the pond. The residents of the upper colony were amazed at the size and solidarity of the scythes held lovingly in their hands, and the unearthly courage and spirit that lit their faces.

They moved fast. The boys ran as if they were buses, ahead of the adults. The sun rose in the sky. Everybody was carrying something, and Thopamma was urging them to gallop ahead. The men moved with giant steps to reach the fields, in their midst Chilre shouted something like a message. As they walked along the banks of the fields, the sunlight fell on them, so that the shadows of what they carried moved along with them.

They stood dumbstruck for a moment as their eyes took in the expanse of the fields and the glistening gold of the paddy crop. No one could have captured the countless emotions that crowded their faces.

Young boys touched the hanging paddy stalks gently, like birds, with unconcealed joy.

By now the tehsildar too had arrived, flanked by police constables. They positioned themselves in the shade of a tree. There was no sign of the illegal field owners. Their womenfolk stood at a safe distance, hurling curses at the harvesters. But the hopes and desires of the harvesters danced along with the paddy crop swaying gently in the breeze.

The tehsildar addressed the gathering, "Look here. No one should make any unnecesary noise. Cut the crop in complete silence. Organize yourselves efficiently by dividing the work. Don't be afraid of being attacked. But you must finish the harvesting today. You must also finish beating the paddy by this evening." His words provided the signal for the epic event to start.

They stepped into the slushy fields. They began cutting the crop at an incredible speed, their scythes waving and swishing, their bangles jangling, wielding their tools with dexterity. The harvesters' footsteps on the slushy ground looked like thousands of drawings. Since they could not use scythes, young boys picked paddy bunches with their hands and stored them in their small bags. The work was divided spontaneously, on the spot. Some collected the cut paddy and heaped it, while others poured the paddy into bags for beating and winnowing. Yet others heaped the stalks in one place. It was a marvellous teamwork, carried out with exemplary speed and skill. Sweat streamed down from their rhythmically moving bodies. Large parts of the field were being harvested at great speed.

Chilre rushed around, as if he was directing everybody, meddling in everyone else's work, all the while scheming ways of filching three bundles of paddy for himself. He screamed, "Faster, faster, you have no time to wipe your sweat! Don't forget that the Sahib wants us to finish everything by this evening."

Those who made bundles of the paddy were amazed. They had never before collected so much paddy. The tehsildar, enjoying the sight of so many people working so fast, and with such enthusiasm, chatted with his colleagues underneath a tree.

In a few hours, the cut paddy rose in huge heaps. Nearby, the paddy was beaten and winnowed in the wind, then packed into bags placed in a neat row. All the time the paddy fields were being emptied of the crop. Women, their saris unselfconsciously tucked up to their thighs, wielded their scythes. No one had the time to enjoy the spectacle of their thighs melting with sweat. The little boys were taking the bags to their homes. Some sneaked away extra bags.

The scorching sun blazed in the sky. The police felt jealous when they saw how quickly the people worked. Even they couldn't have lathi charged with such speed if they had been ordered to do so by their superiors! Nobody knew where the illegal landowners had fled. Though they felt some fear deep down, the harvesters also felt safe working under the protective eyes of the constables. By now, all of them had succeeded in taking away quite a bit of paddy. In spite of this, the paddy heaps grew sky high. As the fields emptied, the winnowed husk turned into a large hill.

That evening, even as they dreamt of her, the bewitching enchantress lay abjectly at their feet. Their bodies and clothes were crumpled and exhausted. They looked different now, the men's arms and the women's waists showed the most signs of exhaustion. Hunger had fled from them, ashamed of itself. The work went on, almost automatically, and most of the fields had been harvested. It was growing dark, but people were still taking the paddy home. Chilre, after stealthily manoeuvring five bundles of paddy to the sugarcane field of the village headman, stood there triumphant, scanning the expansive paddy field that lay there, emptied of everything.

Then there was a disruption, as if to say that there are always forces to hinder or control human effort. The tehsildar was jolted by the picture he saw at a distance. The people greeted the new arrivals with total incomprehension. The arrivals were the Deputy Commissioner of the district, the Police Circle Inspector, other minions of officialdom, and naturally, the illegal owners of the fields. The atmosphere changed with the suddenness of lightning, as if someone unknown had twisted the throat of all that was living and eager there.

The Deputy Commissioner angrily took the tehsildar to task. The illegal landowners watched silently, wincing when they saw the heaps of paddy staring at them. Here and there hostile words were exchanged. The constables who had come there to protect the harvesters were now totally confused.

The tehsildar insisted in his officialese English, "No sir, I did it legally."

The Deputy Commissioner also rapped out in English, as if to silence a subordinate, "Who said it is legal action? It is just a cruel action against village people and I know what kind of idiot you are."

The colony residents didn't know what to do.

The Deputy Commissioner lapsed into Kannada. "Out of love for your own untouchables you have done this and destroyed the village peace. I know what action should be taken against you."

He turned his furious face to the landlords. They reeled off a long list of crimes supposedly committed by the tehsildar. Then the DC ranted that his subordinate had allowed the untouchables to harvest the paddy without his written permission. The tehsildar had indeed written to the DC about it, but had acted without waiting for written permission. The landlords shouted that the tehsildar himself was an untouchable and that his action was partial to the interests of his community.

Then they let loose a flood of abuse against all untouchables.

The harvesters felt trapped. They wondered how to get out of the situation, they tried to steal away.

The upper caste landlords moved forward with energy and opened their mouths wide to hurl a legal point, "Show us the law which says we should give half the harvested paddy to the untouchables!" They complained loudly that the labourers were now getting away, that they had stored the entire crop in their homes, that they had recklessly harvested from adjacent, legally owned fields, that the whole harvesting was a caste motivated affair, and that the tehsildar had to take full responsibility for the outbreak of violence.

The poor tehsildar did not know how to face the accusations heaped on him. The fields, full of slush, stared at them. The harvesting crowd began to melt.

As evening drew near, their problems grew like tails. Three of the illegal landlords had seized land belonging to the untouchables. These farmers had not yet harvested their crop. The landlords now pointed to those lands and said, "See, sirs, how they have not touched the crop in the lands of their own untouchables." The constables remained silent. The Circle Inspector walked up and down solemnly. The landlords cried revenge, demanding that the tehsildar be dismissed and the untouchables punished. Night crept in slowly.

The anti-climax took place like this. Before the harvest, the landlords rushed to Bangalore, hobnobbed with the politicians there, bought their support and then won the support of the DC and other officers. It was a well organized counter-move. The fact that the tehsildar did not have written permission was blown up. The now united landlords placed a proposal before the officers. First, the untouchables should bring back the paddy they had stored in their houses, if they did not want to return the paddy it could officially be counted as levy. It could also be adjusted against the landlords' irrigation debts to the government. The officials accepted these suggestions.

The paddy dream of the untouchables now collapsed, like a silver bird falling to the ground when its wings are clipped.

The landlords who had not been affected also joined their aggrieved brothers. No one knew where the anonymous sender of the petition against illegal cultivators had gone. The entire colony was in the grip of anguish. The poor tehsildar too was nowhere to be found.

The sun had yet to sink below the horizon. The dream of the people was not yet dead. They struggled desperately to salvage it by stashing away as much of the paddy as they could. They filled all sorts of containers, and hid them in all sorts of unlikely places! Mayamma thought up an ingenious scheme. She cooked the paddy in a huge pot, thinking she could save it by claiming it was hers. And she was sure it would be impossible for them to retrieve the cooked paddy. One of her neighbours firmly believed that any constable who dared enter her hut with boots on would start vomiting blood. Chilre's mind was aflame. The local Gnaneshwar Sangha, a youth organization, was unable to stir up any protest. Manchavva dragged a bundle of paddy to the backyard, and hid it in a small vessel covered with odds and ends. As she squatted on the floor, she tried to contain her racing heart.

Everyone seemed involved in a struggle to save something momentous. They covered the mouths of the paddy filled vessels with wet saris to make it appear they were spread to be dried. Some were frustrated that they couldn't hide the paddy in their huts. While the small boys were befuddled by their elders' helplessness, older girls sat crumpled in a corner, overcome with shame and fear. The youth of the colony sat on the steps of a college near the public circle, gossiping, as if what was happening was none of their business.

Suddenly the colony was electrified by a new excitement. They were no longer concerned with a fistful of paddy, they were drawn into something larger, the need to defend their undefined rights. The police constables and officials had begun to invade the colony to retrieve the harvested paddy. The whole colony lay immersed in a sea of darkness, paralyzed. It was as if it was night, or that the sun had died, or as if all vitality and courage could be killed by petty intrigue and humiliation.

The official party entered the colony, determined that the untouchables should surrender the hidden paddy, else they would see that not a grain remained with them. Since the DC was there to supervise the operation, the constables had to act quickly and efficiently. The Circle Inspector too was under pressure to perform his duty well. He was in line for a promotion and had to impress the DC.

He ordered the constables around, shouting, "Rush in. Search every nook and corner and load the hidden paddy on to the lorry waiting outside."

The people began to tremble with fear.

The Inspector roared his order like a government lion, "Come on, charge!"

The helpless constables who had been asked to protect the harvesters in the morning were now ordered to attack them and recover the paddy. They were confused and hesitant, but finally they rushed into the houses. Some of the men stood in their way and pleaded, "Please sir, don't enter our huts with your boots on and insult our gods." Small children scurried away to hide. Old women came forward to touch their feet and plead. Someone broke into a sob. Everywhere the word Rush was heard. When they found they were being resisted, the constables had no choice but to use their lathis.

An enraged Chilre danced in anguish, "Sir, beat us to death. After all, your lathis, boots and guns are meant to be used against poor, small folk like us. Kill us and bury us here. Like that paddy, destroy the colony of untouchables."

The constables rushed like demons into the huts and pulled out the hidden paddy. The widow Thopamma stood there, intending to take them on and teach them a lesson. She was the only midwife in the entire village. She was always there to console and help people when there was misfortune and death. But now the tears collected in her eyes and she hesitated to come out.

The paddy grains fallen between boot shod feet looked forlorn. The constables looked ferocious when they smashed pots with their lathis, or tumbled containers so that the grain rolled noisily on to the floor. They rushed about as if they were mad, hunting for the hidden paddy. Now the people grovelled on the ground. The men ran helter-skelter, fearing imprisonment. The women's dreams had been dashed to the ground like their pots and containers. Meanwhile, the paddy cooking in Mayamma's hut sent out a pleasant aroma that reached the noses of the constables.

In Chamayya's house they threw out coconuts along with the paddy. Only the day before yesterday he had stored the stolen coconuts. Seeing them, someone said, "Look sirs, who knows what else these thieves have hidden inside?" This set off an even more thorough house search, and along with the paddy, they began to seize anything they suspected was stolen. All sorts of things were found in all sorts of houses. The very body of the untouchables' colony was being stripped naked.

The constable with the pot belly shouted, "Bring out whatever else you have hidden. Otherwise the whole village may be arrested. We can find even buried corpses. So you better take things out yourself."

When she heard this, Manchavva dragged out the paddy bundle she had hidden in the backyard, panting, and threw it before them. She wailed, beating her mouth, and then simply vanished. The constable had not yet reached Mayamma's house where she was cooking the paddy in a big pot. Poor Chilre's paddy bundles were stolen by someone who must have watched him hide them. But Chilre did not know this yet. One of the landlords flaunted his shiny moustache and accused them of crime after crime, going on and on as if he was going to recite all the crimes ever committed on earth! The colony's schoolboys grew angry but they blamed the residents. "Who the devil asked them to do it? Let them suffer." Then they fell silent and kept to themselves.

In the search party was an untouchable constable. He went about pretending to perform his duty. The constable who entered Mayamma's hut got angry when he couldn't find the paddy. "So this is your plan, you old hag," he shouted, kicking the pot on the stove. The pot rolled down and the cooked grains of paddy scattered, filling the hut with its mouth watering aroma. As the aroma spread everywhere, Mayamma sobbed and cursed with the same breath, but she couldn't do anything about the split paddy. Some said, as they watched all this, "Even if our children starved, died of hunger and became rotten corpses, we wouldn't want to touch this paddy." They gave up the paddy they had stored so carefully.

The paddy fell outside in a heap. The officials couldn't believe that so much had been stolen! But they were pleased with their success. His hands crossed over his belly, a fuming Chilre stood silent, watching. Then he saw a constable fleeing Thopamma's house.

About four days back, Thopamma had carved beef out of a slaughtered bullock. After eating some of it, she had cut up the rest, strung the pieces into a garland, and hung them out to dry before being preserved. But the pieces had not dried properly and had begun to rot, swarming with worms and flies. They stank horribly. To resist the policeman who rushed into her house, the only weapon she could lay her hands on were the bits of beef. She thrust them on the nose of the policeman and had him running for his life to escape the killing stench. Then Thopamma ran out and gave the DC the same treatment, spoiling his white clothes. Some of the officials ran away, but a few constables rushed at her, caught her and tied her up after a beating. With this success the anger of the officials doubled. They saw what had happened as a challenge to their authority and honour. The Sub-Inspector ordered a lathi charge. Then they beat everyone without restraint so that not a creature was left in the ransacked hovels.

The fact that a mere woman could wield garlands of rotting meat and humiliate him made the Circle Inspector think deeply. He felt the situation must have wider dimensions, beyond the local and the immediate, there must have been a plan to resist the official party. Of course, it was obvious that some external agency must have had a hand in all this. The more he thought, the more convinced he became that the old woman's act was distinctly naxalite in style! And the landlords said a local untouchable youth studying in Bangalore had returned last year to organize a group, the Gnaneshwar Sangha. Their suspicions reinforced, the officials were now convinced the whole thing was a naxalite operation. They began to worry about setting up a different kind of enquiry into the incident.

In the thickness of night, the members of the Sangha were arrested by the landlords. Chilre tried to hide in the darkness. Paddy had taken the village into a complex political conspiracy, the colony was the centre of an armed rebellion. The incident became a serious political issue. Some landlords who had lost in the recent elections tried to give it a new twist. They said there were organized attempts to disrupt the peace of the village and that threats to life had increased. As a result, Thopamma and the others were arrested and taken in a police van to Channapatna. They were described as reckless, violent terrorists. No one knew where the paddy collected by the colony had gone. In any case the residents had lost all interest in it. They were now in the grip of something deeper – the tragedy of living a life that had become a relentless hunt. The visiting official party soon left the village and got busy with follow up action. Thopamma refused to say anything, remained monumentally silent, and prepared for the worst as she was hustled into the van. Chilre planned to get his friends released on bail after selling paddy to the Muslim merchants in Honganur.

Daylight woke like an epileptic in the sleeping colony. Men squatted here and there, smoking bidis as if nothing had happened. The crows cawed as if they were cursing. No one had eaten the night before, and their bellies suffered in the early morning heat, hunger jostling with humiliation. They hoped that the landlords in the upper colony would give them some coolie work, though they also knew that this was impossible. The upper caste men had resolved that very night to teach the colony residents a lesson by not employing them.

As the sun rose, the women mopped up the night's wreckage of broken pots and vessels. The village was buried in complete silence. Then a constable arrived from the town. This scared them, though he was one of those who had come earlier with the tehsildar to protect the harvesters.

He called a few people and they sat in one of the frontyards, talking. They questioned him, full of fear, curiosity and shame.

He told them that when the arrested villagers were being taken in the van, Thopamma had managed to slip out and escape. The senior officers had then sent a constable to the village to capture her immediately. An uncomfortable but sympathetic constable appealed to the people to hand her over if they saw her. He also warned the villagers that the officers may take drastic action against their boys in Bangalore.

Chilre said to him, "Why should you suffer for our misfortune, sir? We know how to ripen our suffering and eat the fruit."

No one had the energy or strength to react. They now knew what that witch, paddy, had brought upon them after her tantalizing dance, they could only squat now, in a stillness marked by exhaustion, hunger, anguish and humiliation.

When he had made sure that Thopamma was not there, the constable left the village. In the eyes of the colony the image of Thopamma grew and grew till it appeared a supernatural force. In their dreams, they now looked hopefully to her arrival.

As time passed, people melted into their own shadows. Mayamma's grandson, unable to bear his hunger, began picking up the cooked paddy grains scattered around the stove. He stuffed his little mouth with them. He chewed hard, spat out the husk, the paddy juice streamed from the two corners of his mouth. It seemed as if he could digest everything.

The whole village was steeped in a profound silence, as it stuffed its belly with all sorts of things. They felt the wind blow from the dried pond fields, where their hopes of a harvest lay dead. And time, bearing its burden of truths in its womb, grew and grew.

"Battha" was originally written in Kannada and published in the author's first collection of short stories, *Buguri*, 1992. "The Paddy Harvest," translated by K Raghavendra Rao was first published in Githa Hariharan ed., *A Southern Harvest*, October 1993, by Katha.

Mahasweta Devi

BAYEN

TRANSLATED BY MAHUA BHATTACHARYA

Bhagirath was very young when Chandi, his mother, was declared a bayen, a witch, and thrown out of the village.

A bayen is not an ordinary witch. She cannot be killed like an ordinary one, because to kill a bayen means death for your children.

So, Chandi was turned into a pariah and put in a hut by the railway tracks.

Bhagirath was raised, without much care, by a stepmother. He did not know what a real mother could be like. Now and then, he did get a glimpse of the shed below the tree across the field where Chandibayen lived alone. Chandi, who could never be anybody's idea of a mother. Bhagirath had also seen the red flag fluttering on her roof from afar, and sometimes, in the flaming noon of April, he had caught sight of her red-clad figure – a dog on her trail – clanking a piece of tin across the paddy fields, moving towards a dead pond.

A bayen has to warn people of her approach when she moves. She has but to cast her eyes on a young man or boy and she sucks the blood out of him. So a bayen has to live alone. When she walks, everyone – young and old – moves out of her sight.

One day, and one day alone, Bhagirath saw his father, Malindar, talk to the bayen.

"Look away my son," his father had ordered him.

The bayen stood on tiptoe by the pond. Bhagirath caught the reflection of the red-clad figure in the pond. A sun bronzed face framed by wild matted hair. And eyes that silently devoured him. No, the bayen did not look at him directly either. She looked at his image as he saw hers, in the dark waters, shuddering violently.

Bhagirath closed his eyes and clung to his father.

"What has made you come here?" hissed his father at her.

"There's no oil for my hair, Gangaputta, no kerosene at home. I am afraid to be alone."

She was crying, the bayen was crying. In the waters of the pond her eyes appeared to swim with tears.

"Didn't they send your week's ration on Saturday?"

Every Saturday, a man from the Dom community of the village went to the tree with a week's provision – half a kilogramme of rice, a handful of pulses, oil, salt, and other food for the bayen.

A bayen should not eat too much.

Calling on the tree to bear witness, he would leave the basket there and run away as fast as he could.

"The dogs stole it all."

"Do you need some money?"

"Who will sell me things?"

"Okay, I'll buy the things and leave them by the tree. Now, go away."

"I can't, I can't live alone ..."

"Who asked you to be a bayen, then? Go away! Go away!"

He picked up a handful of mud and stones from the side of the pond.

"Gangaputta, this boy ...?"

With an ugly oath Malindar threw the mud and stones at her.

The bayen ran away.

Malindar covered his face with his hands, and cried bitterly. "How could I do it? I hurled stones at her body? It used to be a body as soft as butter. How could I be such a beast?"

It was a long time before he could calm down. He lit himself a cigarette.

"You, you talked to her, baba?"

Malindar smiled mysteriously. "So what, my son?"

Bhagirath was terrified.

To talk to the bayen meant certain death.

The thought of his father dying scared the daylights out of him, because he was sure that his stepmother would throw him out.

Malindar said, his voice growing extraordinarily sombre, "She may be a bayen now, but she used to be your mother once."

Bhagirath felt something rise to his throat. A bayen for a mother! Is a bayen a human being then? Hadn't he heard that a bayen raises dead children from the earth, hugs and nurses them? That whole trees dry up the instant a bayen looks at them? And Bhagirath – he, a live boy, born of a bayen's womb? He could think no more.

"She used to be a woman, your mother."

"And your wife?"

27

"Yes, that too," Malindar sighed. "It was bad luck. Hers, yours and mine. Once a bayen, she's no longer human. Which is why I tell you that you don't have a mother."

Bhagirath stared in wonder at his father as they walked back along the mud culvert. He had never heard his father speak in that tone before.

They were not ordinary Doms. They worked in the cremation grounds and the municipality allowed only one Dom family to work there. Malindar's family used to make bric-a-brac out of cane and bamboo, raise poultry on the government farms and make compost out of garbage. Out of the entire Dom community only Malindar knew how to sign his name – an accomplishment that had recently earned him a job in the subdivisional morgue, a government job that entitled him to forty two rupees a month after signing on as Malindar Gangaputta. Besides, as Bhagirath knew, Malindar also bleached skeletons out of unclaimed bodies, using lime and bleaching power. A whole skeleton, or even the skull or the rib cage, meant a lot of money. The morgue official sold the bones to would-be doctors at a handsome profit. The mere ten or fifteen rupees that his father got out of it was enough for him. He had invested the sum in usury and bought some pigs with the interest. His father was a respected man in the community. He went to his subdivisional office in shirt and shoes.

Red-eyed, Malindar stared at the red flag which burned above the bayen's hut like a vermilion dot against the saffron coloured horizon.

"She had everything, when she was your mother, my wife. I gave her striped saris to wear, and silver jewellery. I fed her, I rubbed oil into her hair, her body ... She used to be so afraid of the dark," he muttered. "Did fate have to make a witch out of her? She'd be better off dead. Did you know that no one can take her life except she herself, my son?"

"Who makes a bayen out of a person, father?"

"God."

Malindar glanced around wearily to see if any other shadow hovered near Bhagirath in the midday sun.

A bayen is crafty in her art, like any flower girl in the market. If she is keen on having some child, she walks close by, her face in shadow, in spite of the fierce sun all around. Invisible to mortals, she casts the

28

shadow of her veil on the child as he walks. If the boy dies she chuckles with feigned innocence, "How was I to know? I just tried to make a little shade for him in the heat but then he goes and melts away like butter! Too soft!"

No, there was no shadow of a foul smelling, filthy red veil anywhere near his son. "What is there to fear, my son?" he said, "She'd never do you any harm."

As days went by, Bhagirath's mind began to stray towards the hut. Be it on the paddy field, be it on the pasture with the cows, his mind would rush to the railway tracks, if only to see how terror stricken the bayen was of her loneliness, to see how she put oil in her hair and dried it in the April wind.

He was too afraid to go to her.

Perhaps he would never come back if he did. Perhaps she would turn him into a tree or a stone forever. He only gazed out for days on end. The sky between the Chhatim tree and the bayen's hut seemed like a woman's forehead where the red flag – now limp, now flying in the breeze – burned like a vermilion dot. He had a mad wish to rush to the hut. Then, afraid of his own wish, he swiftly traced his way back home, wondering why no one mistreated him for being a bayen's son.

If you ill treat a bayen's son, your children will die.

Bhagirath's stepmother didn't mistreat him either. In fact, she never showed any emotion for him whatsoever, the chief reason being that she did not have a son. Both her children, Sairavi and Gairabi, were daughters. She had no influence over her husband – first, because she hadn't borne him a son and second because she had such protruding teeth and gums that her lips couldn't cover them. She would say, "My lips won't close at all. It makes me look as if I'm smirking all the time. See to it Gangaputta, be sure to cover my face when I die or else they'll say, "There goes the bucktoothed wife of the Dom."

Jashi did nothing but work all day – cleaning the house, cooking rice, collecting wood, making cowdung cakes for fuel, tending to the pigs and picking lice out of her daughters' hair. She called Bhagirath "Boy." Come eat, boy! Have your bath, boy! – as if theirs was a very formal relationship. If she did not take proper care of him the bayen might kill her daughters by black magic. Also, she knew she would have to depend on Bhagirath for support in her old age.

Sometimes she would sit, chin in hand, her lips baring her prominent gums, terrified that the bayen was working a magic spell on her daughters that very moment or making their effigies out of clay. At those times Jashi looked uglier than usual.

Malindar had deliberately married the ugliest girl in the community because when he had married the loveliest one, she had turned out to be a witch. Everyone knew that Malindar had loved his first wife deeply. Perhaps it was that love which had prompted him to tell Bhagirath everything about Chandibayen, his mother.

One day, they were walking along the railway tracks. Malindar had a parcel of meat under his arms. It was one of his strange weaknesses that he could not kill the pigs he raised himself. He raised them and sold them to others and when he needed some meat, he had to get a portion of the meat from his customer. "Shall we sit a while under this tree, eh?" he asked his thirteen year old son, almost apologetically. Then he sat down, his back against the trunk of the banyan tree.

After a while Bhagirath asked, "This is the place the robbers go by, isn't it, Father?"

Malindar liked to listen to him and often felt himself unworthy of his son.

Those days, the evening trains passing Sonadanga, Palasi, Dhubulia and other places were often robbed. They came in all shapes and sizes, these robbers ... posing as gentlemen, poor students, refugees, settlers or houseowners, to get an entry into the compartments. Then, at a predetermined place and time they would pull the emergency chain and make the train stop in the dark. Their accomplices would rush in from the fields outside. They would loot all they could, beat up and even kill passengers, if necessary, before disappearing. This banyan tree, in particular, was their favourite haunt after dark. This is what made Bhagirath ask about the robbers.

Bhagirath went to the government primary school. Once, his teacher had made them paint the wall magazine. He had sketched out the letters himself and had made the boys colour them. It was from the magazine that Bhagirath had come to know that after the Untouchability Act of 1955, there were no longer any untouchables in India. He also learnt that there was something called the Constitution of India, which says at the very beginning that all are equal. The magazine still hung on the wall but Bhagirath and his kind knew that their co-students, as well as the teachers, liked them to sit a bit apart, though none but the very poor and needy from the "lower" castes came to the school. There are schools, and then there are schools. In spite of this, the fact was that Bhagirath now spoke a bit differently, his accent had changed.

But, Malindar's mind was elsewhere. His eyes scoured the bare fields and beyond, as if in search of something. "My son," he said, "I used to be a hard and unkind man, but your mother was soft, very soft. She cried often. What irony!"

Irony indeed! It was as if God came and turned the tables, in a single day, on the Dom community. Chandi became a bayen, a heartless childhunter. Malindar grew gentle. He had to. If one of a family turns inhuman and disappears beyond the magic portals of the supernatural, the other has to stay behind and make a man of himself.

Malindar grabbed his son's hand. "Why should you not know what everyone knows about your mother," he told him. "Your mother's name was Chandidasi Gangadasi, she used to bury dead children. She was a descendant of Kalu Dom. She belonged to a race of cremation attendants, the Gangaputras. They were known as Gangaputras and Gangadasis, men and women who cremated the dead ones on the banks of the Ganga. Any river was the Ganga to them, in reverence to the great river."

Malindar would carry bamboo trunks and slice wood in the cremation ground while Chandi worked in the graveyard meant for the burial of children, a legacy of their respective pasts. The graveyard lay to the north of the village, overlooked by a banyan tree beside a lake. In those days if a child died before it was five years of age, its body had to be buried instead of being cremated. Chandi's father used to dig the graves and spread thorn bushes over them to save the dead from the marauding jackals. "Hoi! Hoi, there!" his drunken voice would thunder ominously in the dark. Chandi's father survived almost entirely on liquor and hashish. On Saturday he would go round the village carrying a thali in his hand. "I am your servant," he would call out, "I am a Gangaputra. May I have my rations, please?"

The villagers were frightened of him. They would keep young children out of his way, silently fill his thali and go away. One day a fair girl with light eyes and reddish hair came instead of him.

"I am Chandi," she announced, "daughter of the Gangaputra. My father is dead. Give me his rations instead."

"Will you do your father's work then?"

"Yes. I will bury the dead and guard the graves."

"Aren't you afraid?"

"I am not."

The word Fear was foreign to Chandi. She could understand why parents cried when their children died, but the dead had to be buried, they couldn't be kept at home. That was what her job was, simple as that. What was fearsome or heartless about it? It must surely have been ordained by God himself? At least the Gangaputras had no hand in it. Why should people detest or fear them so much?

This was the Chandi that Malindar was to marry.

Even in those early days, Malindar was in the bone business with the morgue official. The bones from the charnel house were used as fertilizer and were expensive as well. Malindar had money as well as courage. At night he used to return home shouting across the fields "I am not scared of anybody! I am a fire eater. I have no fear of anyone!"

One night he came upon Chandi, roaming alone, under the banyan tree, lantern in hand.

"Hey there!" he said. "Aren't you afraid of the dark?"

Chandi burst into peals of laughter which surprised him.

That very April he married her. The next April Bhagirath was born.

One day Chandi came back crying, carrying Bhagirath in her arms. "They have stoned me, Gangaputta, they said I meant evil."

"How dare they?" Malindar stopped fencing the yard and almost danced with rage. "Who dares stone the wife of Malindar Gangaputta?" he roared.

"Now, will you stop raising a row over it, and sit here for a while?"

"Oh, oh, oh!"

"Where is the shirt for Bhagirath?"

Malindar had forgotten.

"Tomorrow, I promise," he said. "A red shirt for my son, a red sari and a yellow blouse for the son's mother!"

"No, no, not for me. It only makes people envious and cast an evil eye."

"Don't I know that? At the primary school, they were always skipping classes. I alone learnt how to sign my name. They were envious. I landed a government job, more envy. I married a golden doll of a wife, a descendant of the great Kalu Dom, still more envy. I built a new hut, and had two bighas of land for share cropping, how could they help being envious? Bastards! Get as envious as you like! I can take it all, I, Malindar Gangaputta. I'll send my son to school — over there, beyond the railway tracks."

As he spoke, Chandi who sat and looked fixedly at him, grew silent.

"I have not the heart to do it any more," she said at last. "I have not the heart to pick up the spade. But it is God's will. What can I do?" In wonder she shook her head and looked down at her limbs.

If there had been a male member of her father's family, he would have done the job. But there was none. She was a Gangaputra, keeper of the cremation grounds. She belonged to the family of the ancient Kalu Dom, he who gave shelter to the great king Harishchandra when he lost his kingdom. When the king became a servant, a chandal in the burning ghat, it was Kalu Dom who had employed him. When the king regained his kingdom and the ocean-girdled earth was his, he began to dole out large territories. "What have you got for us?" asked a voice booming large across the royal court.

It was the ancient Gangaputra. His type could never speak in a low voice nor hear one, because the fire of the pyres roared eternally in their ears.

"What do you mean?"

"You have ordained cattle for the brahmins, daily alms for the monks. What have you for us?"

"All the burning ghats of the world are yours."

"Repeat it."

"All the burning ghats of the world are yours."

"Swear it!"

"I swear by God."

The ancient Gangaputra raised his hands and danced in wild joy.

"Ha!" he shouted. "The burning ghats for us ... the burning ghats for us. The world's graveyards for us!"

Being a member of this particular race, could she, Chandi, reject this traditional occupation? Dare she, and let God wreak his wrath on her? Her fear grew greater every day. She would turn her face away after digging a grave.

Her fear and unease remained even after the grave was well covered with prickly bushes. At any time the legendary fire-mouthed jackal might steal in and start digging away with large paws to get at the body inside.

God ... God ... God ... Chandi would weep softly and rush back home. She would light a lamp and sit praying for Bhagirath. At those times she also prayed for each and every child in the village that each should live forever. This was a weakness that she had developed of late. Because of her own child, she now felt a deep pain for every dead child. Her breasts ached with milk if she stayed too long in the graveyard. She silently blamed her father as she dug the graves. He had no right to bring her to this work.

"Get hold of somebody else for this work, respected ones!" she said one day. "I am not fit for this any more ..."

No one in the village seemed to listen. Not even Malindar, whose dealings in corpses, skin and bone — objects of abhorrence to others — had hardened him. "Scared of false shadows!" he had scoffed at her. If she cried too hard he would say, "Well, no one's left in your family to do this job for you."

It was around this time that the terrible thing happened. One of Malindar's sisters had come for a visit. She had a little daughter called Tukni who became quite devoted to Chandi. The village was suffering from a severe attack of smallpox at the time. Neither Chandi nor her people ever went for a vaccination. Instead they relied on appeasing the goddess Sheetala, the deity controlling epidemics. When Tukni got the pox, Chandi, accompanied by her sister-in-law and carrying the little girl in her arms, went to pay homage to the goddess. The temple of the goddess was a regular affair set up by the coolies from Bihar who had once worked on the railway tracks. There was also a regular priest.

As fate would have it, the little girl died a few days later, though not in Chandi's house. Everyone, including the girl's parents, blamed the death on Chandi.

"What, me?"

"Oh, yes, you."

"Not me, for God's sake!" she pleaded with the Doms.

"Who else?"

"Never!" she thundered out, "I swear upon the head of my own child that I've never wished any ill of Tukni, or of any other child. You know my lineage."

Suddenly those people, those craven, superstitious people, lowered their eyes. Someone whispered, "What about the milk that spilled out of your breasts as you were piling earth on Tukni's grave?"

"Oh, the fools that you are!" She stared at them in wonder and hatred.

"All right," she said after a pause, "I don't care if the rage of my forefathers descends upon me. I quit this job from this very day."

"Quit your job!"

"Yes. I'll let you cowards guard the graves. I have wanted to leave for a long time. The Gangaputta will get a government job soon. I need not continue with this rotten work any more."

Silencing every voice, she returned home. She asked Malindar if he would get a room at his new place of work. "Let's go there. Do you know what they call me?"

It was just to calm her down, just to pacify her with a joke, that he said with a loud laugh, "And what do they call you? A bayen?"

Chandi started trembling violently. She clutched at the wooden pillar that supported the roof. Excitement, rage and sorrow made her scream at him, "How could you utter that word, you, with a son of your own? Me, a bayen?"

"Oh, shut up!" Malindar shouted.

It was dead noon and the time for evil to cast its spell on human beings. It was a time when terrible rage and jealousy could easily take hold of any

35

empty stomach and uncooled head. Malindar knew well the ways of his people.

"I am not a bayen! Oh, I am not a bayen!!"

Chandi's anguished cry travelled far and wide on raven's wings through the hot winds that reached every nook and corner of the village.

She stopped crying as suddenly as she had begun. "Let us run away somewhere when it's dark," she pleaded with him.

"Where?"

"Just somewhere."

"But where?"

"I do not know." She took Bhagirath in her arms and crept near Malindar. "Come closer," she said, "Let me lay my head on your chest. I am so afraid. I am so afraid to have thrown away my forefather's job. Why am I so frightened today? I feel that I'll never see you or Bhagirath any more. God! I am afraid."

It was here that Malindar stopped speaking and wiped his eyes. "Now that I look back, my son, it seems as if it was God who put those words in her mouth that day."

"What happened next?"

For a few days Chandi just sat as if dazed. She pottered about the house a bit and often sat with Bhagirath in her arms, singing. She burned a lot of incense and lit lamps about the house and had an air of listening closely to something or the other.

Two months passed by uneventfully. No one came to call Chandi to work. There had hardly been any work either. They lived very peacefully, the three of them. Chandi became whole again. "There ought to be some other arrangement for the dead children," she said. "The present one is horrible."

"There will be, by and by," Malindar said. "Things are changing."

"How am I to know if I did the right thing? You see, some nights I seem to hear my father raise his call."

"You hear him?"

"I seem to hear his Hoi, there!, just as if he were chasing the jackals off the graves."

"Shut up Chandi ..."

Fear grew in Malindar. Didn't he sometimes fear that perhaps Chandi was slowly changing into a witch? Some nights she woke up with a start and seemed to listen to dead children crying in their graves. Perhaps it was true what people were saying? Perhaps it would be best to go to the town after all.

The Dom community did not forget her. The Doms were keeping an eye on her, to her complete ignorance. Covertly or otherwise, a society can maintain its vigil if it wants to. There is nothing a society cannot do.

That's how one stormy night when Malindar was deep in drunken slumber, his courtyard filled with people. One of them, Ketan, an uncle of sorts of Chandi, called him out, "Come and see for yourself whether your wife is a bayen or not."

Stupefied, Malindar sat up and stared at them with sleep-laden eyes.

"Come out and see, you son of a bitch! You are keeping a bayen for a wife while our children's lives are at stake."

Malindar came out. He could see the burial ground under the banyan tree humming with lamps, torches and people who stood milling around in silence.

"Chandi, you!"

There she was, a sickle in her hand, a lantern burning beside her, a heap of thorn bushes stacked on one side.

"I was trying to cover the holes with these."

"Why, why did you come out?"

"The jackals had suddenly stopped their cries. Something in me said, there they are! Right at the holes, pawing for the bodies."

"You're a bayen!" The villagers raised their chant in awe.

"There is no one to watch over the dead."

"You are a bayen!"

"It's the job of my forefathers. What do these people know about it?"

"You are a bayen!"

"No, no, I am not a bayen! I have a son of my own. My breasts are heavy with milk for him. I am not a bayen. Why, Gangaputta, why don't you tell them, you know best."

Malindar stared, as if entranced, at the dimly lit figure, at the breasts thrust out against her rain soaked clothes. His mind was seared with pain, something whispered within him, "Don't go near, Malindar. Go near a snake if you will, a fire even but not now, not to her, though you may have loved her. Don't go, or something terrible will happen."

Malindar stepped forward and looked at Chandi with bloodshot eyes. He let out a yell like a beast, "O-ho-ooo! A bayen you are! Who was it in the grave when you were nursing with milk? O-ho-ooo!"

"Gangaputta! Oh God!"

The terrible cry that tore out of her seemed to frighten the dead underground, her father's restless spirit and even that of the ancient Dom, Kalu, whose cry would rend the sky and the earth when a human being was banished from the human world to the condemned world of the supernatural.

Malindar rushed to get the drum that had belonged to his father-in-law and ran back to the graveyard. He shouted as he beat the drum, "I, Malindar Gangaputta, hereby declare that my wife is a bayen, a bayen!"

"What happened next?" asked Bhagirath.

"Next, my son? She was forced to live alone at Beltala. As afraid as she once was to live alone, she is all alone now. Hush, listen how the bayen sings."

A strange strain of music floated up to them from afar, accompanied by the beat of a tin can. The song seemed to have no words at first but gradually the words became distinct.

Come sleep, come to my bed of rags,
My child-god sleeps in my lap,
The elephants and horses at the palace gates,
The dog Jumra in the ash heap.

Bhagirath knew the song. It was the song that his stepmother sang to make her daughters sleep.

The song entered his soul, mingled in his blood and reverberated in his ears like some inscrutable pain.

"Let's go home, son ..."

Malindar led a dazed Bhagirath back home.

A few days later Bhagirath rushed to the dead pond at noon. He heard the sound of the tin.

The shadow of the bayen trembled in the water. The bayen was not looking at him. Her eyes lowered, she was filling the pitcher.

"Don't you have another sari? Would you like a sari that is not torn like this one? Want my dhoti?"

The bayen was silent. She had her face turned aside.

"Would you like to wear nice clothes?"

"The son of Gangaputta had better go home."

"I ... I go to school now. I am a good boy."

"Don't talk to me. I am a bayen. Even my shadow is evil. Doesn't the son of Gangaputta know that?"

"I am not afraid."

"It's high noon, now. Young children shouldn't be at large in this heat Let the boy go home."

"Aren't you afraid to live alone?"

"Afraid? No, I am not afraid of anything. Why should a bayen be afraid to stay alone?"

"Then what makes you cry?"

"Me, cry!"

"I have heard you."

"He has heard me? Cry?" Her crimson shadow trembled in the water. Her eyes were full. Her voice cracked as she said, "Let the son of Gangaputta go home and swear never, never to come near the bayen. Or ... or ... I will tell Gangaputta!"

Bhagirath saw her turn back and race away along the mud culvert, her hair swirling about her face, her crimson sari fluttering in the air.

He sat alone for a long time by the pond, till the waters became still again. He couldn't recall the song.

On her part, the bayen sat in silence in her hut, thinking she knew-not-what. A long while later she raised herself and drew out a broken piece of mirror.

"I am only a shadow of myself!" she muttered incoherently. She tried to run the comb through her hair. It was impossibly matted.

Why did the child talk about nice clothes? He was too young then to remember now. What should it matter to him, good decent clothes for her?

She frowned hard in an attempt to collect her thoughts. It had been a long time since she had thought about anything. Nothing was left but the rustle of the leaves, the whistling of winds and the rattling of the trains – sounds that had muddled up all her thoughts.

Somehow she had a concrete thought today – the child was in for some terrible disaster. Suddenly she felt a very wifely anger at the thoughtlessness of Malindar. Whose duty was it now to look after the child? Who had to protect him from the witch's eyes?

She rose, lit a lantern and took the road. She hurried along the railway tracks. There was the level crossing, the linesman's cabin. Malindar, on his way back from work, would turn here and take the mud culvert. As she walked towards it, she saw them. There were people doing something with the tracks. No, they were piling up bamboo sticks on the tracks. The five-up Lalgola Passenger train was due that evening with the Wednesday mail bag. It meant a lot of money. They had been waiting for the loot for a long time.

"Who are you?"

She raised the lantern and swung it near her face.

The men looked up, startled, with fear dilated eyes and ashen faces. She had never seen the people of her community look so frightened before.

"It is the bayen!"

"So you are piling bamboos, ah? You would rob the train, eh? What, running away from fear of me? Ha! Throw away these sticks first, or you are done for!"

They could not undo what had been done – clear the tracks, prevent the disaster. They could not. This is how society is, this is how it works. It was like when they had made her a witch with much fanfare and beating of drums.

The rain lashed her as she picked up the lantern. She was so helpless. What could she do? If she were a witch with supernatural powers, would not her servants, the demons of the dark, obey her bidding and stop the train? What could she do now, helpless as she was?

She started running along the tracks, towards the train, waving at it wildly in a vain bid to stop it.

"Don't come any further, don't! There's a heap of bamboo piled ahead!"

She continued to scream till the roar of the train drowned her voice and the train's light swallowed her up.

Chandi's name spread far and wide for her heroic self-sacrifice that had prevented a major train disaster. Even the government people came to hear of it. When her body left the morgue, the Officer in Charge, accompanied by the Block Development Officer, came to Malindar's house.

"The Railway Department will announce a medal for Chandi Gangadasi, Malindar. I know all about you, you see. She used to live alone, but there must be someone to receive it on her behalf. It was a brave deed, a real brave deed. Everyone is full of praise. She was your wife?"

Everyone was silent. People looked at one another, scratched their necks in embarrassment and looked down. Somebody whispered, "Yes sir, she was one of us."

This announcement astonished Bhagirath so much that he looked from one face to another. So they were recognizing her at last?

"Well, the government cannot give the cash award to all of you at the same time."

"Give it to me, sir." Bhagirath came forward.

"And who are you?"

"She was my mother."

"Mother?"

"Yes sir," said Bhagirath, and the officer started taking it all down. "My name is Bhagirath Gangaputta. My father, the revered Malindar Gangaputta. Residence, Domtoli, village Daharhati ... my mother ...," he paused and then, very distinctly, "My mother, the late Chandidasi Gangadasi ... (Bhagirath broke into loud sobs) ... my mother, the late Chandidasi Gangadasi, sir. Not a bayen. She was never a bayen, my mother."

"Bayen" was originally written in Bangla. This translation by Mahua Bhattacharya was first published in Geeta Dharmarajan ed., *Separate Journeys*, March 1998 by Katha and Garutmän.

Urmila Pawar

A CHILDHOOD TALE

TRANSLATED BY JAHNAVI PHALKEY
AND KEERTI RAMACHANDRA

W rite something for children, said the letter from the respected editor of a children's magazine. Arre baapre ...! It was not going to be easy to become a little child and write for children, so I put the letter aside and became engrossed in the growing work, but ... who knows when, my childhood stole upon me and perched itself on my neck like a ghost. It didn't just sit upon my neck, it turned the hands of the clock back, thirty five years, and dumped me in enemy territory – among my enemies of thirty five years ago!

When I was a child I considered all older people enemies. Probably all small children think this way, but my enemies were of a different kind altogether. I had four major enemies. Enemy number one was my father, number two, my mother, three, my brother and my fourth enemy was my teacher, Herlekar guruji. These four enemies laid the foundation of my life and I am what I am today, because of them.

There were a few insignificant people, whom I looked upon as my enemies, because they always picked on me. They carried tales about me and believed that my mother should not send me out of the house at all. "This brat of yours plucks the tondli from the bunds ..." Or then, "You wretch, if you throw stones at the bor tree or the standing crops, I will break your leg and let you have it." Or, "You there ... go away ... go far away ... you might touch me ..." In this way they showed their dislike of me.

I didn't bother much about these minor enemies, but I had to deal with the four big ones every day. The four of them waited to pounce on me. Enemy number one, my father, died early and I was released from one of the fearsome foursome. But of course the terrible threesome remained.

I was studying in the third standard when my father died. I remember him very well. If someone had asked me to draw a picture of him, just the two colours, black and white, would have been enough. Father was thin, short and dark, a white dhoti, white khamis, a black coat, a Gandhi topi on his head – this was his attire. His eyes were always wide open, glaring. They were black and white, his teeth were white ... where was the need of another colour?

You know how the tiny crabs scuttle around on the sand? Father walked like that, constantly running around here and there. In the hot weather, in the rainy season, even when it was neither rainy nor sunny, Father always carried a black umbrella. It seemed like the umbrella was his third hand. It often landed soundly across our backs.

Since Father was a schoolmaster of those times, he was obviously a "beater." He did not just beat us, he lost control once he started. He was the only educated person in our wadi, and just how much do you think he had studied? Up to the seventh class! What was so great about passing the seventh standard, who knows. Some old heads from our community made much of him because he was educated despite belonging to a backward caste. And he puffed up with pleasure at their praise. He went around telling everyone to study, to get an education, as if he was advising a treatment for arthritis. When he came home, he would make us sit with our books in front of the lantern till we felt our necks would get twisted. If we didn't, he would thrash us. Our foolish mother would merely watch him.

Once, however, my aunt from the village actually managed to embarrass him. My father had gone to the village and had started beating her son, his nephew, for not going to school. Said my aunt, "Let him not study. What's it to you?" But my father ignored her and slapped him a couple more times. My aunt split open a ratamba and rubbed the bright red slices on to her son's bottom. Then she began to scream, "The uncle has beaten up my child and now he's bleeding ..." And beating her mouth with her palm, she began to howl. The elders in the village started abusing my father. Scared, he ran home, like a coward.

There was one interesting thing, though. My father was the priest of our community. He would examine the panchang, conduct the Satyanarayana puja, and solemnize weddings. These rituals had been performed by his father, his grandfather and his great grandfather before him. Father carried out these duties in addition to his job at school, so he was hardly ever at home. When he did come home, he would bring a coconut and some rice tied in new cloth. Mother would untie the bundle in front of us children as we stared at it with crow's eyes. Dried dates, pieces of coconut, almonds, walnuts and all kinds of other things were mixed with the rice. We just waited to attack the bundle. One of us would snatch the cloth and cry out, "A khamis for me. I want a gavan." When a sufficient number of cloth pieces were collected, khamis and gavans of assorted pieces were stitched together and our bodies clothed in new dresses. So what if one sleeve was of one colour, the other of another! There would be a paisa or two, or some small change in the rice which we tried to grab, but Father would tap us sharply on the head and say, "Is that your father's money?" Whose father did it belong to, who knows!

Don't even ask how miserly my father was. He wouldn't spend a paisa, even on himself. Not even to have a "single cha" in a hotel. If his dhoti was torn, he stitched it and wore it. His torn shirt he hid under the coat. If we ever asked for money for something, even a pencil, he would get angry. When he was angry, he looked like the demon in the moon, because of his white and black eyes.

He enjoyed torturing us children. When he came home he would make us drink castor oil. At night, by the light of the lantern, he would unwrap the small chinapud packets, mix them with jaggery and roll into berry sized balls. If one swallowed those balls after dinner and drank castor oil in the morning, then not just the worms in one's stomach, even their grandfather would be dead. Perhaps the worms inside us died just looking at the bloodshot gleam in Father's eyes as he sat rolling that mixture between his fingers. Actually, we did not even need to drink the castor oil in the morning. But we had to.

Once, I just couldn't swallow the chinapud pellet so I started bawling. My father got up and gave me one kick on my chest. I fell backwards and the tablet slipped right down my throat. Immediately he burst into a guffaw. I was furious. I wished that he would never come back from whichever school he went to.

Next to our school was a Maruti temple. I felt very secure because of the temple. Whenever I did not feel like going to school, I would camp inside the temple with my school bag. Often I would say, "God, please don't bring my father home."

God must have heard my prayer. I was in the third standard when my father fell ill. Mother used to say that the blood had become water inside his stomach. Once when I went to the hospital, he was covered with a white bedsheet. I could not see Father, only his stomach which stuck out like a pregnant woman's. We went and stood by his pillow and he started crying like a little child. He kept repeating to mother, "Educate the children."

That day I felt that Father should not die. He should live. He had been so keen that my older sister should also study. Though he couldn't afford it, he had kept her in somebody's house so that she could be educated. But she turned out to be thick headed and she was married off. I was not going to be like that. I wanted to say to Father, I will study, I will go to school, but you don't die. But he died. It was a Friday. We sat around his body all night. Everyone had remained awake through the night. The next day, Saturday, we had morning school. I don't know what came over me, but I packed my school bag and asked mother, "Aai, can I go to school?" She only turned her face away. Never before or after that, did I ever show such enthusiasm for school.

Father was gone. Aai went around looking like a poor wretch. I thought this was a good sign, for she wouldn't scream at me or tell me to go to school. I would be free to run wild. But that was not to be! Before going, Father had given Aai the mantra, "Educate the children." That was it. Mother started behaving like she was possessed. I began to think Father was preferable to her, in the role of educator.

Aai was also skinny like Father, but tall and fair, with a permanently mournful expression. She wore a tattered nine yard sari that only came up to her knees. Our house was right on the road. Children could be seen going to and from the school. Aai sat in the courtyard weaving baskets – big ones, small ones, wide ones, and shallow ones. Even when one woke up in the morning, she could be seen sitting in the courtyard weaving a winnowing fan or sieve. One could see her like that till one went to sleep at night. In between she would meddle around near the kitchen fire. That's it. If it was father's legs that moved, with Aai, it was her hands.

Sometimes the children would stand on the road and watch her weave. They would stare at her. I would feel embarrassed. Their mothers looked like beautiful goddesses in their lovely clothes, jewellery and sweet, loving smiles. But Aai was always angry and yelling at me, "Go to school ... Study!" She could not read a single letter, and she spoke incorrect Marathi but she bossed around like a teacher. If, for some silly part I had played in the school fair, I won a prize – a pencil, or a box of chalk or a ruler –

47

I would take it to my mother. She would show no appreciation, no pleasure, merely say dryly, "That's good!"

When it came to stinginess, she outdid my father. She cooked rice and a watery dal for meals. Occasionally, a vegetable was made, but it was just enough to cover a tamarind seed. She mixed bran with flour and served us these bhakris with prawns, dry fish or something salted and roasted. Even on festivals she made no sweet. When Father was alive, once in a while she made kheer with jaggery and broken rice, but now she stopped doing that. She only shed tears. My friends' mothers would give them such tempting food in their tiffin boxes. My mouth watered, but it made no difference to Aai.

Leave alone indulging the palate, we did not even know what it was to dress up. Once a week Aai washed our hair with washing soda and boiling water, scrubbing the scalp and also the ears. When the hair was dry, she oiled it and ran a fine toothed comb hard through it so it picked out lice and nits. Then she pulled the hair back and plaited it tightly like a firmly twisted rope. During this ritual, I would see glow worms and fireflies dancing before my eyes! Then she would tie the end of the plait with the border, torn off one of her saris. For a whole week the plait would hang on my back like a scorpion's tail. My friends would have bows of colourful satin and plastic ribbons in their hair. They would deck themselves up and preen in front of the mirror. But if we even peeped into the mirror, Aai would say, "Why do you look into the mirror again and again? The face of the person before you will tell you how you look."

Aai looked very simple and straightforward, but she was a big liar. She was also very theatrical. Sometimes an angry customer shouted, "Where is the basket that we had asked you to make? You said you would give it today, why isn't it ready? Now give back the advance we had paid ..." On such occasions, Aai would declare me ill. She would whine and plead, "This little one of mine was very sheeck. I didn't know if she would live or ... that's why I couldn't, but I will definitely finish your work today. Forgive me this one time," she would cry. When in fact, I was fine and healthy. At times, women from the village, including my aunt and her

---

Sheeck: a vernacularized pronounciation for sick.

daughters-in-law came to borrow four to eight annas. Aai had the money but didn't give it. She lied. Cried even.

If she had to deliver the baskets to somebody's house, she called out to me in a sweet tone, "Dhaktyaa ..." As I was the youngest, she fondly addressed me as dhaktya. When I heard that tone, I knew what she was up to. She would call me several times but when I did not respond she would hit me. The same Aai who had sounded so loving a moment ago, would turn into a teeth gnashing witch and shout, "You whore, you just want to eat ... don't want to work. Get up now or I will scald your face. Go and deliver so-and-so's supa, and give Tutu her haara."

This Tutu was the granddaughter of king Thiba of Burma. The British had imprisoned him in Ratnagiri. He had a daughter called Payagi. Everyone called her Phaya and Tutu was her daughter. The granddaughter of the king lived in a hut, collecting cowdung cakes. Aai used to tell us that when the king and Tutu's mother died, nobody from Burma came to take her back, and nobody paid any attention to her here. Tutu wore just a long skirt and a blouse. She was fat and short with a yellowish complexion, a broad face and a flat nose. I did not like Tutu at all.

But Tutu made very beautiful flowers from coloured paper. She used to sprinkle glitter on them and sell them to the village women who came daily to the Ratnagiri market. They bought the flowers from her and wore them in their hair.

Tutu was my mother's friend. Sometimes she came over to chat with Aai. Their hands and their mouths both worked at the same time. Tutu made flowers. Aai wove baskets. If Aai started scolding me, Tutu would also abuse me. Where was the need for her to do this? But she did. She said, "This girl should be sent to herd somebody's cattle. Or then, give her to my Digya." And her broad face would spread out in a smile. I used to get really angry with her. Someone should kick her back to Burma, I'd think, or at least a dog must bite her, hard.

When she talked to others Aai seemed very gentle, cow-like. "Yes, ji. Yes, ji" she would nod and smile innocently, but when she shouted at me, she would get new strength, her movements became quick, like lightning. If I was ill, if I had a high fever then she would cuddle me for a while, put saltwater towels on my forehead. Her touch felt nice. But she was very restless. She would keep muttering, I have so much work ... weave the wretched baskets, prepare fodder ... She would peck at the words like a hen.

Oh yes, I was telling you that Aai would send me to deliver the baskets to people's homes. Those people would make me stand outside the door, sprinkle water on the baskets and supas before picking them up. They would drop the money onto my palm from above. Was their hand going to burn and turn black if it touched mine, I wondered? If there was a child from my class in the house, I'd feel so ashamed, it was worse than death itself. And I would tell myself, today I will teach my mother a lesson. I won't go to school!

But as soon as I reached home, mother would know what was in my mind. She was a proper mind reader. Putting a lump of jaggery on my palm, she would say, sweetly, "Go, go to school ... When you come back I will give you money to buy chana." I believed her each time, but she was an absolute liar. She would keep putting me off, "Not today, tomorrow ..." and keep cheating me. If I persisted, she would lose her temper and punish me. Then I too would be angry. I would think up all sorts of different excuses for avoiding school. I would say I was going to school but sit in the temple instead.

The temple priest would come there, bathe the Maruti idol, perform the puja, and give us prasad. I liked the pujari very much. He was very fair, like the marble statue of Ram. I loved to look at his black eyes, black hair, the pinkish ear lobes and soles of his feet. He usually wore only a half-pant and had a sacred thread across his bare chest. A long red mark was drawn vertically on his forehead. And his smile was very sweet.

Once we were in the temple, playing. The pujari was performing the puja. A long time went by but the pujari did not come out. We sat there, on the temple steps waiting for the prasad. Much later, he opened the door and Ulgavva, the daughter of a Kombati came out looking scared, as if she was about to cry ... Right behind her came the pujari but he hurried away without giving us any prasad. I do not know why, but ever since then, I began to fear the pujari.

Why would Ulgavva be crying, I wanted to ask my mother that day.

Kombati: one of the lower castes in Maharashtra.

But then my secret that I was at the temple and not at school, would have been out. Aai would have beaten me and my enemy number three, my brother, would have joined in.

Once because I did not want to go to school, what I did was, I hid my only nice frock in the corner behind the grinding stone among some rags. As usual, Aai served me dal and rice and said, "The school bell has rung. Hurry up." The school was quite close to our house. But even if it weren't, my mother would have heard the bell and the school prayer from anywhere.

"I can't find my frock," I whimpered. She guessed what I was up to and called my brother. He was getting ready for school. Both of them began to search for my frock ... This brother of mine was only four years older than me. Of the four children before him, one brother was dead, the older sister was married and lived with her in-laws, while the remaining two were very docile. They never hit me but they didn't pamper me either. I liked that. This brother, though, had taken a vow, almost, to beat me, like Afzalkhan's decision to kill Shivaji. He was strong, not fat but wiry. His hands used to really hurt. He was very quick to grab me and present me before Aai. No matter how fast I ran, he always caught me. I wished a dog would bite his leg as well ... Well, then, these two searched all the corners of the house, they shook out the quilts hanging on the clothesline, they looked among the tattered gunny bags, ropes and coils of string in the loft. As they searched, they chattered continuously and threw angry glances at me.

I too was getting angry with my brother. When it was time for his school, shouldn't he have left, quietly? But no. Nobody even scolded him for being late because he was in high school. If his teacher ever shouted at him, he would immediately blame it on me ... What a brat I was, how I troubled my mother and skipped school ... How he had to take me and make me sit there ... His stupid teacher listened to him. You are doing the right thing, he would say. That's why I say they were all my enemies!

I wished that Herlekar master from my school would really thrash these two. I would paint this scene in my imagination. At that moment too, I was saying this to myself and eyeing the grinding stone in the corner, when my brother came forward and kicked aside the heavy stone and saw the frock lying behind it. Then what happened? He pulled it out as if it were a bag full of gems from Alibaba's cave. With a glint in his eye, he held it up, "Aai, look!"

"You miserable wretch, why do you torture me like this?" Aai shouted. Then both gave me two hard slaps, made me wear the frock and holding me firmly by the neck, my brother took me to the school. He looked like a mankapya, a ghost that would break my neck, at that moment. This "slit-neck ghost" does not have a head. It has eyes on its chest and walks with its hands and legs spread out, kicking aside anything that came in its way. That's how my brother was moving, dragging me through the ditches on the road, the gutters, thorny bushes, whatever else there was on the way ... This mankapya stood me outside my classroom and called out to the teacher from the door itself "Guruji, mother has requested you to let her sit in the class. She will not be late from tomorrow ..." That's all he said, pushed me in front of the fire eating demon of a vetal and disappeared.

This vetal was my enemy number four, Herlekar guruji. He was cast in the same mould as my father. Even to look at. If Father were to have worn trousers and a khamis, he would have looked exactly like Herlekar. There was a difference between them, but very little. Herlekar guruji was a little taller and his eyes were red. Just looking at those red eyes would make me tremble and almost wet my pants.

There was my father who would beat me if I did not study, but Herlekar guruji would punish me even if I did. If I sat very quietly in the classroom, he would say, after he had finished writing the tables on the blackboard, "Get up! Clean the blackboard," or "Go throw out the garbage," "Collect the cowdung from the verandah and take it away" ... He always made me sit in the last row.

You should come to school on time. Step into the classroom as soon as the short recess bell rings. You should be inside immediately after the noon break ends, guruji warned us sternly. If I made a small slip, that was it. I was soundly thrashed. He used to beat the others as well but a little less. My mother, she had issued a proclamation to the teachers in the school to beat me. She was convinced that if I had to gain knowledge, I had to be beaten. Because she knew for a fact that Father used to beat his students. Besides, she had heard me sing, very tunefully, *Chadi lage cham cham* from the movie, *Shyamchi Aai!*–

So, as I was saying, when mankapya handed me over to the vetal, the vetal thundered, "Hold your ears and stand!" Then he shouted, "Bend forward!" He was not yet satisfied so he said, "Get up, go collect the cowdung from the veranda and throw it away."

Stray animals from the area would drop dung in the school courtyard, because it was open. Each class took turns to pick up the dung. When it was our class, it was always me. I had to do it. Because we had this wonderful cow called Kapila. Aai had brought her from the village to pray to the thirty three crore gods in Kapila's stomach. Guruji said it was Kapila who always dirtied the school courtyard, that's why it was my duty to gather it. But today was not the turn for my class, yet Guruji was making me do it.

I saw my Friends – what friends, they were actually my enemies – looking at me and giggling. I don't know what happened to me but I did not move. Guruji yelled, "Can't you hear me?" I continued to stand still. I realized that Guruji was going to hit me ... He got up ... I could feel the heat of his anger but my legs would not move. Aai used to say that when you see a python in front of you, you cannot move. I felt like that ...

Guruji came close, very close and slapped me hard across my face, screaming, "Get out of here." I started bawling, and ran straight home, howling. Aai was sitting in the courtyard, weaving her baskets. When she saw me crying, she stood up and asked, "What happened? What's the matter, why are you crying?" I could say nothing, just continued sobbing. When Aai saw my swollen cheek with the mark of guruji's five fingers on it, she lost control. "Guruji hit you? Just wait, I will show him ..." she declared and started abusing him. "Should I go to the school?" she muttered to herself.

I badly wanted Aai to shout at Guruji, fight with him, but I didn't

---

Shyamchi Aai: *Shyamchi Aai* was a film based on the autobiography of Sane Guruji, a social reformer. The song that is referred to *Chadi lage cham cham* literally meaning the(teacher's) rod hits cham cham is enacted by the little boy playing the young Sane Gurujoi, mimicking the teacher in absence.

want her to go to school for that. To tell you the truth, I was ashamed of her torn sari, drawn tightly above her knees, her unkempt hair ... As I sobbed, I watched her, my eyes swollen from crying.

She paced up and down, suddenly sat down, picked up her work, then put it aside and got up. She brushed off the husk from her sari, then as if she remembered something, sat down. This happened twice or thrice. I continued to sob. Then she put alum and turmeric paste on my cheek and asked, "Why did Guruji hit you?"

"I ... because I did not collect the cowdung," I mumbled through my tears.

"Why did he ask you to collect the cowdung?"

"Guruji says Kapila drops dung ..."

"OK you sit here and when you see your teacher going home after school tell me. I will deal with him." Aai sat down. What is she going to do to Herlekar guruji, I wondered. If she comes face to face with him, she will not even open her mouth. Her tongue and her hands work only when it comes to me.

I started feeling sleepy in the afternoon. But I jerked my eyes wide open. Again Aai put the alum and turmeric paste on my cheek. Soon the afternoon passed and the evening bell rang for the school to end. My heart was thudding. When I saw Herlekar guruji approaching amidst the children, I felt even more scared. Slowly, the words slipped from my tongue, "Aai, Guruji."

The moment she heard the words, she threw down the half woven basket, straightened her sari and stood, like a female cobra, with its hood outspread, ready to strike. Just as Guruji appeared she drew her sari on her head and said, "Wait a minute, Guruji ..." Guruji rolled his eyes quickly and looked at her. Arrogantly he asked, "What is it?"

"My daughter studies in your school, right? What did she do today? I mean you beat her so much, see, look at the child's cheek," she said and called me to her and held my face in front of him. I did not have the courage to look at Guruji.

"That ... that ... your white cow ... drops dung in the school ..." he stammered.

"Our cow drops dung, eh? You saw her dropping dung? Guruji, you are so well educated, yet you talk like a small child? Look here, I am not a respectable woman. I live under this tree, by the roadside, with my children, like an exile. Why? So that they can study ... become important people. And you harass the girl like this? Aai was speaking incorrectly, ungrammatically. In a loud voice she was threatening Guruji, "Look here, after this, if your finger so much as touches my daughter, I will see to it that you can never walk on this road ..."

"All right, all right, I too will see ..." Guruji replied as he moved backwards. Then in a flash, he disappeared. By this time many people had gathered around us, staring at my mother's gesticulation and my swollen Hanuman-like face.

After that day, many things became easier ... Collecting dung and Guruji's beating were no longer a part of my fate and destiny. I started going to school on time. But the main thing was that I began to look upon my mother as a tremendous support. And my life got some direction.

"Gosh Seshvachi" was originally written in Marathi. "A Childhood Tale" translated by Jahnavi Phalkey and Keerti Ramachandra was first published in a SPARROW booklet.

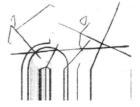

Narain Singh

MARRIED TO SEPARATENESS

TRANSLATED BY GEETA SAHAI, RUPALEE VERMA AND
KATHA FICTION EDITOR

Last week's expedition was to a village. This being his in-law's village, my friend Ram Vichar Pande also came along. Our talks with the boy's grandfather went something like this.

"Where is the girl's mother from?"

"Bhojpur ..."

"Which village?"

"Sonpatia."

"Whose house?"

"..."

"Why are you silent Thikedar Saheb? What is the name of the girl's maternal grandfather?"

"What can one say Thakur Saheb? Truth is, no one in Dilip Babu's in-laws' family is alive today," Pande, who was sitting cross-legged on a low stool crushing the tobacco in his left palm with his right thumb replied, signalling me to keep quiet.

"Arre, Pande Babu, when alive, his father-in-law must have had a name, an identity. Even now some heir, some distant relation must be alive, or do you mean to say that the entire village has been left childless? Just four kilometers away from Sonpatia is my in-law's village. To this day I remember so many of them ... Girija Babu who had an elephant, ex-MLA Deviki Misir, and that Jugal Teli ... who became a millionaire by opening an oil factory in Buxar. And ... then ... there was that chamar, Shivbachan and his gazetted officer son Mohan Ram, whose daughter was picked by some babuan and kept at his place ... some twenty, twenty five years ago ... ho ... ho ... ho ..."

Pande had started thrashing his tobacco noisily and Babu Mansukh Singh's loud laughter turned to stormy fits of sneezing. When the atmosphere became normal again, Pandeji looked at me, helplessness writ large on him, and tried to pick up the original threads of the conversation. He said, "Arre, our Vidhayakji had asked us to come to you, malikaar. Hasn't he mentioned anything to you?"

"Which Vidhayakji?" The old man put up a good show of being surprised.

Babuan, babu, saheb, malikaar are forms of respectful address equivalent to the English "sir." **Chamar**: community of tanners; derogatory nominal of identification for the scheduled caste; an untouchable.

"How many vidhayaks do you have as sons-in-law, babuan?" Pandeji mocked with a laugh, taking full advantage of being the son-in-law of the village. Caught out, the cunning old man gave a sheepish laugh and said,

"Oh, you mean Kamalji? Now where does he have the time? Patna today, Delhi tomorrow. Oh, yes ... I remember now, he did mention something about marriage once. Anyway, marriages can be finalized only after proper enquiries ..."

I thought it was time to end this discussion. "Babu saheb, you are my elder. Why hide anything from you? Mine was an inter-caste marriage. To that same Shivbachan's granddaughter ... gazetted officer Mohanji's daughter."

No one spoke for a while.

The ensuing silence made the atmosphere heavy. Pandeji started making the motions to rise. Perhaps he had seen the body of the old man in front of him tense up all of a sudden and his moustache beginning to quiver fiercely. Though he tried to curb his anger, the old man sounded incensed. "Arre, so you are that saviour. You dare to come here, right at the door of Ujjain, for a son-in-law for Shivbachan's granddaughter? Courageous indeed! Better leave the way you came ... And listen, even today there are those who keep stock of seven generations of a family. Mere wealth cannot purify the grain, Thikedar Saheb."

Till long after my silent retreat, I was plagued. Barbed dismissive retorts assailed my mind. Ai budhe, your son-in-law, Kamal, had come to my door, begging with all ten fingers of his hand folded. During the elections I too could have shown him the door. Why didn't you ask him to take into account seven generations of my family then? Your own daughter was then begging, spreading her aanchal in front of that Shivbachan's granddaughter a number of times, "Shyama behna, you are a banyan tree, and you still support the garden plants. Walk through the village with me just once, and see how the Dalit votes fall in my husband's fold. And what is your worry? Your daughter's marriage? Worrying about the marriage of such a beautiful, educated girl? Wherever she goes, she will spread light. Here, come closer. Listen. My brother's son is in Delhi, doing his MBA. If you like the boy, consider the marriage final with just paan and flowers." When all this was happening, which planet was your Ujjain, your icon of pure blood, orbiting?

Yet I won't lie. I have questioned myself scores of times, Would I have taken the decision I took twenty two, twenty three years ago if I had known that this would be its consequence?

"When the clan is destroyed, the sanctity of the sanatan kul dharma, the traditional Hindu religion and religiousness, disappears and when dharma is destroyed, all families are destroyed and sin overpowers everything. He Krishna! Surrounded by such sins, the women of the clan are defiled. He Varneya!, such corruption of the women leads to the debasement of the family. Such mixing of clans becomes the reason for leading the destroyers of the family and the family to hell. Since such degeneration leaves none pure enough to perform the rites of pind kriya and jal kriya, the ancestral spirits are disturbed from their peaceful abode."

That decision, taken twenty two, twenty three years ago, was it merely the outcome of youthful passion?

I have had to ask this question of myself seeing Dilip's troubles. His worries are mine too. A young, beautiful daughter, studying MA, at home. Every week Dilip leaves the house in search of a life partner for her as though he is going on a mountaineering expedition. And the return ... as if unseasonal gales and rain have forced him to turn back midway itself. He once told me how I could not understand the pain of being the father of a daughter.

Very true. Every pain is unique in its own way. I agree. I cannot understand his pain. But the pain of being a girl, having a girl, can he ever understand that?

The other day Dilip was very sad, so much so that I started being scared of him. When I asked him, he told me the entire story. It did not surprise me. I had helped Kamalji and his wife because my husband asked me to and not with the motive of arranging a match for my daughter. I had not seen the boy and I was not one of those people who would give their daughter away in marriage to a stranger just because

---

Pind Kriya and Jal Kriya: Religious ceremonies performed for purification of the soul, after the death of a person.

he happened to be wealthy and of an illustrious lineage.

I wanted to make Dilip understand, "This is not something to be so troubled about. The child is doing her MA ... She would be going in for an MBA or a PhD ..."

"There would have been no hurry Shyama, but for a recent incident ... One day I saw her with Deepak in AC Market. Both of them happily eating ice creams and laughing ... That very day I decided that the sooner one is rid of this problem the better." Purposely, I swallowed the word Problem and asked him, "Is eating ice cream a crime?"

"I mean ... with Deepak?"

"Why? What's wrong with Deepak? He is good at studies ... is in the last year of engineering course, is the son of Ram Prasad, your closest friend."

Hearing this, he was exasperated. Perhaps he wanted to say something, but for some reason the words stuck in his throat. As soon as I had an inkling of what he actually wanted to say, I felt I had been pushed off a mountain top.

That night just refused to pass. It was as if I had received the news of the death of someone very dear to me. Dilip had divined my sadness. Perhaps that was why he was repeatedly trying to take me in his arms, cajole me. But it was as though my body was devoid of life. I felt whatever had been happening till today, was all artificial, unreal. Even his entreaties seemed faked. Still, it was difficult for me to be upset with him for long. I thought this was the right moment and asked him, "Suppose Shweta and Deepak have started loving each other, then ...?"

At my query, all his bodily actions stopped abruptly. His face, in that dim light, seemed blank. Maybe a little ugly too. "Love ...? Now? At this immature age it can only be physical attraction," he intoned, eyes closed, as though delivering a dialogue from a play. I felt, if I was in his place, I would have been given the same lines. Still, each of us were acting out our assigned roles.

"Was it the same with us too?" It was as if I had recited the next dialogue in the play. My voice, so very soft, was to him so forceful that his inert, passive body had been recharged with life. He shot up and retorted in a slightly raised voice, "Had this been the case with me would I have been here on this bed, with you today? Would I have left everything – my well wishers, friends, family, society, and the job I held — all of it just to be here with you? Cleaning up your children's dirt and shit?"

I turned my face away from him because within me, there was a terrible explosion happening. The play had turned into reality. Or was it the feeling of emptiness one experiences after the play is over, echoing within me like an inaudible scream. This was the limit. He remembers, in minute detail, every single thing that he had to give up to get me. Does he want to extract their price, with interest, from me today? Is he repenting his decision? Should I also do the same? Bring to mind what all I lost, whatever I gained?

While other men of his caste kept themselves free of any kind of commitment or responsibility after enjoying a physical relationship with women of other castes, Dilip proved himself completely different from all of them. But if Dilip is proud of this act of his, why should I not think that I have more cause to be proud of than he does? I was a graduate while he had not even cleared his matriculation properly. My father was a senior government officer, while Dilip was an orphan working right from his adolescence as a depot clerk in a private colliery on the recommendation of a local politician. My marriage had been fixed up with an engineer while it was almost impossible for him to get a girl from a good family within his caste. Well, given Dilip's attractive personality and his mannerisms, any girl would probably have run away from home, just like I had done ... What all had he not done to attract me? When I used to leave home for my studies, I would see him waiting at the bus stop every single day. He would be wearing a pant and shirt resembling the colour of the salwar suit I had worn the previous day, standing there with his eyes glued in my direction. Today, when my memory takes me back to the past, I think, so much of that which was mine had been left behind.

I remember how Babuji had brought the police to that small cell-like dwelling of Dilip's and berated me.

"How will you adjust with this drunkard, this vagabond? Even now, nothing is lost. That engineer boy is still prepared to marry you ... despite knowing everything ... come back."

That is, my society was ready to take me back but Dilip's world had turned completely away from him. He had lost his job and his belongings were thrown out of the room. All those who were his — his relatives, including his brother and sister — had broken all ties with him.

So who has more reasons to be proud of oneself and one's society? Him or I? And today that same Dilip, despite being insulted again and again, still wants to return to that old, rotten, decaying society of his!

"Nature is against the growth of mixed bloodlines. Even otherwise the third, fourth and fifth generations of such mixed bloodlines have to suffer pain which keeps increasing progressively with each generation. Not only are they deprived of their traditional ancestral qualities, but due to the deficiency of high quality and density of blood, their will power and self-determination also keeps declining."

What made me think these improper thoughts about Deepak? He is Ram Prasad's son. And Ram Prasad? Forgive me friend, I am not in my senses. Otherwise would I have been disturbed at seeing my daughter in the company of my close friend's son? Would I have raised questions about his caste or mine? That time, twenty two, twenty three years ago, when I was told to resign from my job and my belongings were thrown out of my house because of my marriage with Shyama, comes to mind now. Straightaway I had gone to the local leader and requested him, "We belong to the same village. Going by those ties, you're like my uncle. You were the one who had arranged for this job. Now do you want to cut the very tree you planted with your own hands?" I was hopeful that with my humility I could repair the damage.

"You have caused me a tremendous damage, Dilip." He replied, sighing deeply.

"Who ... me?" I asked hesitatingly.

"Yes, you! Listen, my image is that of a man true to his clan. If one of my men elopes with a girl, and a Dalit one at that, can you imagine the repercussions? You do know, don't you, that I have to fight the forthcoming elections?"

"But Shyama has stated categorically in front of the police and her family that I had not asked her to elope. She is a consenting adult and we have had a court marriage," I tried to clarify.

"That is where the trouble started. Who asked you to make the relationship public? Does one strut about, bowl hanging down one's neck, after eating? How did the thought of marrying that characterless girl enter your head?"

"Characterless?" The tenor of my voice changed. Truth is, the heat of that explosive word had melted the humility inside me. The hatred for this person, hidden till then, came out with a force. I lost my temper and forgot all about being humble.

"Yes, characterless. Do you think it is the Sati Savitris who opt for love marriage?" This man was abusing my wife continuously and that too right in front of me. How could I have kept quiet?

"And what do the Sati Savitris, the girls with character do? Have an affair with one and marry another ...?" After that his curses and swearwords completely drowned my voice.

For many days I nursed my wounds. Where else but at that very same Ram Prasad's quarters. His house was my sanctuary for several months. He used his position as a Junior Engineer to get me my first contract. I had no capital. Ram Prasad arranged for that too. And today whatever I have – this big car, this huge bungalow, these trucks, the high status in society because of these, the fact that that very same political leader who is now the Vidhayak here frequents my house, claiming the familiarity and kinship of old – I owe it all to Ram Prasad. How can I ever forget Ram Prasad's role in my life?

Forgive me, Ram Prasad. Thankfully, my thoughts about your son remained unsaid. What can I do? My value system cannot change overnight. Surtvala, Sankar, Surtaan. One wants to escape from the negative connotations of these words. In childhood, the period full of curiosity and innocent ignorance, even without wanting many things can be known. In the subconscious mother's voice still echoes ... Playing with that surtaanva? Eating with that surtvala ...?

My classmate Ram Prasad is from the chamar caste. My childhood could still somewhat understand why it was forbidden to eat and play with him. But not being permitted to play or eat with Manohar and

---

Surtvala, Sankar, Surtaanva: Various ways of referring to persons of mixed caste.

Kamta, my father's distant cousin's children, was simply impossible to understand. "Mai re, what caste is this surtvala?" I would ask irritably. Later, the priest who had come to our house on purnima, the full moon day, told me in his expansive style, "Surtvala is a community where men have bought girls from some poor girl-selling families because they couldn't find a suitable girl from their own caste. The lineage of this marriage are the varnsankar or the surtvala, the mixed blood clans. This person of mixed blood, is not only inferior to a man of pure blood, but is also destroyed soon. This person just cannot face any crisis. Look around you in the village, at the kind of stories that the calamity afflicting these families tell you."

After leaving Ram Prasad's place, I rented a house. Some years later, when I had constructed my own house and was making preparations for grihpravesh, the housewarming, this priest came to visit me. He was in town to perform some puja in the house of the vidhayak, that same leader of my village. After I had offered him the honours due to a guest, he said "Beta Dilip, I have come to ask you for a favour. I want to send a calf to the village. Do you know of anyone who could?"

"You want to send a calf from here? Why? Is there a shortage of calves in the village?" I asked.

"Vidhayakji has given it as a gift. Well not exactly a gift. I myself asked for it. He was not saying yes readily, but his wife, being more spiritually inclined, agreed. Truth is this calf is so special that anyone who sees it will be tempted. I am sure it will grow into a kamdhenu."

"Why? What's so special about it, Baba?" curious, I asked.

"First of all, its whole body is of one colour, pitch black. Then it is a hybrid. A cross between a Jersey bull and a native cow.

I reassured him that while he stayed at his son-in-law's house in the town I would come up with some arrangement to send the calf to his village. As he was leaving, he said with a show of affection. "Why yejman, you married on the quiet. Do you intend calling another pundit to perform the grihpravesh too?"

I was in a dilemma, "Will you agree to have a puja in my house?" I said. There was a hint of sarcasm in my voice. Ignoring this he said very naturally, "Why? What crime have you committed? We do not forsake even those patrons who slaughter cows ... Bahman or shudra, whose marriage ... whose funeral rites have we not joined in? And you, you are Ram Khelavan's son ... The kings of yore, god knows how many wives they had. Moreover, our dharmashastras, the sacred texts, lay down that there is never any fault in a young unmarried girl no matter what caste she belongs to. Hasn't Gosainji commented, Samrath ke kuch dosh nahin gosain ... the strong (samrath) are devoid of faults ... take Indira Gandhi for example."

So many memories. Snippets of conversation. During school, nibbling on guavas stolen from an orchard, with classmates, sharing gossip, arguments.

"Arre yaar, bahman, chhatri, bania, harijan is fine, but where did this bhumihar caste come from?" someone would ask.

"Don't you know ... they are the cross-breeds of bahman and chhatri castes." Another would answer jokingly.

"Then the man must have been a bahman," a brahmin boy would claim.

"No, he was a chhatri," promptly a kshatriya boy would cut in.

It is hard to understand this distorted vision. Our village priest, Gita's Arjun and Nazi Germany's Hitler – how come all of them speak the same language when it comes to purity of blood?

"Thus we see that a person of mixed blood is not only inferior to one of pure blood, but his end is also faster. Pure castes survive, facing innumerable crises, while mixed bloodlines are ruined by the mildest adversity. Nature, through pure blood, gives birth to great reformers and statesmen. Through the process of creation she helps the growth of capabilities in the pure blooded people while limiting the procreation of the mixed bloodlines, thereby leading them towards extinction."

I close *Mein Kampf,* the autobiography of Hitler, and along with it, my eyes too. I wonder, how in the attempt to maintain the purity of blood who knows how many communities and races are on the verge of disappearance. And the Indian breed – accepting and absorbing

---

Bahman, chhatri, bania, harijan: Colloquial ways of referring to the four major castes in India – brahmin, kshatriya, vaisya, shudra.

within their selves the continuous flow of foreign blood, from the Aryans, Shaks, Huns, Arabs, Afghans, Iranians, Turks and Mongols — and its burgeoning population is now a cause of worry to the entire world ...

My eyes open at the sound of footsteps. Dilip. He is looking tired, face unshaven, moustache drooping. Pure bloodline ... Suddenly laughter bubbles up inside me. After the invasions of the Aryans, Greeks, Shaks, Huns, Uzbeks, Arabs, Afghans, Iranians, Turks, Mongols and the English and after being ruled by them for thousands of years, how much of pure blood would have been left flowing, in whose veins, in what proportion? And those kings of yore ... What did they do? Wherever they went, if they chanced upon a beautiful woman they added her to their harems. The old king died, the new one ascended the throne. Except for a few young women and the reigning queens, he drove out all the remaining women, old and spent, in the harems and the fort, kids and all. The ousted women, along with their children, would wander like nomads and form their own settlements at various places, and their children would call themselves rajputras or rajputs, the descendants of kings.

I feel like asking Dilip Which king was his clan related to, which kingdom did he rule, which throne did he ascend, in what century BC? But looking at his face, I feel sorry for him and ask instead, "What happened?"

"What can happen. Whatever usually does. It is the same old excuses, evasions ..." he replies, and falling flat on the bed tries to regain his poise. This is the right moment, the opportunity I had been looking for, to say what I have been wanting to say for a long time.

"Can I say something?" I prepare the ground. He looks up, as if to ask. Why is my permission being sought? I complete what I started, "Why don't you get Shweta married to Deepak?"

For a second, sparks shoot out of his eyes and his tongue slips, suddenly, unthinkingly. "Are you in your right mind? Marry my daughter to a chamar?"

I thank god. After a long wait, Dilip has finally landed in my net. He has said exactly what I had wanted him to say. Without delaying, I say, "You can marry a girl from a chamar's house, but you can't give your own daughter in marriage to a chamar. Why? What was your reason behind marrying me? ... Seeing the reflection of your victory in the eyes of the vanquished? Why are you silent? ... Or are you drowned in remorse because your true self is finally revealed?"

For a while he keeps looking at me, pitifully. Then suddenly, like an innocent child, he clings to me. I realize that, head on my shoulder, he has started sobbing loudly.

"Kulaghati" was originally written in Hindi and published in *Hans*, in its special issue *Ardhshati*, 1997. "Married to Separateness," has been translated by Geeta Sahai, Rupalee Verma and Katha fiction editor.

M T Vasudevan Nair

SUKRITAM

TRANSLATED BY VANAJAM RAVINDRAN

As the month of Karkitakam cleared, we gave up all hope of finding Cheriyatti. That was when a woman was seen trudging along the narrow path at the foot of Thani hills. With slow steps, she came into the courtyard of the Kanancheri house. Then, throwing off the tattered cloth that covered her from head to foot, she let out a heart-rending cry, a sound like the splitting of tender bamboo shoot. "Amma ..."

Atti and her four brothers rushed to the front door and stopped, speechless. There stood their dear Cheriyatti, young Cheriyatti, who had been lost in the forest. Atti trembled, overcome with joy: "Oh my daughter! You've come back at last," she exclaimed, as soon as she found her voice.

Cheriyatti's uncles recovered from the shock and ran in different directions to let the nattukoottam know of their niece's return. The people, relieved that their paradevata — household deity — had not completely abandoned them, turned to the south and offered short fervent prayers.

Our people have faced grievous dangers in the past. But those seem trivial compared with the menace that recently swept through our land with thundering hoof beats, raising clouds of dust.

The news that an invading army was coming down the pass from the North had first reached Tampuran, the ruler of our desam. At once he ordered all three of his palanquins to be prepared. He left in the first one, taking the royal ornaments and the idol of Goddess Bhagavati with him. His consorts followed in the other two palanquins. Escorted by their retinue, they were swiftly borne across the borders and over the Chammini hills to foreign lands.

Soon after, terror-stricken messengers came running from the furthest limits of the land to inform the nattukoottam of the impending danger. They talked of marauding invaders, mounted on fierce fire spitting beasts, who were fast closing in, leaving devastation in their wake.

Nattukoottam: literally the citizenry; but in the social context of the Kerala of the 18th-19th centuries, the representatives of all important families or tarawads who virtually ruled the desam, a cluster of villages.

The leader of the nattukoottam sent out his messengers immediately. They beat their drums and ordered the people to gather their jewel boxes and the keys of their granaries and, if possible, seek refuge with their cattle in the Chundolakkala forests beyond the Thani hills. The messenger-warrior who reached us first, travelling as fast as wind, was later awarded the grand title – "Parakotti Ammaman" or "The drum beating uncle." With time this was shortened to "Paramman" and the ritual of making offerings to him came into vogue. And then the practice of slaughtering fowls in his name, on the night of the new moon in the month of Medam, started.

As soon as the invading army entered the land, they dragged out, and sent to the gallows, the native warriors who had hidden in the banana groves and behind the haystacks. The four fields on the river bank later came to be called the "gallow fields." Seeing the dense clouds which augured the onset of the monsoons, the invaders decided to move southwards to avoid any flash floods. And we, realizing that the enemy had departed, returned to our homes.

This incident was recorded on copper plates. Years later, our children, studying the history of their native land based on these plates, were taught: The ruler of Thavinjanadu deigned to meet the Nawab. Much later this same statement was recorded by one of our research scholars who chanced upon the copper plate inscriptions preserved at Orumanassery. The fact, however, is that in those days our land was bereft of a ruler and we cannot say with certainty who the ruler referred to is. And we do not want to find out either. For we are the historians and the history. What we do know is that Thavinjanadu is a corruption of "The nadu (land) deserted by the Devi." But enough of this. Let us move on to the glories of our temple.

The people performed the ritual cleansing of their hearths and homes, soon after they returned. The nattukoottam quickly assembled in the shade of the twin banyan trees. They had barely got the palm leaves ready on which to reckon their various losses, when young Kalia came rushing in. "Cheriyatti of the Kanancheri tarawad is not to be found," he gasped.

"Young Cheriyatti not to be found!"

The nattukoottam were shocked. Their very universe trembled!

They remembered how distressed they had been when Atti, the only sister to four brothers did not have a child to carry on the tarawad. Eager to hear the patter of little feet there, the community had made a concerted effort to invoke the deities, by providing load rests for porters, constructing shelters along the highways to provide drinking water for tired wayfarers. Atti prayed and fasted for forty one days. Finally, she had been blessed with a daughter. Though the baby girl was named Ittati, she was fondly called Cheriyatti – little Atti – by her mother and uncles. It was when this little child, the favourite of all the land, had blossomed into a young maiden, that the marauders passed through the area and turned it into a wasteland.

An enquiry was conducted. Atti and the eldest woman of the community were summoned by the nattukoottam. Atti informed them that Cheriyatti had definitely been among the women and children who had gone into hiding. The girls had always stayed in groups. But one day Cheriyatti had gone for a swim in the forest spring, accompanied only by her young pinati. When the child did not return, no one had been worried. Cheriyatti had friends of her age among the other Ettuveettukar families and she often spent time with them. But she had not been with them!

"O my land! The Devi has abandoned you!" the chief of the nattukoottam let out an anguished cry.

The monsoons came again. Messengers brought news that our Tampuran, who had fled from his desam, had been given land by the Perumbadappu Raja. And he was going to build a temple and install the deity there.

The monsoon ended, but the tears coursing down Atti's cheeks would not be stemmed. We were beginning to despair because both the astrologer and the singing soothsayer had not been able to get a clue to Cheriyatti's whereabouts through their divination. It was then that the young girl suddenly appeared.

Pinati: women who waited upon the female members of prominent tarawads.
Ettuveettukar: the eight (ettu) illustrious tarawads.

The nattukoottam assembled in the Mancheri courtyard. Atti looked at her young daughter, hiding behind a carved pillar, staring at her toe nails, absorbed in some beautiful dream. She called out to the girl, "Speak my daughter, speak. Whatever happened to you, my child. Let the menfolk hear."

When she came out after her dip in the spring and was changing her clothes, Cheriyatti recounted, the pinati had whispered that a stranger was standing behind the thickets. No sooner had the pinati said that, the stranger appeared in front of Cheriyatti – a soldier! Seeing his lecherous eyes and outstretched arms, she ran as fast as she could to save her honour, crying out, "Oh, Devi, protect me."

Inflamed by desire, the soldier followed, in hot pursuit of his prey. Hunted like a gentle deer, she fled till she fell at the feet of a stranger.

"Who? Who was he?" asked the nattukoottam in consternation.

"A hunter, a hunter from the forest."

Cheriyatti continued her story. The hunter hid her in a bower of dense creepers till her besotted pursuer gave up and went back the way he had come, sorely disappointed.

Cheriyatti lived in the hunter's hut till she was free from danger. The hunter, said Cheriyatti, had fed her honey and wild fruit and had given her a mat to sleep on. He had stood at the entrance of the hut with his spear and his bow and arrows, guarding her from wild animals and enemy soldiers.

"Tampuratti, where's my daughter? Where's the pinati, respected masters?" asked a vanian agitatedly, from where he stood, some distance away.

Atti's fourth brother was furious. How dare a vanian speak to them like this? He promptly drew his sword. If the chief of the nattukoottam had not pardoned the vanian for his thoughtless misdemeanour he might have been killed! Glad that his life had been spared, the vanian promptly withdrew from there and listened to their interrogations from afar.

Tampuratti: the respectful way of addressing a woman of a Nair household. The men would be addressed as Ejamanan or Tampuran.

Vanian: a person belonging to the caste whose traditional profession was extracting oil from seeds.

The hut was at the other end of the forest, said Cheriyatti, so the news of the enemies' withdrawal had reached them much later. The hunter then took her back along the shortest and least tortuous route, she walking in front and he, behind her. When they reached the outskirts of their land, he had turned and gone back the way they had come.

Having said all this, Cheriyatti covered her lotus-like face with soft, delicate hands and sobbed and sobbed, till she slumped at the foot of the pillar, exhausted. The nattukoottam dispersed after deciding to reassemble at dusk.

That night a grand feast was prepared at the Kanancheri tarawad to which the members of the other seven Ettuveettukar tarawads came.

The leaves were laid for the first batch of guests – the women and children. When food was about to be served, a venerable old grandmother asked, "Tell me, oh you, my wise brothers, is it proper to allow a girl, who has eaten food from a hunter and shared his mat, to enter the nalakaya, this inner courtyard?"

Not one of us had thought of this in the hurry and scurry of preparing the feast. Our ruler, who should have advised us on such matters, was elsewhere. So the alternative had to be Cheramballi Cherunni Ejaman, the oldest member of the community. He would be able to give us an answer to the old lady's question.

Promptly Cheriyatti's uncles and a member of the nattukoottam ran to the Cheramballi tarawad. After long and deep deliberation, Cheramballi Ejaman said, "No, my nephews, it's not proper. It is not proper."

The guests, who had come to the feast, left without even a sip of water. Overnight the news spread and scandalized women said, "Just imagine, the virgin of Kanancheri in the bed of a hunter! Oh, our paradevatas, let not evil befall our children!"

We had always conducted ourselves honourably, living in awe and fear of our virtuous and illustrious ancestors, so that our land would be protected. The karanavar of the Kanancheri tarawad knew this very well. Pacing the courtyard restlessly, he summoned his sister.

Karanavar: the head of a tarawad – the senior most ammaman (uncle).

"Light the lamp upstairs," he ordered her.

Standing before the lamp the venerable old ammaman, still in his wet clothes after his ablutions, prayed fervently, invoking all his valorous ancestors – Thasammaman, Kandamman, Koppamman, Cheriya Koppamman, and the rest of them. His body trembled as he touched the lighted lamp and made a vow. Then he came out, as if in a trance, and asked his sister and the younger generation of the tarawad, "Do you want the tarawad disgraced? Do you want the land ruined?"

His voice had assumed a different tone. It was as if all our ancestors were speaking through him.

Cheriyatti, lying half asleep close to the wall, woke up with a start. Standing in the doorway were her mother and her uncles. Her mother was weeping bitterly. Realizing the gravity of the situation, Cheriyatti said, "Amma, the family should not be disgraced. The land must not be reduced to rack and ruin."

The Kanancheri karanavar's anger subsided. He looked at the others around him and heaved a sigh of relief.

The nattukoottam assembled under the twin banyan trees the next day. No one from the Kanancheri tarawad went to the meeting. However, one of Atti's brothers, spurred by curiosity, went and stood a short distance away from the assembly, pretending to look at the bamboos in the paddy field. But they spoke very softly, and although he strained his ears, he could hear nothing.

"Why not build a little hut for her somewhere behind the house far away from the tarawad precincts?" suggested one of the younger men of the family. The karanavar did not respond.

When Atti was consulted by a cousin, she muttered through her sobs, "But my sister, that doesn't remove the stigma."

The karanavar cried out in lamentation, "Oh, the spirits of my forefathers, my dead karanavars, don't subject me to this trial."

Then he narrated the story of Cheriyatti, right from the days of Atti's fasting and praying. At the end of it all, he plaintively asked his ancestors, "Oh, why should this have happened to my darling child, who not long ago played in this very courtyard, wearing her gold chain and the consecrated thread round her tender waist!"

Cheriyatti's voice was then heard.

"I will shift to the uralppura," she announced. Her eyes dazzled like lightning in the darkness of the room. Her entire body glowed, and she thrilled to a strange sensation.

"But the disgrace! It won't end with that either, my child ..." Atti diffidently reminded her.

"Kanancheri Cheriyatti doesn't need anybody's advice. She knows how to safeguard the honour of her family," she stated.

"Oh Mother, Maha Maya!" Protector of the destitute ..."

As soon as the nattukoottam heard about this, the whole community buzzed with excitement. People thronged to see Cheriyatti seated cross-legged on a rough blanket in the uralppura. As if absorbed in some beautiful dream, the maiden was oblivious of the crowd before her. Seeing the radiance on her face the people folded their hands in prayer and bowed to her.

"This spot, where this Devi is now seated, before her great sukritam, will henceforth be known as the Uralppura temple. It's only after paying their obeisance here that the worshippers will go to the temple down the hill," declared Aromanejaman who had trudged with great difficulty to see Cheriyatti in this posture.

The news of Cheriyatti's divinity spread far and wide and people from the neighbouring desams hurried towards the Kanancheri uralppura.

"The night of the fourth day is auspicious for the ceremony," said Aromanejaman, after protracted calculations. "The time after Moolam when Avittam starts."

It was her mother who conveyed this decision to Cheriyatti. As she turned to go, the girl called her back and said, "Amma, please tell Valiyammaman not to have it done in the temple pond. For three or four days after that, the people will have problems bathing there."

The leader of the nattukoottam enquired, "Will Kothan deliver everything on time?" And then, with a sense of great pride and self-righteous indignation, he said, "The neighbouring desams may have forgotten the

---

Uralppura: a room away from the main house, for pounding grain in an ural or wooden mortar.

age-old rituals. Our ruler may not be with us, but we haven't given up our customs. What people now do is resort to deception. They remain outside of the tarawad for a certain length of time, then enter the house at the auspicious moment. What new fangled practices! I wonder what will happen to us at this rate? Certainly it was not without reason that our old karanavars laid down these rules. As long as I'm alive, things will be done as they should be. After that ... I can't imagine the state of affairs."

He heaved a deep sigh of regret.

"But what about the weeds in Kummanikkulam? Suppose the legs get entangled in them and the head resurfaces?" someone asked.

"Weren't you there when Aromanejaman said that nothing untoward should mar the event? Remember it is after many years that such a day has dawned, an occasion to perform such an auspicious deed. And that too by the flower of the Kanancheri tarawad!"

Down came some able bodied men, promptly jumped into the pond. They took out all the tangles of moss lying at the bottom.

Aromanejaman was being given a blow by blow account of what was happening. His niece, half concealed by the door, said very humbly, "Had it not been so late at night we could have watched it too."

"No. The womenfolk cannot go to see it! After all there are certain restrictions," the old man reprimanded her. She passed on whatever she had heard to the women in the neighbouring tarawads.

All the people of the desam had to observe a fast that night. After the midday meal, the women were to engage themselves in prayer. This had been the custom since time immemorial.

In the early hours of that morning, the stonecutter and his wife had delivered two granite blocks with holes cut in the centre. As remuneration for this service, he was entitled to a measure of rice and a pair of woven towels from the Kanancheri tarawad every year for the rest of his life. And the nattukoottam gave him a word of praise for the neat way in which the holes were cut.

As the time for the auspicious moment drew near, Cheriyatti was ceremoniously prepared by two pinatis whose food and clothes were paid for by the tarawad. Except for Cheriyatti's earrings they removed all her other ornaments and handed them over to her mother. A Nair, whose privilege it was to carry the lamp, walked in front. Atti stood gazing at her daughter in the light of the lamp. Cheriyatti stepped down to the courtyard. Her eyes wore an expression of pride and dignity. The menfolk started following Cheriyatti who walked behind the lamp bearer.

Around the Kummanikkulam had gathered men of all ages – barring the very young. Anyone who could walk or limp was there. Many of them carried lamps and torches.

"Where's the rope? Who had undertaken to bring it?" asked a voice.

"It's got lost in the crowd," shouted the leader of the nattukoottam. Cheriyatti stood on the bank, in a clearing of wild pandanus plants.

"Where's Aromanejaman?"

"I wasn't there on the last such occasion. According to the sastras, who is to tie the rope around the ankles?"

Some said it was the chief of the nattukoottam. Or was it the karanavar of the Kanancheri tarawad?

One of them, who had a sense of humour, said, "Let it be the karanavar himself, for isn't he a member of the nattukoottam as well? In that case no one can say later that rules were violated."

Slip knots were made at the end of the two ropes tied to the two slabs of stones. The karanavar said to Cheriyatti, "Child, stand with your feet inside the loops."

She did as she was bidden. While the slip knots were being tightened, the karanavar said, "Don't be afraid, there's nothing to fear. It's not the old Kummanikulam. All the muck has been removed."

Some of the youngsters were getting impatient.

"Why is the karanavar not tightening the knots?"

"If this old man can't do it, one of you can. He only needs to touch it."

However, such an exigency did not arise. The karanavar stood aside after he had carried out his task.

Cheriyatti, who was standing alone, looked around at all the spectators. The Nair in charge of the lamp brightened its wick and, as the light fell upon her face, the people observed a smile of supreme satisfaction.

"The timid ones sometimes have to be prompted. Do you think we will need to do that?" asked a man in the crowd.

No, there was no need for that at all. Cheriyatti gazed at the crowd with her shining eyes, as if anointing and blessing them, then jumped into the pond.

For a brief moment there was utter silence. Then the people dispersed, thankful that no inauspicious happening had marred the sacred act.

The nattukoottam also dispersed after deciding to return in the early hours of the next morning – by which time the water would have settled – to perform the rest of the rites.

That night, not only the Kanancheri karanavar but also all the other worthies of the place had the same strange dream. A fierce looking hunter, clad in elephant skin, wearing a chain of skulls around his neck and carrying a shining axe and a rope, suddenly descended from the skies and plunged into the Kummanikkulam waters. Then he rose and leaped back to the skies he had come from.

The nattukoottam, on reaching the banks of the Kummanikkulam early next morning, did not utter a word about the dream to one another. The untouchables, who were assigned the task of taking out the dead body, found, to their surprise, that it was not there.

The Kanancheri karanavar knew that it was a futile exercise. "That's enough," he said. "It won't be found."

The head of the nattukoottam turned to the pond and prayed. He muttered, "Sukritam! Mahasukritam!" And then said impatiently, "Come on, now. We have to discuss matters pertaining to the building of the temple. Hurry up."

The nattukoottam followed their leader to the shade of the twin banyan trees. They were in high spirits. As if renewing their memory of the dream, in one voice they exclaimed, "Amme, Bhagavati!"

"Sukritam" was originally written in Malayalam and published in *Vanaprastham*, a collection of short stories by the author. This translation by Vanajam Ravindran was published in *Indian Literature*, 1995 by Sahitya Akademi. It was published in Meenakshi Sharma ed. *The Wordsmiths*, March 1996 by Katha.

Arupa Patangia Kalita

DOIBOKI'S DAY

TRANSLATED BY KRISHNA BARUA

"Take it, babu, take it! Give me twenty rupees and take it! How long am I going to sit and watch over this one fish?" Tying the roe-filled kurhi with a thin strip of tender bamboo, Doiboki wound up her wares with deft hands. She called across to Mano and her friends at the other end of the bazaar, "Are you there, Mano?" but there was no response. They must have gone home. Now she was on her own, with the descending darkness. But then, how could she have sold such fine fish for the price of water? The traders who used to pay her a fair price had suddenly turned stingy, behaving as if they were parting with their own flesh. Apparently, they had to pay someone a huge amount of money. Doiboki put a tamul, a piece of betel nut, into her mouth and cursed them roundly. "Bloody mekhela wearers! Swallowers of their own sputum! They want my fish free! Damned, miserable, low caste specimens of humanity whose corpses are consumed by vultures!" Doiboki felt a little better after her outburst.

Candles and small kerosene lamps lit up the bazaar. Doiboki's neighbour Raghubir, the potato and onion seller, had stuck two candles in his neat arched piles of onions and potatoes. He looked at the candles, his hands folded in a silent prayer, then turned towards Doiboki. "What's the matter, Doiboki Bai? Aren't you going home today?" Doiboki slapped her thighs in disgust. "Why, would you like me to stay and admire your beautiful face instead?"

She looked around her. As usual, Jaduram had arranged his greens and vegetables in neat little piles and was sprinkling water on them. It was time for the babus of the town to arrive. Ganesh, the masala dealer who usually sat between Raghubir and Jaduram, had not come that day and Jaduram

---

Mekhela and sador: the traditional dress worn by Assamese women.
Through the story, there are references to several varieties of fish. These are — **kurhi:** medium sized freshwater fish; **kawoi:** small fish which lives in tanks, water bodies, flooded fields but not in running water; **darikana:** a small freshwater fish; **singi:** a small fish which lives in muddy waters and has sharp bones near it's mouth; **magur:** a scaleless, dark fish, which lives in still, muddy waters; **kandhuli:** medium sized, flat, scaly fish of silvery colour which lives in freshwater; **barali:** big, scaleless, freshwater fish found in rivers, large tanks and water bodies; **sang:** small fish living in muddy holes; **puthi:** very small, reddish, stillwater fish with scales; **pabha:** flat, scaleless, white-skinned, freshwater fish; **mirika:** big, scaly, silver coloured, freshwater fish; **goroi:** a big freshwater fish of the carp family.

had filled up the vacant space with his lemons arranged in order of size and hue. He had spent the entire day playing around with his vegetables, arranging and rearranging them like a child with its toys, Doiboki thought. A scathing comment rose to her tongue but she swallowed it in time. "What's happened to Ganesh today, oi?" she asked instead.

Raking the small heap of ridge gourds, Jaduram whispered, "How could he come after the death of all those army men? When the bomb exploded on the bridge, Ganesh's village was instantly overrun by the military. Life has become impossible for them."

A sudden shiver ran through Doiboki. She had heard similar stories.

It was growing darker inside the bazaar. Doiboki began to feel a little uneasy. Had the trader bought her basket of fish, she would have been home by now and lying on her cane mat, after an evening meal of rice. Mano and her friends had asked her if she wanted to go home with them but she had refused, hoping to earn a little more money. Luckily, it had not been a total loss. She would have some money left over even after buying her rations. If she could save a little more money, she would cut open her bamboo saving box and then she would be able to take her mother-in-law to the town hospital to get her cataract removed. Doiboki was already late today. Perhaps the old woman was trying to cook the evening meal, groping for things because of her dim eyes. Luckily, Doiboki's eldest daughter was there to help the blind woman.

Doiboki bought half a kilo of potatoes. She had been lucky today, otherwise when did one buy potatoes? The old woman liked to have mashed potato with salt and mustard oil mixed in. Yes, it had been a lucky day. She had bought two kilos of rice; there were some three or four kilos at home as well. And her son must have caught some fish.

Doiboki made her way out of the bazaar carrying her bundle of rice and potatoes. Transferring the money from the tucked-in ends of her mekhela to her blouse, she took long, rapid strides. The old woman must be nagging the children at home – Has your mother come? I wonder where she's gone and died. The children troubled their grandmother a great deal, Doiboki thought, her heart quickening with tenderness.

The streetlights had been on for a long time. The shops were ablaze with light. Stepping into the glare, after having been in the weak flickering

83

light of the oil lamps in the bazaar for such a long time, made Doiboki feel as if she was being stripped, exposed. There were two buttons missing from her blouse, and her mekhela, held up by a single knot, barely covered her thighs. The inadequate, narrow sador appeared to shift every now and then, as if to deliberately expose the blouse with its missing buttons. Doiboki felt as if all the men were gaping at her and ... did someone whistle at her? She moved the basket under her arms to her head along with the bundle of rice and potatoes. Then, crouching in the shadow cast by the basket, she started walking quickly – her head bent low, her mekhela slapping against her legs, satap, satap!

Soon she was outside the town, walking on the kuccha road that led to the riverside village at its southern end. There were fewer people now and not much light. The rice fields on either side of the road were wet and dark and glow worms, clustering like shoals of small darikana, winked in the dark. Somewhere a pack of jackals howled. A young rikshawalla sang his way towards the town, his empty riksha rattling down the road. Doiboki lifted her head to the sky. It was swollen with darkness like a pregnant river during the monsoons, with not a hint of light anywhere. The night was hot and sultry and after some time she took off her blouse. Weakened with sweat, the fabric gave way. Irritated, she tossed it into the basket, pulled her mekhela up over her breasts and carefully tucked the money back into its folds. The cool breeze soothed her body.

Cars and other vehicles seldom plied on that road at night. A little ahead lay the naamghar, the village prayer house. Doiboki had first seen the naamghar when she was a child – running wild without a stitch on.

It sat in a large compound with two vast tanks – Ganga and Jamuna – in front of it. These tanks never dried up, whatever the season. People travelled long distances to collect water from them to keep near their thaponas, their altars, at home. Right at the centre of the compound was an immense banyan tree whose reflection painted the waters of the Ganga and Jamuna green. In these waters lived two gigantic algae-covered turtles – Doiboki and Jashoda. When morsels of food were thrown into the water and the turtles called out to, they would appear on the bamboo platform that led down to the tank. Doiboki had heard about these turtles but never seen them. How could she? Dark-skinned people whose skins smelt of fish were forbidden to enter the naamghar. Her friends used to tease her incessantly, calling her "The turtle of the great tank." Had her mother named her after one of the turtles? As children, Doiboki and her friends went to the naamghar at least once every day. People would sometimes offer the scampering bunch of urchins mah-prasad. But it had not been the lure of the mah-prasad alone that led them there. They were curious – What was it that lay inside the great house, surrounded by trees and tanks, to which passersby bowed so reverentially?

Doiboki quickened her pace. Beyond the naamghar, near the sharp bend of the river, was the bridge that led to the village. Nets billowed in the breeze here, and the place reeked of fish. Once she set foot on the bridge she would be safe, in her village, with its familiar comforting sounds – brawls, blustering drunkards, crying babies, the curses of battered wives.

A creeper of lightning shot across the sky. In the sudden flash she saw a black and yellow striped bakraj snake slither across the road just as three trucks loaded with army men appeared, scattering the quiet darkness. Doiboki stepped to one side. She clearly saw the back wheel of the truck crush the snake. The skies rumbled once more and lightning flashed. The sight of the mangled snake pierced Doiboki like a singi, sharp and painful. The fearless woman was suddenly gripped by a strange terror. Had her husband been alive today, would she have had to step out at night, for such a lousy little sum? Remembering the sturdy man who had passed away after only a week's fever and diarrhoea, hot tears rolled down her cheeks like drops of water slithering down the slippery surface of a magur.

The naamghar was surrounded by vast, open stretches of land. There were huge fields in front of it, and passing by the place, even in daylight, a timid person would find his heart pounding. Usually when Doiboki and her friends approached the naamghar they would see the ladies sitting in front of it, singing their naam and bhajans. No woman was allowed to set foot inside the naamghar. The sorais and sakis offered by them were taken inside by the naamgharia while the well dressed women knelt and prayed at the steps by the entrance. In summer, Doiboki and her friends would stretch out under the shade of the banyan tree near the naamghar, hoping that one of the women, after finishing her naam, would give them a plantain leaf filled with mah-prasad. Once in a while, one of them might call out, "Doiboki, my daughter and son-in-law have come. Could you bring over some good fish?"

Now, as Doiboki neared the naamghar, even the faint steady glow of the oil lamps in the distant huts seemed to disappear. There was darkness everywhere. Doiboki took out a tamul and thrust it into her mouth, remembering how once she would cross this same bridge with friends. In the light of the setting sun, their skin would glisten like ripe jamuns.

She had never been out so late before. Blast those traders! If they had only paid her a fair price as before, she would have had no problems. Doiboki's head throbbed at the thought of the price they had offered for the live, roe-filled kurhi. About to spit out a heartfelt curse with the betelnut juice, she stopped. In the field opposite the naamghar she could see some sharp beams of light bobbing up and down like silvery kandhulis somersaulting in shallow waters. Doiboki quickly, quietly, sank to the ground. The thunder and lightning seemed to grow fiercer. Looking beseechingly at the naamghar, Doiboki folded her hands, praying... "Hei Bhagwan, what is this?" In the flashes of lightning Doiboki could clearly see some soldiers wading in the water, like villagers chasing fish towards enclosures with their fishing gear. A great barali seemed to wriggle in their hold. She heard cries of pain – as if someone was being tortured. Doiboki shivered helplessly, images of the mangled bakraj enveloping her. The beams of light had once more turned into somersaulting kandhuli.

The barrier, sustained by years of tradition, suddenly snapped. She rested her hand on the gate of the naamghar. The crowd of men were coming, under cover of darkness, towards the road. But even as she was about to push open the gate, Doiboki hesitated one last time, fear tripping through her body. What was she doing? Could she enter the temple of the Lord? She saw the bamboo fencing in front of her. Like a wall of stone. She knew all about the golden boat that floated on the waters of Ganga and Jamuna at night. Whoever saw the boat vomited blood, and died. But ... if anything were to happen to her now, the old woman and the children ... Doiboki pushed the gate open, ran in blindly. She stumbled and fell under the peepal tree.

The military men were on the road. A sudden beam of light licked her body. A stern, harsh voice floated up to her, "Kaun hain?" Doiboki crawled into the furrow. Boots clip-clopped on the road. Jeeps roared to life. For a moment, as the many vehicles sped off towards the town, it was as busy as day.

There was an anthill somewhere inside the furrow of the peepal. Her fall had disturbed the ants and some came crawling out now. They stung. Doiboki quickly moved out of the hollow, shaking her sador briskly, the smell of the black ants and their eggs filling her senses. Lightning danced on the waters. Intense fear, combined with the heat of the night, made her feel as if her skin had been roasted. She looked around for water to slake her thirst. If she couldn't get a drink of water now, she knew her heart would burst. Even so, she told herself, she didn't dare drink from Ganga or Jamuna.

Yet she saw herself moving slowly towards Ganga.

There was a sudden noise in the water, which was soon lost in a sharp rustle somewhere near the edge of Jamuna. Doiboki's heart was pounding. She remembered Pado Kaity's brother who, while returning to the village one night, had heard the two turtles splashing around, khalap khalap, and had walked in impulsively to take a look. On that moonlit night, Doiboki and Jashoda appeared near the bamboo platform when he called out to them. But as soon as he threw some of the roasted gram he had on him, Pado Kaity's brother had turned blue, as if from the poison of the revered one around Siva's neck.

The rustle from inside the hollow had died down. What could there be in the hollow where she had left behind her fish smell to mingle with the odour of the ants? It was said that everyone was afraid to touch Pado's brother's dead body. What happened to his corpse? Had the crows and vultures gorged on the stale flesh? She had never asked.

Doiboki pressed her arms around her body and found it soaked with perspiration. She wiped her face with her palm. It reeked of roe-filled kurhi. Carrying this odour, she had dared to ... She licked dry lips. Desperately, she looked around for some water to drink. She walked down the steps of the bamboo platform to the water's edge and bent down to cup her hands. But she just could not bring herself to do it.

How could she use these hands, polluted as they were with the smell of fish to …

Doiboki sank down on the platform, the cool waters lapping at her feet. Then, like sang suddenly springing free of the fishing line, Doiboki's hand shot out and brought up some water. She drank thirstily and even sprinkled some on her head, "Bhagwan, forgive me if I have sinned." Then she stood up abruptly, her feet creating small ripples on the waters that lapped the bamboo platform.

There was not a sound anywhere. The thunder had stopped. The sky was a heavy black, the colour of her body. The trees and leaves were absolutely still.

And in that silence, a sudden splash in the water. Salap salap. Doiboki strained her ears. This was not the sound of fish beating their tails against the waters. She shivered. Who had told her the story? Where had she first heard it? Sometimes in the middle of the night, a golden boat floated on the waters of the tanks of the naamghar. Two great, green-backed turtles always swam by its side, guarding it like sentries.

People said that the sudden death of her sturdy husband was a mysterious affair. On a dark, moonless night, dripping with rain, the reckless man had gone out of the house, oblivious to all warnings. The fields opposite the naamghar had been inundated with shoals of kawoi. When he returned in the morning, his basket was laden with fresh red, glinting kawoi, each the size of a man's palm. That was the first day the man had shat blood nonstop. People had whispered that he had seen the golden boat on the waters of Ganga and Jamuna on that moonless night. How else could a healthy man be reduced to such a state, in the space of one night?

Seeing the blobs of blood in the courtyard, his mother had beaten her breasts and cried, "Gluttony, it was sheer gluttony! Oh, why did he go out on that moonless night, on his father's death anniversary, to fish in that haunted field? So what if it had been flooded with fish?" Doiboki seemed to hear her mother-in-law's voice breaking out of the silence, distorted by pain and grief. "Greed, sheer greed!" Her mother-in-law had hurled veiled taunts at her. And now, with the money tucked in the folds of her mekhela burning her like red hot cinders, clawing at her like sorat leaves, Doiboki told herself she had been greedy too.

The noise in the waters grew louder. Drops of water splashed on to her feet. Her eyes had grown accustomed to the darkness and she could clearly see a huge turtle waiting near the bamboo platform. Like a kawoi jumping out of a bamboo basket, Doiboki bounced back on to the bank. Trembling, her eyes fixed on the pond, she knelt down. The turtle continued to wade in the ankle-deep water on the platform.

Tears blinded Doiboki. She was afraid to look at the tank. Was the golden boat floating in, unmanned and rudderless, a cursed sight that made people vomit blood and die? The sound of another splash ... Two great, algae-covered turtles would be guarding the golden boat.

She ran towards the naamghar without pausing to look back, but stopped at the door. Even the ladies sang their naams from the steps – the ladies who were as beautiful as the vermilion-coloured senduriputhi, as fair as the smooth milky white pabha, whose clothes glittered like the shining scales of a mirika – they too said their prayers here. Doiboki had seen them since she was a child.

She sank to the ground, her head buried between her knees. The noise in the waters had ceased. She looked reluctantly towards the naamghar. A crowd of glow worms winked within it in the dark.

Doiboki started walking away, slowly. The wind had whipped up by now and the rain that had been threatening to descend came down in a great deluge. The large trees began to sway and Doiboki was forced to retrace her steps. She stood at the spot where the ladies sang their naams, soaked to the skin. The tin roof of the naamghar rattled. Hailstones the size of lemons began to pelt her. She knew that a part of the naamghar near the entrance was kept open; only the sacred area, the monikut, was locked. When she could not bear the assault of the hailstorm any longer, she took a small step inside, but came out immediately to stand under the hail that threatened to crush her. Finally, her exhausted body could take no more. She crept into the naamghar.

Inside, there was not a drop of rain, only a refreshingly cold breeze that washed over her. She squeezed the water out of her clothes. Instantly, the smell of raw fish filled the place. And then she heard it, the rustling sound once again, this time from inside the monikut. The thing must be out looking for her!

She stared at the monikut. There was a huge lock on its iron grill. Through the grill she could see the floral gamosa on the thapona. By its side, two wicks flickered in the oil lamp that must have been lit that evening. In this light, soft as two glow worms, Doiboki saw the many flowers made of gold and silver placed on it. She went down on her knees before the thapona.

Suddenly, a lamp that burnt on a mound of earth outside the monikut, guttered out. There was a muffled noise, as though something had jumped off the roof on to the huge drum in one corner of the naamghar. Doiboki shivered. She could hear, once again, the rustling sound of the revered one near the drum.

She tried to concentrate on the many smells that floated in the naamghar – the mild sweet fragrance of the incense sticks and camphor, that of mustard oil, the smell of burnt-out cotton wicks in ancient oil lamps mixed with the fresh smell of the mopped mud floor, the smell of the soaked gram and moong prasad – but for her only the stench of raw fish stayed, overpowering all else. Her rain soaked basket reeked of fish.

Doiboki's heart started to pound. What had she done? She had spread the odour of fish in that holy place which barred its doors even to those women, fair and fragrant like the gardenia. She flinched like a magur on which salt had been sprinkled. Her head reeled. She had left home at the crack of dawn, after a meal of leftover rice soaked in water. Now suddenly, without warning, she retched, then began to throw up noisily. Hastily, she mopped up the slimy, sour smelling vomit with her sador, afraid even to look at it. Surely there was blood, clots of blood, yes, certainly there was blood. Wearily, she lay down on the floor and, in her semiconscious state, she heard the same rustling sound. She saw two green-backed turtles splashing around a golden boat that floated on the waters. Then everything blurred. Only blotches of blood and a sador soaked in blood, unfolding to its full length ...

"She's breathing."

"She's moving, she's moving."

"She's not dead, not dead."

"She's sitting up. The woman is sitting up."

Doiboki woke up to a babble of female voices. She rubbed her eyes and looked around her. She was right in the middle of the great naamghar, a crowd of women peering at her from outside. The hailstones that had pelted her had disappeared. Where was the sador soaked in blood? She looked at the crumpled sador on her body. It was stained with huge patches of dried vomit. Where were the gigantic turtles and the golden boat, the long one that rustled around? And the gold and silver flowers glittering in the soft light of the oil lamps?

Doiboki rubbed her eyes and looked at the monikut. The gold and silver flowers, the brass oil lamp, the big sorais of bell metal glittered reassuringly in the daylight. She fell to her knees, her head touching the ground reverentially in prayer. Then, arranging her sador, she came out of the naamghar. Her head was throbbing. Still unsteady, she reached the spot where the women sang their bhajans and slumped heavily to the ground, just a little distance from the monikut.

"Isn't this Doiboki the fisherwoman?" one of the women, who was as beautiful as the vermilion-coloured senduriputhi, cried out in astonishment. The menfolk were to have a meeting at the naamghar that evening, so the ladies had come in for their daily prayer in the morning instead of the afternoon. And the sight of an unconscious woman in front of the monikut created a stir among them.

What were they to do? The women were not allowed to enter the naamghar and the naamgharia lived quite some distance away and would take time to arrive. A messenger was sent off to inform him. And the news – A fisherwoman had entered the hallowed, jagroto naamghar – spread like wild fire. People stormed the naamghar to stare at the fisherwoman who was indeed sitting at the entrance to the holy place, her head between her knees.

"I often buy fish from this fisherwoman."

"She lives in that village." Someone pointed to the village at the other end of the bridge.

"How did she enter the naamghar?" The question was asked by many, in many different words. "Why *won't* our country be destroyed by fire? A lowly fisherwoman has entered God's holy temple!"

"There will be disaster. Our country will surely burn," old Banamali Sharma wailed, beating his chest.

"Even the women who share our beds are not allowed to set foot in the holy place, and now this fisherwoman has ..." spluttered Krishna Mahanta.

"Were you not afraid to enter the naamghar with a woman's impure body?" Baruani's voice quivered with a strange dread.

"She will die. She will surely throw up blood and die!" cursed Saikiani, snapping her fingers.

Doiboki tried to get up but sat down again. Her head was spinning. She could feel the bile rise in her empty stomach. Pressing her forehead with one hand, she suddenly threw up. The floor was soaked with the foul smelling, yellow vomit. And finally, when the pain in her stomach subsided and her body felt lighter, she stood up with folded hands and tried to say, "The army, the hailstorm ..." But as she stood up a hundred rupee note, a fifty rupee note and several ten rupee notes fell out from the folds of her mekhela.

"Where did she get all that money?" shouted Mahantani, who had never had even a hundred rupees of her own to spend, nor earned a single rupee in her life. "She must have surely stolen the money and taken refuge inside the naamghar."

"Who knows if the gold and silver flowers ... Naamgharia, why don't you take a look and see if anything is missing."

"Yes, how does one trust these low caste people? She must have had some ulterior motive for entering the naamghar."

Doiboki picked up the notes. Someone spoke up in slightly jocular tones, "Ladies, why don't you feel her body? See if she has hidden anything anywhere."

The throng laughed.

Doiboki's fulsome, dark, magur-like body peeped out of her dishevelled clothes. The eyes of the men seemed to lick her skin. Baruani, thin and flat as a bamboo strip on a weaving loom, suddenly saw her husband staring intently at Doiboki's ill-covered bosom. She pounced on Doiboki, grabbing her by her hair. "How can anyone trust a woman with no sindoor, no conch bangles? Who knows what lover she may have brought in with her?"

"You are right. Whatever her motive, she must certainly have been accompanied by someone."

"Come on, spit it out! Who was with you?"

"Where has he gone?"

The abuses hit Doiboki harder than the lemon sized hailstones. The sharp-tongued fisherwoman was reduced to silence. Suddenly she saw a small dark-skinned boy on the bamboo bridge at the entrance to the naamghar. At the sight of his sturdy limbs, she felt her heart break. Everybody said that the boy was the image of his father. The child took one look at his mother and started running across the bridge.

Holding her nose with one hand, one of the ladies rummaged through Doiboki's basket of rice and potatoes. "What have you got here?"

Doiboki's head throbbed. How dare they call her a thief; her hard earned money, spoils; and accuse her of stealing the potatoes and rice she had bought for the blind old woman. Doiboki bristled. She stretched out her hands like the sharp fins of a magur about to be trapped. Her dark body empowered by the poison of the singi, she pushed away the woman rifling through her bundle.

And then ... a familiar odour wafted up to her in the breeze. She looked up. The people were looking over their shoulders, at the bridge on the river.

Their dark bodies glistening in the sun, groups of people were storming towards the great naamghar, clustered together like a nest of goroi fingerlings.

Coming into her own, Doiboki slapped her thigh in her customary fashion, "Yes, I'm a woman. We're impure. We menstruate. We give birth to babies. I fish for a living. I've sinned by entering the great naamghar. But I'm not a thief. Last night in fear of the army, the hailstorm ..."

Her words were cut short by the blows that began to rain on her, her dark body blackened by the shadows of the people – those very people who would abuse her if her shadow so much as fell on their paddy spread out to dry.

The dark, sturdy little boy came running into the naamghar, shouting, "Ma, Ma!" Somebody gave him a push. And from the dark depths of the crowd, Doiboki let out a heart-rending scream. "Don't kill me, oi ... the old woman, the children ..."

Like a fishing line descending on a nest of goroi fingerlings the scream wound its way towards the dark-skinned people clustered on the bamboo bridge at the entrance to the naamghar. And like tiny kawoi emptied on to the ground, they poured into the naamghar from which they had been barred since the days of their forefathers.

The blind old woman, holding on to this one and that, groped her way in the direction of Doiboki's screams, "Doiboki, oi, let's see someone harm you. You are my child, as good as a son. This blind old woman who in her prime could stop a fully grown rohu with a swipe of her pole, is not yet dead, Doiboki, not yet dead!"

"Doibokir Deen" was originally written in Asomiya and published in *Gariyoshi*, October 1997, Guwahati. "Doiboki's Day" translated by Krishna Barua was published in *Katha Prize Stories 8*, December 1998, by Katha.

K P Ramanunni

WHAT IS YOUR CASTE

TRANSLATED BY GITA KRISHNANKUTTY

A resounding laugh. Talk punctuated by vigorous gestures. He would appear among them spinning around like a ball of fire. "How long is it, man, since I saw you. Haven't you been going out at all since your wedding?" He would hug people he'd met only at literary seminars, like long lost friends. Winding his arms around their shoulders, shaking them from head to foot, he would take accurate aim at the little worm creeping down the collar and flick it away. "You didn't spend anything on the wedding. Come on, let's go to Apsara." Pulling, goading, exchanging jokes. Fake threats. In short, the man we are in the process of describing was simple and straightforward, with no sadistic tendencies, no secretiveness. Besides, the confidential information that he belonged to an excellent taravad and was in some way a distant nephew of V M Nair made writers and readers of stories like us even happier.

But, for the last few days, Ravi Master, the man whom we've just finished describing, had sat closeted in his room in the lodge, forlorn and deeply depressed. Unaccustomed to quaffing even a glass of water without company, he had divided a tall bottle of Green Label into twelve one inch portions with equal measures of soda and was working his way through each, all by himself, at half hourly intervals. A photograph of Koman Valia-ammaman, his granduncle, which he'd discovered after much rummaging in Amma's old wooden box, stood on the windowsill. The sun and moon shapes carved by silverfish on the photograph hinted at the light years that separated space from time past. Ravi Master scrutinized the photograph of his Valia-ammaman, seated in a wooden chair with a stricken expression on his face, and tried to read his body language. His granduncle's right hand seemed to be gripping an invisible walking stick. There was unwarranted force in the way he squared his wide shoulders, the rounded, arrogant ears defied deafness.

Comparing his own reflection in the mirror with Valia-ammaman's physique and expressions, Ravi Master felt more and more damned. The architectural principles that had created Ravi Master, Koman Valia-ammaman, as well as Trivikraman Nair, the Tehsildar of Kanhirapally, had followed a special system of measurements: A backbone that was girderlike, the triangle that took shape, when they stood hands planted on the waist, that was an exact mirror image of the entrance to the courtyard of the traditional four winged taravad home, the nalukettu.

"It is not you who determine the way you stand or sit or walk, Ravi Mastere, but your genes. The same DNA that fashioned you, fashioned your father, your uncle and your granduncle. The stylish way they hitched up their mundus as they walked towards the paddy sheaves, and the swagger with which they sat in the taravad hall have repeated themselves through history, hence it is that the Kanhirapally Nair and the Nairs of your taravad look so alike."

Ravi Master remembered Neeli Raman describing the Nair physiology on the veranda of the Taluk Office. He determined to shatter the shackles of tradition in a flood of intoxication and wrench out the man, that Sisyphean rock. He poured a tall whisky, but did not drink it at once.

His words and actions had to be further analyzed in accordance with Neeli Raman's theory of the "subconscious Nair mind." Ravi Master went over the whole episode once again, playing the scene on the day of the seminar over in his mind, when he had welcomed each speaker to the Town Hall. His intention was to study the discrimination that had insinuated its way into his attitude towards each of them, according to their caste. He began by recalling the manner in which he'd greeted the Dalit woman speaker from M G University and the royal blooded thampuratti who was a professor in a college, belonging to the princely family, the kovilakam – "Hullo, Neeli Raman," "Hullo, Sudha Varma," – and then examining how condescending was the "Hullo, Neeli Raman"; how much more deferential the "Hullo, Sudha Varma."

It was the literary and cultural seminar held a month earlier that had created the need for this ordeal by fire self-examination. The literary organizers of the place had entrusted the preparation of the programme to Ravi Master with the sole intention of placing a man with no vested interests at the helm of affairs. Working round the clock, denying himself sleep, he had hurried through his work at school, correcting the children's answer papers and preparing pamphlets for the Science Parishad before springing enthusiastically into the preparations for the seminar. From choosing the cloth for the banners to personally inviting the speakers, he had had to shoulder every responsibility. Already slim, Ravi Master opened now into three, four slender petals, each petal rushing around simultaneously, one to arrange for a microphone, another to post the programme notices, to get the badges ready ...

It was while officiating as the moderator for the lengthy discussion on the cultural implications of caste during the last session that it happened. When Neeli Raman, with her dark skinned cast iron face, her lips molten as if turned red-hot in a furnace, and her incredibly white teeth, got up to speak, Ravi Master had a premonition that she was going to put a spanner in the proceedings. And, no sooner did he pass her a note under the microphone stand, telling her that she had to keep to the stipulated time limit, she had barked,

"Stop interfering, Nair! Hasn't this been going on for centuries, this business of keeping people in order?"

Instead of rhetoric, sounds like the cracking of green bamboo poles rent the air. When inappropriate words are pronounced on a dais, it shatters in a material sense and something indefinable and uncultured happens in its place.

The waves of sound that burst from Neeli Raman's abuse devastated all the modern arrangements in the Town Hall. The decorative lamps that burned at high voltage began to flicker and grow dim, the tube lights went out and a spluttering like that of mustard seeds and chillies in hot oil disturbed the clarity of the loudspeakers. A murky darkness, like that found in ancient houses, cast shadows over the faces of all those seated on the dais and in the hall. The young Dalit woman who had shyly pinned her delegate's badge on the curve of her breast had mutated into the power and fury of a colonized forest. The realization that the situation in the Town Hall was a volatile one, terrified Ravi Master. Clenching his hands between his legs, as if safeguarding something very valuable, he called out,

"All you need to do is to call my name. Don't be impertinent."

It was the most moving declaration of protest a Nair could have made against caste. To think it was he, a true comrade in the Communist movement, that a young woman had insulted in public, calling out his caste.

The image of his father, who had adorned the puja room of his taravad home with portraits of Marx, Lenin and AKG, rose before him, veins jutting out of his neck in support of the Kuthali Estate Farmers' Revolt. Flags, banners and pandals put up for the protest workers had blossomed all over their estate and its vicinity. The games that the police, the landowners and the goondas had indulged in had been bloody and terrible. It was only when Communist martyrs, spattered with fiery red, felled by guns and lathi charges, lay scattered on the ground that the demonstration had come to an end. When Achan, his father, had come back home, his face sunburnt and unshaven, Amma had sat him down on her sickbed. He had heard her say all sorts of things to Achan as she struggled to breathe. That very day, Gangadharan Master had ushered Ravi out of his class, before he could finish drawing the map of India, and had taken him home. Amma lay unmoving in a strange sleep in which she was not tormented by breathlessness or any other suffering. Since that day, every time his father had gathered him up in his arms and rushed out, he had participated fully in countless processions and demonstrations, holding on to Achan's fingers and shouting, "Inquilab!"

When Sudha Varma, Dr Thomas, M R Mallisserry and Aboobacker, all seated on the stage, looked at him surreptitiously from the corners of their eyes, the man who had been a Comrade from infancy lowered his head, as embarrassed as if the red flag had suddenly turned into a pattukomanam, a red loin cloth. He realized that he would no longer be able to control the discussion in a disciplined way.

By that time, Neeli Raman, her mouth too close to the microphone, had begun her speech.

"Isn't what I said right?" she asked, running her eyes over the high caste people in the audience as she detailed the sufferings that subordinates had endured for centuries. Her question roared through the silence that had blocked the great throats of the loudspeakers. When Neeli Raman shot a look from her half-moon eyes towards the stage, Ravi Master knew it was aimed not at the coordinator, but at the Nair that he was.

A complaint about a Dalit being insulted by having his caste called out is wicked, a mockery. It is like opening your mouth wide and clicking your tongue, uttering the distasteful sound, "tchh." However, knowing that a high caste man suffers because his caste has been called out evokes everyone's respect and compassion. And, as soon as the meeting was over, intellectuals like Thomas, Mallisserry and Kannambilly crowded around Ravi Master and embraced him, as if he were some sort of hero.

"Oh, Ravi Mastere, imagine calling someone like you by the name of your caste! Where is our country going to ... nothing but caste and religion everywhere."

And it was the buzz at the drinking session at the Amalapuri that evening.

Kissing Ravi Master's cheek with drooling lips to express his respect and admiration, in memory of the Nair woman he had once been in love with, Mallisserry the Ezhava proclaimed,

"Whatever caste ... or religion, all we want is that human beings be good."

"Go ... go ... go ..." Pouring out the last peg into all the glasses, Kannambilly, professor and left wing intellectual, conducted a rite of exorcism, "Hindu, Muslim, Nair, Theeyan, Cheruman, may all kinds of evil caste spirits leave us and be doomed by the sorcery of liquor, may the real person within us emerge – dead drunk!"

The clamour and camaraderie of the cultural seminar party ended in some dark ravine of inebriation where space and time followed no order. Having heard the proclamation of strategy – Humanity, Humanity, Humanity! – echo around them, they all went back to home and hearth without straying from their path: Thomas to Thresiamma, Mallisserry to Radhamani and Aboobacker to Fathima. Only Ravi Master, who was not yet married, though the silver clouds of noon had descended on his beard, went back to his pillow that smelt of oil, in the old Paradise Lodge inhabited by teachers and clerks.

He came to slowly, to the snakelike touch of sticky vomit and cigarette smoke, feeling something more than a headache clinging to his consciousness. Ravi Master realized it was Neeli Raman's call, singling him out as a Nair, a leech that brought out drops of blood on his skin.

It was Lambodaran Master at school the next day who first teasingly called him a Nair. When he went back to the lodge, the lively, dissolute Mani Kurup repeated it. One by one, as they came to hear of the frightful comedy that had taken place at the seminar, all those close to Ravi Master began to have a dig at him. However skilfully he dissolved the comedy into laughter and drained the laughter into intoxication, he found no peace of mind. Master, leave it alone, urged Sankarankutty and Habibullah, inmates of his lodge and colleagues at his school, making light of it. But it kept coming back, like regurge, to give him nausea.

It was at this point that Ravi Master decided, bolstered by the large peg he usually had at dusk, to talk directly to Neeli Raman and ask her to explain why she had called him a Nair. It was a mystery to him how she had discovered his antecedents, the horrible truth which only found mention in the appropriate column of his SSLC book, a secret that not even his close friends knew about.

Sankarankutty and Habibulla were quite startled when he suddenly threw down his cards, abandoning the game that evening and muttered, "Certainty and clarity are what we need in all things. Even if I have to go to Kottayam, I will do so and I will confront her there."

"This is sheer madness, Mastere," they said to him, scolding him for the way he had changed since the seminar. But take the bus he did, to Mundakayam from the Kottayam bus stand, and got off at Chittadi. The ghat road that went up from the left stretched on for quite a while before ending in the rubber estate. A craggy path from there on wound and twisted itself along the edge of the estate. The house that the arrow drawn with a thick felt pen indicated became visible as soon as the path ended.

Clutching the piece of paper with the drawing he had got from the University hostel, Ravi Master, who had set out in search of Neeli Raman's house, realized the hardship of uneven pathways. The kilometres spanned out when he climbed the slopes, and knocked at his knees when he descended them. Rebellious stones rolled around under his feet, threatening his equilibrium, yet he hurried on, anxious to come upon Neeli before the courage of the small peg he had drunk petered out.

"What is it, child, where are you from, is it to see her?"

Neeli Raman's father, Kochuraman, welcomed Ravi Master. His missing teeth, a symbol of the childhood of the human race, flashed a smile. "Neeli ..." His call swept through the house in search of her, while Ravi Master waited in the courtyard, taking a bird's eye view of the place —

the upside down hills, the rubber forests, the little stream that mined silver in the buried abyss. He realized that the stamp of these surroundings had entered the Town Hall along with Neeli's body and that this was why her mild assault had suddenly turned the atmosphere savage.

Neeli Raman appeared from within her house and stood there with no trace of the aggressiveness she had shown at the seminar. When she said in a happy voice, "Who is it? O, Ravi Master!" he retorted a little viciously, "No, Ravi Nair!" and plunged headlong into the subject.

First of all, he wanted to know how she had discovered the fact that his father and mother were Nairs. Second, she must convince him that she had a reason for insulting him, progressive that he was from head to foot, by calling out his caste.

Neeli Raman stood smiling all the while. Only her eyes shifted from where they sat, face to face with the wooden ledge in front of the house — to the mountain ranges, the rubber forests and the sky that hung upside down in a yogic sheershasana posture between them.

The place was so peaceful, so soporific, that it relaxed all the tautness in him. When he realized that Neeli was in no mood to talk, he too dissolved into the phenomenon of nature, seeking there for deeper replies to simple questions.

Neeli Raman laid out a lavish spread for Ravi Master with rice, boiled and flavoured buttermilk, tapioca, steamed sardines. Then a walk circling the High Range that sent a pleasant ache of fatigue creeping up his knees. As the ghat evening gathered, with the kind of enormous shadows that people living on the coast never see, Kochuraman poured out mature palm toddy for him.

Whenever Ravi Master brought up the questions that were the object of his journey, Neeli Raman replied, "I'll show you."

That was how, the next day, they went to see Trivikraman Nair, the landlord of old, in the Tehsildar's office and how, on the grounds of the physical similarities between Trivikraman Nair and Ravi Master, she lay down her case — points one, two, three — for having called him "Nair" in the seminar hall.

When they got back to her room, Neeli explained the deductions she had made from her research on the physiology and psychology of caste. The changes in the anatomy of different castes who, over generations, had been engaged in different kinds of jobs, the diversities in their mental makeup. As organic parallels to all these, the great variations that occur in the production of adrenalin, the expansion of the thyroid glands and the predilection for salty, sour or sweet flavours – why, the way the influence of caste determined sexual deviations! She wound her way through proofs and statistical data with the impartiality and accuracy of a scientist. And all the time, her regret for the human suffering that lay behind historical truths gleamed moistly in her eyes.

Having become a believer after listening to all this, Ravi Master began to fill in the answers to the questionnaire she had given him as a final test, and arrived with absolute exactitude at the column marked "Nair."

After an analytical study that ran into hours, they leaned back in their chairs on either side of the table. The optimistic belief in the oneness of man had disappeared with the two pegs Ravi Master had had that morning. Sorrow darkened his face like blood splatters a sacrificial stone on which history has dashed its head. Neeli Raman too noticed this and became melancholic.

They became continents of distress and the vastness of the table between them turned into a sea and danced like one possessed. Then, suddenly melting, Neeli Raman lunged forward. Locking her fingers into the bridge over the sea, she caught hold of Ravi Master.

"Never mind. Accept the truth first. Then we can rebuild it differently."

Returning on the Kannur Express, Ravi Master spent the night relearning his life in the context of his past. Gingerly he touched the eyes, the nose, the chest, the genitalia, of his alter ego, that Nair Siamese twin who existed alongside his progressive self. The prototype for the resemblance between Trivikraman Nair, the Tehsildar of Kanhirapally, and himself was not his father. He knew now that it was his mother's uncle, Koman Valia-ammaman – the village authority, Adhikari Koman Nair – who used to go around cruelly wresting his share of the produce from the tenants, the stud bull who established his ownership over tenant gatherings by impregnating them. He recalled Amma saying that his laugh, his quick temper, his insistence that if he planted a banana tree, it had to bear fruit the same day, were all inherited from Koman Valia-ammaman.

"What's this, Comrade? Just because a woman called you Nair do you have to change completely?" asked KEN, an old friend and comrade-in-arms, who had hurried to see Ravi Master on getting wind of the fact that all was not well with him after the infamous incident at the seminar. Sankarankutty and Habibulla had reported a couple of days ago that, what with the trip to Kottayam, the phone calls to Neeli Raman and all that, things were no longer under control.

Ignoring the question, Ravi Master opened the half-filled bottle on the table with a feeble smile and poured out two pegs each for himself, Sankarankutty and Habibulla. He filled the fourth glass with soda and pushed it towards KEN.

"Tell me, Ravi Master, what then is the problem?" Sankarankutty asked quickly, anxious that KEN's question should not be an isolated one. Engrossed in adding soda to the drinks and downing his own, Ravi Master ignored him. However, it transpired that the effect of those large pegs was incendiary. They merely fireballed into one huge outburst.

"Valia-ammaman, Koman Valia-ammaman!" Ravi Master screamed suddenly, his closed fist breaking an invisible mud pot on his chest. He looked fearfully at the corner of the room, as if a corpse had just risen from the burning ground. Sankarankutty and Habibulla rose from their chairs, their muscles twitching with shock. Ravi Master spoke unblinkingly, single minded as an arrow.

"Koman Valia-ammaman, here is your nephew, your spitting image, your heir, flesh of your flesh, an exact replica of your qualities. A caricature of the feudal character ... a carbon copy of arrogance. And ... and ..." His tone, which climbed inch by inch to a threatening crescendo, ended in an angry outburst that drove Koman Valia-ammaman away – "Chi po!"

Exorcized, or at least exhausted, Ravi Master embraced KEN and lamented like a son who has not been able to give his forefathers peace even after performing all the recommended rituals in the most sacred places.

"However deeply one is involved in progress, evil spirits stay on with one, Comrade. Do you know who I am? The infant ghost of Adhikari

Pandikakalathil Koman Nair. The same likes and dislikes, the same impatience, the same tendency to brag, why even the same ISI stamp at the back of the neck and on the lower chin."

He detailed the conclusive evidence of Neeli Raman's research, begun in mockery, about the decisive influence of caste and tradition on a person's makeup. Although KEN tried to rebut his argument, fighting with words like *human*, *history* and *class politics*, he felt that nothing held water for Ravi Master. If only a human being were like what the Comrade said! Even as he cried out, Ende, Thrikavilamma! a sigh spun like a whirlwind around him ... no, a human being is not like that.

Once Sankarankutty and Habibulla realized that they would gain nothing by argument, they changed their tactics and handled Ravi Master as if he were out of his senses, completely drunk. Using phrases like, "Have this buttermilk and water, now," "Pour a couple of buckets of water on his head," they made ready to discipline Ravi Master, to rescue KEN from his clutches, and send him home on his scooter.

From that day on, Ravi Master was treated with ridicule or disbelief by all the other lodgers. Gathered in the Teachers' Union Office, his colleagues, including Sankarankutty and Habibulla, concluded that the way the Comrade was going was clearly dangerous.

The Union Secretary, whose eyes were surrounded by a forest of warts, spoke in a hushed voice, "We must keep an eye on the Comrade." And from then on Ravi Master's daily routine was monitored down to its smallest detail. "Oh look, that's the fifth peg you've finished today!" they would say, their words taking on the protective tone that guardians use for children and the mentally disturbed. However, no one dared to talk to Ravi Master on one subject – the explosive topic of caste. Only Mani Kurup, coming in one day, riding high on his liquor and a woman hunting session, said –

"So, Master, you've begun to believe in caste? I don't know about men, but I've known for ages that women have caste. Women like your Kottayam character, Master, are good for rheumatism, and it is a fact that body aches and joint pains will disappear in a second. Then, there is the aristocratic, tender touch of Namboodiri women, the deadly games that the sensual Thamburattis of royal birth play, the gymnastic skill of Nazrani women. I'm not going to die, Master, until I know the women of every caste mentioned in the gazette, ha ha ha!"

Ravi Master had no idea where the alarming HIV decisions concerning caste, that had come about so unexpectedly, would take him. Only in the telephone conversations with Neeli Raman did he experience the thrill of light spreading through worlds that had been plunged in gloom.

"I believe an American company has discovered a chemical weapon that seeks out and kills only certain tribes." He called Neeli as soon as he read the report in *Science Today*.

"I read it too. I've written to ask for more details. But isn't the caste species nambidi kanakkova, that includes people like our C R Parameswaran, being annihilated here without the use of chemical materials of any kind?"

When Neeli Raman laughed at the other end, the gurgling of the mountain streams gushed towards him through the receiver.

"Look, Pulaya woman, you are going to receive a bonus for having worked in the sun all this time. Even when the ozone layer weakens, the melanin pigment in the black skin resists ultra violet rays. While fair-skinned people like us go through hell with cancer, dark-skinned ones like you will escape." The suicidal Nair within Ravi Master, dreaming of his own death, suddenly spoke.

"But Nair, long, long ago we became as immune to being driven away and spat upon as we did to ultra violet rays. So we do not immediately realize it if someone attacks us. The superiority complex I display is a kind of anticipatory bail," Neeli replied.

"Do you want Adhikari Koman Nair's crooked intelligence? I have plenty of it in stock."

"Mm. Many other things will have to change hands before that."

Ravi Master's telephone conversations with Neeli Raman provoked the inmates of the lodge to the kind of insecurity and malice that people feel when listening to a foreign language. He was seen as isolated from everyone, like a planet that has left its orbit. Sankarankutty and Habibulla felt themselves growing smaller every time they made fun of their colleague or scolded him in an attempt to change him, for Ravi Master would respond only with a low laugh, making no attempt to conceal the contempt that dribbled from the corner of his mouth. Or with a deep sigh. Or a long silence. In reality, this was an alien personality poking fun at them, wearing the guise of their old Comrade.

Unable to bear the insult and fear any longer, his colleagues laid the problem open for discussion once again in the Union Office.

"Why not have a psychiatrist look at him?" The Union Secretary, clearly distressed, blinked his warty eyes.

"What we should do is catch hold of him and give him a couple of blows. All this dressing up as an intellectual and having philosophical discussions with a pulaya girl!" Sankarankutty was losing his patience.

But what they finally accepted unanimously was the crafty warfare of middle class trade unionists rather than direct combat.

Ravi Master did not receive any of the telephone calls Neeli made to the lodge – his calls to Kottayam were intercepted by Neelakantan, the owner of the booth near the school. And all the letters from M G University were intercepted at the Post Office.

Meanwhile, Ravi Master spent all the time available to him trying to discover a concept resembling Mendel's Genetic Theory. He used himself, Koman Valia-ammaman, and Sekhara Ammaman as the three prototypes. Placing Koman Valia-ammaman in the F1 generation, Sekhara Ammaman in F2 and himself in F3, he was attempting to draw a chart of the metamorphosis of certain inherited characteristics.

Ravi Master first assumed that cruelty towards those at a lower level and slavishness towards those at a higher one would be one characteristic. This he named C. Hence, Koman Valia-ammaman's actions – from the high point of standing next to the tenant while the paddy was being boiled and measuring out the produce from the tenants' field, to the depths of being spat upon on his face and standing obsequiously in the illam, the Namboodiri residence, where he held the post of manager – would be noted down in the F1 generation column as C1. Sekhara Ammaman, who had been a Police Inspector, had, on the one hand, killed someone who had been in his custody and on the other, ceded even his wife for his master's pleasure. Since the quality marked C appeared much more sharply in the F2 generation than in F1, it would be noted as C2. Ravi Master, who was in the F3 generation, would become C0 since he had only done trivial things like enforce discipline on certain Class IV employees, pick up the school Inspector's handkerchief when it fell down and so on. (Even so, it had to be understood that the characteristic is still latent in C0 and that 0 never indicates emptiness.) In a cultural revolution like that in China, the factor C would swing around, harass people on top, gladden people at the bottom, become C1 and appear in the F4 generation. If, on the contrary, the Emergency was going to be repeated, C, in its qualitative strength, would become C3 or C4 and appear in the F5 generation. This was the methodology that Ravi Master used to analyze the way in which traditional components were transformed in accordance with new circumstances, in the Nair species.

Once the hypotheses, theses, charts, graphs, footnotes and research papers were complete, he grew taut with eagerness to share them with Neeli Raman.

Ravi Master presented himself over and over again at the phone in the lodge, in Neelakantan's phone booth and in the yard of the Post Office. It may very well have been because of the genes of the old sambandam man, Kadupottan Namboodiri, who used to visit the women of Ravi Master's taravad, that he did not understand their evil machinations. And so the phone boy with his sheepish smile, Neelakantan's phone booth with its calamitous sounds, and the post peon who turned his head the other way, continued to play their tricks on him.

"What's happening, no replies to my letters, nor can I get through on the phone," he said to himself, yearning to rush to Kottayam.

As the days spun out, the hideous activities they were engaged in began to worry Sankarankutty and Habibulla. The mountains of intercepted letters and telegraphic messages, the endless phone calls—it became a habit for Postman Madhavan to complain about disciplinary proceedings and for the phone boy, Sunny, to grumble about "the Kottayam Problem."

Likening Neeli Raman to the fearful witch in the horror stories his grandmother had told him, Sankarankutty asked Habibulla, "Will that yakshi come searching for him here?"

"Mm," snorted Habibulla, who belonged to a high caste Mapilla family and made regular offerings of payasam to the temple of the brahmarakshasu, "Let her come, we'll somehow get rid of her."

Ravi Master's colleagues sighed tragically on the day they learnt that Neeli Raman was in. Listening in on the phone, Sankarankutty's face grew progressively more shrivelled like a pickled tender mango and his voice gave way, as he broke the news, with the solemnity of imparting the announcement of a dear one's death, to the other teachers in the staff room. The news soon reached Sukumaran Nair, the Union Office Secretary and Habibulla, who had gone to look into some matter concerning the side business in readymade garments that he ran. Professor Kannambilly lost his temper and KEN was plunged in thought.

"Didn't he walk into her lap, this boy from an excellent family? She'll never let him go."

"She's a southerner, remember? And a Kottayam woman too!"

"She has sexy eyes, the yakshi. I noticed them on the day of the seminar."

Ravi Master's respectable friends were lavish with their sexist comments, comments that we all tend to make but which are seldom dwelled upon later.

As soon as the phone boy, Sunny, brought the news that Neeli Raman and Ravi Master had arrived at the lodge, Sankarankutty, Habibulla, the Union Secretary, Professor Kannambilly and the others rushed there. Sunny, who was waiting on the veranda, indicated with a single kathakali gesture that they were both inside the room.

Feet moved stealthily through the corridor, tapping out the multiplication tables that multiply four by two. In front of Ravi Master's room the twin door panels were glued to each other by a thread of light. Since a half-closed door is also a half-opened one, it follows that a fully closed door is a fully opened one. Therefore, since they saw everything inside the room clearly, Sankarankutty, Habibulla, the Professor and the Union Secretary said to themselves,

"What a pity! In the end, she got Ravi Master ..." (Echoing the standard lament of those who chance upon the bones and hair that the yakshi, having devoured her victim, strews under the palm trees of history!)

Tchh (The first muffled question). Tchh tchh (The loud question). Tchh tchh tchh tchh tchh tchh tchh tchh (The long scream of fury).

What Sankarankutty's fingers tapped out on the door was the rhythm pattern of his great grandfather Shoolapani Variar's agitation, a world famous magician in his time.

"Should we break open the door?"

"Isn't this insolence?"

"Open the door quickly, man."

Each one grew angrier and more impatient, as if in an agony to empty his bowels, unable to stand it any longer.

"Ravi Mastere, Ravi Mastere!" Kannambilly pushed the two cries out of his throat like some ritual.

At this point I would like to request the readers to stop reading for a minute and conduct a small soul searching exercise. In the impatience of all those who want to have the door opened at once, is there not, beyond mere pleasure, a slightly murderous intent? A woman, and that too one from another caste like Neeli Raman, to come in search of Ravi Master, get into his room and shut the door? Is there not in this something that weakens the unconditional support of readers for the hero and heroine?

Kada kada

Kada kada kada kada kada.

Although each member of the four man army banged on the surface of the closed door in turn, the heartwood of the shutter, saturated with heavy monsoon rains, held on.

Ravi Master and Neeli, who were compassionately discussing the results obtained from their research on caste, grew tired of the irritating noise. Ravi Master closed his notebooks and records, lay down flat on his cot, and closed his eyes. Neeli sat beside him looking at him emotionlessly.

"Stop your insolence, Nair!"

No sooner did Ravi Master begin to laugh at the image he had in his mind of himself than he was transformed into a vast sky that could perceive the entire Nair horizon.

After a long time, he felt as if the scent of rain drenched earth had enveloped him completely. The slippers that were wrongly placed, the unbuttoned shirt, bore witness to the fact that he had reestablished the bonds he had so resolutely cut off with the earth.

"We have many things to exchange with each other, Ravi Mastere," Neeli's liquid voice flowed gently into his right ear. Remembering that, since the earth was round, the sky could situate itself not only above but underneath as well, Ravi Master lay flat, not moving.

Lacking the strength to touch them and be polluted, the clamouring elements beyond the door moved away into the distance.

"Jadi Chodikkuka" was originally written in Malayalam and published by *Kala Kaumudi*, August 1999, Kottayam. "What is your Caste" translated by Gita Krishnankutty was published in *Katha Prize Stories 10*, December 2000 by Katha.

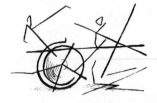

Critical Commentaries

by

HEPHZIBAH ISRAEL

H S SHIVAPRAKASH

BRINDA BOSE

UMA CHAKRAVARTI

OORAKALI: A READING

HEPHZIBAH ISRAEL

"Oorakali" belongs to a body of Tamil writing that consciously seeks to express an alternate poetics and politics in an alternate voice to what has long been considered mainstream Tamil literature. The polemics of mainstream versus alternate literature (and therefore culture) within Tamil literature is, in this context, particularly relevant since the dividing lines are drawn around the parameters of caste, such that the mainstream and established body of literature has been produced by the upper Brahminical castes and the alternate literatures by non-Brahminical lower castes. However, this division is a comparatively recent development in the two thousand year old history of Tamil literature, with the corpus of alternate literature having gathered enough strength and impetus only over the last few decades, posing a challenge to canonized literature.

Broadly classified as "Dalit literature," the significance of the alternate voice lies in its power to disrupt and question complacent notions of cultural and literary traditions as unidimensional categories. By speaking from the counter-space of subaltern culture, the alternate voice, refusing to be ignored, subsumed or suppressed into oblivion, makes more visible the multi-dimensionality of language, literature and culture.

Language, occupying as it does, points of intersection between culture and literature, has become one of the most contested sites in the struggle over the right to define and produce culture. While "cultured" Tamil used by the upper castes has for long been considered the language that befits literature, the dialects and the more colloquial Tamil spoken by the lower castes have been condemned as barbarous on the grounds that they lower or even destroy Tamil culture.

There are two possible strategies to deal with such a scenario – one, for those who wish to write to acquire a command over "cultured Tamil"; and two, to deliberately use folk language as a mode for self-expression, and thereby undermine accepted definitions of "good" literature. While many early Dalit writers felt compelled to do the former, either because they too believed in the sanctity of high Tamil, or because they were handicapped by the belief that only this option would bring them recognition and a place in the canon, there has been a slow change in their outlook. Though it took some time for them to see through the liberal humanist rhetoric based on the politics of aesthetics, and that Litertaure with a capital "L" should not be mixed or confused with socio-political issues of caste conflict, Dalit writers have now begun to recognize that the content and forms of high culture can neither fully accommodate or adequately express Dalit sentiments. There has been an increasing realization among them that there is a need to develop new and different forms that will suit the voicing of Dalit sentiments. More Dalit writers in recent years have thus begun to adopt the strategy of consciously using folk language and adapting it, making use of its very rawness to produce a powerful and vital body of literature. The response of the guardians of high culture to this has been either to reject any such Dalit endeavours as unthinkably uncouth or simply to ignore its very existence, both being equally detrimental to Dalit movement and self-esteem.

The Dalit literary movement has been slow in building up into a recognizable body, partly because of disagreement within the ranks of Dalit writers. Those who were more easily co-opted into the mainstream, by and large wanting to avoid being labelled "Dalit writer," claimed that they were first and foremost writers and that their writing was not to be viewed from the caste angle. However, there has been a gradual shift in

115

perception. So one of the important achievements of the movement has been that these writers are now more amenable to having their names associated with Dalit politics and concerns.

According to Irathina Karikalan, the writer of "Oorakali," it is equally important that there be literature that supports Dalit literature, produced by writers who may not themselves be Dalits, but who empathize and engage with Dalit issues and predicaments. Since Dalit literature can only be produced by Dalits, he suggests that most of his own writing, including "Oorakali," the story under discussion, should be seen as falling within this category of writings in Tamil. Though non-Dalits can seldom approximate the mental or emotional responses of a Dalit to a particular situation, he concedes that they may be able to come close to describing physical conditions and experiences, and thereby wake social conscience. Thus, he sees himself and other writers like him as engaged in the important task of producing this "support literature" that provides both literary and political reinforcement to Dalit literature.

"Oorakali" is a short story that is set in the villages around the small town Vriddachalam in the district of Cuddalore or South Arcot of Tamil Nadu. Most of this area around Vriddachalam supports an agrarian economy where in recent years only the Dalits and Vanniars (a caste just above the Dalits in the hierarchy) are left to farm the land. Most of the Brahmins/upper castes have left the area in the last couple of decades or so for towns and cities. Of the castes that remain, Dalits, though still not landowners, work on farms. Those of the present generation of Dalits who live in farms near towns, either take on jobs in factories or on construction sites. Traditional wages such as a sum of money, bags of rice and daily food in exchange for a year's bound labour continues, though Dalits have begun to prefer daily wages instead. In many regions, they are still expected to remove night soil. However, many of them would prefer not to perform some of the traditional roles such as the lifting and cleaning of dead bodies. When it comes to the question of social acceptance, their children can attend schools with upper caste children, but they would probably still be served tea in different cups in the village teashops.

The alleviation of caste burdens at either the political, economic or social levels is relatively much lower here than in the southern districts of

Tamil Nadu. Attempts at the "upliftment" of Dalits have been severely handicapped by infighting among the different political cliques for greater power and recognition.

Given this scenario, "Oorakali" is a good example of a short story that helps to contextualize and highlight not just political and social problems of caste per se, but also the political underpinnings that govern and shape Tamil literary taste and decide the direction it will take in the future.

The title of the story – "Oorakali" – is in itself interesting, referring as it does to a specific caste in Tamil Nadu. It is a caste name used mostly in the district of Cuddalore (other names such as "Pannakaran" are used in other districts). The oorakali, amongst the lowest in the caste hierarchy, had to collect the cattle of the entire village, take them out to graze in the surrounding woods and pasture lands, and in general were responsible for their well being until they drove them home to their pens in the evening. In exchange, the village was supposed to provide the oorakali and their families with food and clothing. Most often than not, this was barely adequate for their survival, the extra portions handed out to them during festivities and ceremonial occasions being the only relief in their otherwise dreary existence.

This traditional role, however, began to lose its importance as traditional methods of cultivation began to give way to more mechanized forms of agriculture in the sixties and seventies. As the use of oxen and cows in the field became obsolete, fewer cattle were maintained by villagers, so much so that each family had gradually reduced the number to a cow or two for milking, which were given into the care of young boys appointed individually.

The oorakali were among the first casualties and rejects of the grand national agenda of setting villages on the path to modernization and progress. Rendered jobless, they survived by hiring themselves and their children out to landowners for a fixed sum of money to work their tractors and motors. This change can be observed in almost all areas of Tamil Nadu where at present it would be difficult to come across an oorakali.

With Oorakali and his children as the protagonists of the story, the kind of folk Tamil used in the original is both appropriate and significant. For, this language immediately acts as a cultural signifier to the average Tamil reader, pointing to the lowest caste groups of the Tamil social structure. As already mentioned above, not using the more Sanskritized Tamil that is both spoken by the upper castes and is the language of the written text is a strategy by which the author chooses to make a larger political statement in the present context of Tamil literature. Such a Tamil would be ordinarily considered so low and degraded a form, that the very idea that it could be used for literary expression would be radical and seen as a crass assault on the reader's sensibilities. But the story uses precisely these assumptions to advantage, its language and subject shocking the reader by confronting him/her with stark social realities on the one hand, and revealing the inadequacies of cultural elitism to express these realities, on the other.

This kind of implicit signalling of subaltern culture, however, becomes immediately problematic when it comes up for translation. Since English, the target language, does not have any such equivalent signification, the moment the source language is rendered in it, the effect of the Tamil original is nullified and flattened. The English language can, at the most, give class signals to the reader so that the experienced reader can, with ease, distinguish the Queen's English from middle class English, working class English or Cockney English. If one were looking for parallels, Cockney would in fact come closest to the kind of Tamil spoken by Oorakali. But the entirely alien context of the Cockney English, both cultural and spatial, makes it unsuited for the purpose of translation in the present instance. There is no choice but to use standard English, and hope to provide compensation by other means of usage. The English translation, thus, tends to delete from the text its original political intent, and fails to communicate the many political and cultural nuances that invest the original with dynamic energy and potency. The examples cited below illustrate ways in which certain words in the original highlight the problems of translating caste into another/alien language and culture.

The Tamil text uses several words that denote a particular caste or a group of castes that do not have English equivalents. On such occasions, it was better to use the Tamil original in Roman transliteration and attempt at explaining the connotations by way of footnotes. The most obvious example is "oorakali," the caste name retained both in the title and body of the story in the English translation. The English "cowherd" comes closest in meaning to it, but would be unable to convey the whole range of caste relationships and dependency within the village structure. Since "oorakali" would mean nothing to a non-Tamil reader (whether Indian or otherwise), it seemed best to footnote it, giving important information on how this caste interacts with the other castes and the kind of interdependency between them. It is also significant that the Source Language or SL text continues to use "Oorakali," a caste/group identity rather than the personal name – Mandayan – that it mentions in passing, when referring to the cowherd. Moreover, the text shifts with ease between the twin usages of "Oorakali" as a personal name and a caste identity. The semantic effect is to remind the reader that the life and fate of the individual cowherd cannot be separated from that of his caste's. In the English version, the addition of the article "the" to Oorakali served to distinguish the reference to caste identity from the personal. Interestingly, there is one instance at the beginning of the story where "oorakali" is also used to refer to the cattle that he grazes, which links his personal identity with his livelihood. This has been translated as "the oorakali cattle" which though a literal translation, is able to convey the speaker's connection with his caste occupation.

"Padaiaatchi," likewise, had to be retained and footnoted since there is again no equivalent in English. It refers to upper castes in general, but in this instance, specifically to the Vanniar caste which is one immediately superior to the Oorakali's. Similarly, "Nattar" is used in the translation since it refers to the male head or representative (by virtue of being the oldest/wealthiest/most powerful) of an extended family within a caste. Translating it into "male head" without this context would have been meaningless in the English version.

However, there is an instance where in spite of there being an English equivalent available, the original Tamil is used. Except for the first reference to her as "washerwoman" to give the reader a clue, all subsequent references to her are as "vannathi." This helps the Indian reader to understand that she is not merely a woman who does the laundry, but has additional caste roles – such as midwife and nurse – traditionally assigned to her caste.

The easiest to translate was "Paappaar" into "Brahmin," because it is a pan Indian word with a more or less fixed signification (so much so that it is probably the one Indian word that would be understood even by a non-Indian reader who has reasonable knowledge of India). Unfortunately however, the slightly derogatory inflection that is implicit in the Tamil "Paappaar" is lost in the translation.

All references to the village, its streets and its people in the Tamil have been translated into English as "the villagers," "the village streets," and "the village people." It was necessary to footnote these as well, because within the Tamil context of caste, they do not refer to the village in general as the English would suggest. On the other hand, all references to, very specifically, the areas of the village and its streets meant exclusively for the upper castes and the "village people" are not to all the inhabitants of a particular village, but only to the upper castes. These are then clearly distinguished from another set of words within the story – "parasaadi," "paratheru," "pariah kutta"– which refer specifically to the outcastes, the areas to which they are restricted (areas that would be outside and far from the area of the upper castes) and the outcaste streets and huts.

Translating "Sami" into English posed another challenge. "Sami" is a respectful form used either to address another human who is of a higher status and importance (equivalent to lord or master), or God. Again, "s(w)ami" is a word that would more or less be understood by most Indian readers. Hence transliterating instead of translating the word seemed acceptable. However, the fact that it may "mean" little to a non-Indian reader does make such translatorial decisions uncomfortable.

Translating a text such as "Oorakali" that is produced out of and within the complexities of caste, makes prominent another important factor in

the process of translation – the reader. Although it is a cliche to reiterate that ultimately all translations must cater to and satisfy the reader, one cannot but be aware of the complication of addressing a multiple and varied audience, especially given the wide cross-section of Indian readership which would be heterogeneous while sharing some basic cultural affinity. The translator's job is hampered by not having a single, homogenous target audience, where it is either not possible to give precedence to one over the other, or s/he is unable to choose one over the others and keep the translations focussed on them. For each decision to be taken on a culturally loaded word, the translator has to keep in mind what signals it might or might not convey to different kinds of readers.

The potential audience for "Oorakali" can be identified as three different kinds of readers – the anglicized Tamil reader who cannot read the Tamil original, but can recognize a few Tamil words, the non-Tamil Indian reader who would also most probably be anglicized and hail from an urban setting, and, the non-Indian reader who is assumed to be uninformed about Indian culture.

It must be acknowledged that most Indian readers who will approach the original through English, would by and large be unfamiliar with the intricacies of the caste structure as it exists in the rural areas. Most urban/ metropolitan Indian readers, Tamil or otherwise, would be more aware of caste as a social category (for the purpose of marriage alliances, for example) rather than as an occupational category. However, the use of original caste names in the translation was a decision taken based on a desire to root the story in its specific social and cultural context whereby it is a two-way process – that is, not merely the story reaching out to an alien reader, but the reader being brought closer to an alien context as well.

TRANSLATING THE TEHSILDAR

H S SHIVAPRAKASH

The problem with present day Dalit literature in Karnataka is that it does not have a well defined Dalit context. This was not the case twenty years ago, when the large scale emergence of the first generation of Dalit writers coincided with a new hope of restructuring society during the post-Emergency years. Various groups of anti-Congress, non-Congress socialists, leftists and Ambedkarites started working hand in hand in media, theatre, and literature. This brief but feverish period of intense activity gave birth, among other things, to Dalit-Bandaya movement,[1] consisting of new Dalit writers and their fellow farers – socialists, leftists and liberals committed to the vision of a more equitable social and political order. The two Dalit writers who benefited most from this atmosphere were the verse writer Siddalingiah and the prose writer Devanooru. Siddalingiah's impassioned, fiery, poetic narratives were complemented by Devanooru's introspective, dainty, and prosaic narratives. Both of them created a refreshingly new idiom that received a great deal of richly deserved critical attention. While Dalit Sangharsh Samiti[2] was gearing itself up to transform Karnataka society, these writers had already created a new literary language.

The togetherness of new literary aspirations and socio-political projects could not hold out long. Siddalingiah has not kept his magnificent promises to the muses. Devanooru has turned a more self-conscious and self-conserving artist as is clear from his well crafted "Kusumbale" which lacks the ideological urgency of his earlier works. The Dalit-Bandaya school now exists as a state wide organization, but no more as a movement. The chief gain of the school had been that it threw up certain challenges both to the creativity and the critical practices of writers outside the school. Even Adiga – villain of the piece from the Dalit-Bandaya perspective, a pioneer of the Naviayas (modernist) movement which dominated Kannada literature between the 1950s and the 1970s, and a highly influential literary figure of his generation because he did not believe in writing only protest literature – was forced to write a poem on Dr Ambedkar, whom he identified with the pantheon of ancient rishis. But the spirit that inspired literary as much as social transformation now seems to be lost to the school.

Dalit Sangharsh Samiti has been to a large extent absorbed into the existing social order. That is not to say that woes of Dalits are at an end. Not a month passes without some outrage or the other against Dalits. Dalit activists are doing their best to mitigate such horrors. Another agonizing fact about the Dalit situation today is that Dalit identity is no more one. Several Dalit groups are now asserting their separate cultural identities. This, on the one hand, has weakened the force of Dalit organizations. On the other, it has strengthened the hands of anti-Dalit upper caste lobbies. The confrontational gesture of Dalits is now somewhat toned down. Only massive blows to Dalit self-respect like the Badannalu massacre of Dalits during 1993-1994 or the more recent desecration of the Ambedkar statue in Bangalore in 1996 have the potentiality to bring together diverse sections of Dalits. Dalit Sangharsh Samiti remains an important organ to safeguard Dalits against the atrocities of a casteist society. But it no more speaks a revolutionary language.

This situation has created new problems and opened up new possibilities for Dalit self-expression. Today's Dalit writer does not have the historic opportunity of gifted writers like Siddalingiah or Devanooru

123

that catapulted them to immediate recognition. They are trying to write, consciously or unconsciously, something different not only from non-Dalit writers, but also from their immediate predecessors. In an atmosphere of increasing awareness of sub-caste and sub-cultural identities, they are trying to document specific memories and moments of the bewilderingly changed and changing present.

The absence of overpowering visions, utopian or dystopian, makes the present day Dalit writing a very difficult task. When imminence of utopia vanished, some Dalit writers like Devanooru and K B Siddhiah had to introduce the theme of immanence of utopia. K B Siddhiah's poem, "Bakala" seeks to depict the meaningful agony of the primal Dalit sage Bakala, who resorted to intense austerities following the bloody holocaust of the Ramayana and Mahabharata wars.[3] Glimpses of another type of immanent utopia appear in the impassioned speech of Kuriyaya, a remarkable character in Devanooru's "Kusumabale." But such moments of transcendence are very rare in today's Dalit literature, as it is in Kannada literature as a whole.

Mogalli Ganesh, the most talented of the second generation Dalit writers, had to contend with a different present than that of the first generation Dalit writers. His formative years received no inspiration from a dominant literary movement or millennial revolutionary hopes. He could fall back neither on the nihilism of the modernists, nor on the idealism of the socially committed writers. Instead, he had the first hand experience of the anguish of Dalit life. This direct dealing with Dalit reality, combined with an assiduous appreciation of Dalit folklore, helped him write a literature that was refreshingly new.

For this reason Mogalli Ganesh stands out among Dalit writers of today. Most of the younger Dalit writers bring in a lot of historically and sociologically manufactured material into their writings that have the rough hewn authenticity and astuteness of the autobiographical. These facts notwithstanding, they do not succeed most often because their experiences, no matter how caste specific, are not able to strike a chord in the hearts of readers, most of whom are non-Dalit. Mogalli makes them work because he is good at turning problems into metaphors and events into images that then outgrow their caste specific world. Forceful images and metaphors speak to that instinct deep within us that longs to unify eclectic phenomena. Another strength of Mogalli's best stories, the one under discussion in particular, is that it conveys the feel of the present day socio-political angst common to both Dalits and non-Dalits: the bankruptcy of reforms, no matter how well meaning. The tehsildar in this story acts out this well meaning bankruptcy.

The story exposes the ugly underside of socio-political reformism. A good deal of the story is a report of a real life-like event, which in itself is valuable. But, unlike in most Dalit stories, the language of journalistic report is played off against non-rational dimensions of language, the so called figures of speech. It is the tension between its two languages that constitute the peculiar impact of Mogalli's story.

The story begins with the sensuous evocation of how the Dalits of a certain village are preparing for the mock harvest. The description is charged with festive gaiety, despite the forebodings of a muttering old woman who believes that her people have sacrificed the honour of their ancestors by digging up and selling some sacred relics of a glorious past. Notwithstanding this, their hectic preparation takes on dimensions of a cosmic communion when, in the language of the non-rational, "... the stars in the sky's garden looked like paddy grain, hung for drying, or scattered for sowing." (13)

Soon follows the language of journalistic report, appraising us of the background of what happens in Olegere: how a well-meaning tehsildar empowered Dalits through a promulgation which allows them to harvest the land which had been violently encroached upon by upper caste farmers. As the starving Dalits get ready for this "harvest," the encroachers, with the support of the Deputy Collector and the police, gang up to wreak vengeance on the Dalit colony. In the last section of the story, the suggestive non-rational language and the cut and dried journalistic report language clash in the description of the way the police descend on the Dalits in order to recover the produce of their "illegal" harvest. The tehsildar's good intentions bring shame to him. However, it is the Dalits who bear the brunt of it all. The police leave their colony completely ravaged.

The poetic description of festive preparations and the prosaic description of everyday power equations converge in the representation of the primitive quagmire of the instinct of hunger in the story's cryptic conclusion, when Mayamma's grandson stuffs his mouth with scattered grains of cooked paddy – "It seemed as if he could digest everything." "And time, bearing its burden of truth in its womb, grew and grew."(24)

In present-day India, translation is a most crucial and responsible activity. Crucial, because it has to negotiate between a bewildering heterogeneity of cultural and sub-cultural expressions of an exceedingly plural society. Responsible, because it should respect the culture's (or sub-culture's) right to self-expression, which cannot happen if one's objective is reduced to producing an eminently readable (therefore, saleable) translation. Literary texts, particularly those emphasizing culture or group specificity, are inscribed with specific worldviews and attitudes to things. These should not be too smoothly made to fit into the worldviews and attitudes built indiscernibly into the target language. The emphasis today, I think, should be on meeting the significations of source texts on their own terms, rather than translating purely on the terms of the target language – a danger that dogs translation, especially into a language of hegemony like English. In my opinion, even eminent translators like A K Ramanujan have walked into this death trap, trying to Anglicize the source texts excessively.

What is being underlined here is the fact that, in an uneven and plural society like India, the activity of translation cannot be an activity free from ideology. To iron out a source text by capturing only the universal significations of a target language like English, amounts to tyrannical suppression of the right to self-expression of the sections of our people whose texts are being translated. The Dalit and other forms of socio-culture specific writing in Indian languages are expressing themselves mostly in various regional and group dialects. They are compelled to reject standard mediums of expression, so as to be true to themselves. The story under discussion is part of this picture.

"Battha" is not written in a sub-cultural dialect throughout. But the standard Kannada is punctured again and again with non-standard expressions, images, metaphors and idioms. It is an extremely difficult task to do justice to the text's translation into other Indian languages, let alone into English.

In the light of the above remarks, I will now attempt a brief analysis of the translation of "Battha" by Shri K Raghavendra Rao. The force of the source text does communicate to a considerable extent in this translation. But what one misses is the exact flavour that accounts for the original's cultural essence.

The problem begins with the title of the translation. The source text is entitled "Battha" (Paddy). The translation of it as "Paddy Harvest" puts an altogether erroneous emphasis. As I see it, the main point of the whole story is not the harvest, but an unquenched longing of an impoverished but irrepressible community for their right to paddy crop. If there is a harvest in the story, it is only a mock harvest.

Why then does the translator make the harvest episode central to the story by interpolating it unwarrantedly in the text? To be able to conjecture a reply to this question, I would like to focus on passages in the translation and the source text depicting the tehsildar.

> The tehsildar, who always responded promptly to such developments, used all his powers and acted immediately. This efficient officer welcomed such challenges. He thought tackling them was historically necessary to bring about justice in the country. (14)

This translated passage makes it sound as if the narrator is all praise for the tehsildar. However, the narrator's attitude to the tehsildar is much more complex in the source text. No matter how well meaning, the more he tries to help the Dalits, the more he actually harms the Dalits. These nuances are clearly elaborated in the equivalent of the above passage in the source text. To substantiate my point, I have attempted a more source friendly translation of the above passage:

> The tehsildar of that taluk who was in the habit of responding to such developments quick like an arrow,

swung into action forthwith, and made an official
promulgation by exercising all powers within his limits.
According to the young and efficient officer, undertaking
such challenging tasks was indeed as important an act
as meting out social and economic justice to the whole
of India. (Translation my own)

Without pretending to have improved upon the earlier version, I am
only trying to reproduce the irony in the source text. In this passage, the
source writer is exposing the officialese, whereas Raghavendra Rao has
neutralized the significance of this passage. He has replaced the Kannada
adverb "sharavegadalli" (at the speed of an arrow) with the English adverb
"promptly." Though the adverb used in the original is a cliche, it is not
so in the story's context. "Like an arrow," the well meaning step of the
tehsildar wounds the interests of Dalits. Further, according to the
original, the tehsildar cannot use "all his powers." He can exercise his
powers only within the limits of his position of bureaucratic hierarchy.
For, he is not merely efficient; he is also young and therefore
overenthusiastic and inexperienced. The gentle sarcasm about the
officer's inexperience and over-enthusiasm vis-à-vis his duties, clear in
the source text, is missing in Shri K Raghavendra Rao's tame translation.

I now proceed to focus on the only two English dialogues in the source
text. They are spoken by the tehsildar and the Deputy Collector. They
occur at the point where the Deputy Collector, a supporter of the upper
caste people, attacks the tehsildar for his haste. We all know that, in India,
people exercising bureaucratic authority resort to English to make their
point forcefully. I reproduce these dialogues exactly as in the original.

The tehsildar, opening his mouth, as if to sound
determined, said: "No, Sir, I did it as legally." As if to
say, "Shut up your mouth," the collector thundered:
"Who said it is legal action, it is just a cruel action
against village people. I know what kind of idiot you
are." (Translation my own)

Two bureaucrats having this exchange in the midst of Dalits and their
oppressors, both groups strangers to English, is an important social,

political and linguistic detail in the story, suggesting how administrative authority and English go together in India. The translator has slightly corrected the wrong English adverb "as legally" into "legally" and reproduced the dialogue in translation as in the original. The linguistic dimension of the exercise of authority is virtually lost sight of in this rendering. This, in spite of the translator's prefixing the dialogues with "in his official English."

A little later we read:

"The landlords shouted that the tehsildar himself was an untouchable, and that his action was partial to the interests of his community.

Then they let loose a flood of abuse against all untouchables." (18)

The word used about the tehsildar in the original is not "asprushya" (untouchable) but "holeya," one of the several untouchable castes of Karnataka. This significant detail of sociology of castes is taken away by the translator. He has misread the source text, for he has misread the sociology of untouchability in Karnataka.

The last thing we hear about the foolhardy tehsildar is:

> The entire colony was in the grip of anguish. The poor
> tehsildar was nowhere to be found! (19)

As I read it in the original, however, it translates somewhat like this :

> The colony was now made to writhe in restless agony.
> The tehsildar had now vanished from the whole scene.
> (Translation my own)

The fact that the tehsildar was wise enough to disappear and save his skin when blows fall, is missing in Shri K Raghavendra Rao's translation. It should be clear by now that the translator conveys a more positive image of the tehsildar than is warranted by the important significations in the source text. Put another way, the translator, unlike the source writer, betrays a sneaking admiration for the tehsildar. Because the translator's responses to the source text are guided by his tacit and unconscious or

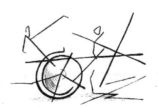

129

political choices, he views the whole story from an angle more favourable to the reformist minded tehsildar. However, the whole point of the source text is to lay bare the ugly underside of reformism from the viewpoint of the oppressed, but irrepressible Dalits.

The title of the story in translation reveals the same problem. "The Paddy Harvest" sounds a lot more rosy and romantic than the bare, "Paddy." What Dalit consciousness seeks to de-glorify, non-Dalit consciousness is trying to glorify. This is an imperative of the dialectics of castes in India. I could have also shown how several ethnic significations of the source text are lost in this translation. But, because such losses have frequently been detected and debated on in translation studies, I have chosen to demonstrate briefly the usually neglected loss of socio-political significations in literary translation.

Notes

1. The Dalit-Bandaya movement, a progressive literary movement, emerged during the post-Emergency years to challenge the then literary establishment dominated by the naviayas (modernists). It was carried forward by a broad coalition of writers belonging/beckoning to various oppressed groups within society – the working classes, the backward communities, the Dalit and the religious minorities.

2. The Dalit Sangharsh Samiti was an organization formed by the "untouchable" castes of Karnataka with the aim of preventing the oppression of the Dalits and protecting their political and social rights. When it was launched in the late 1970's, the organization's immediate inspiration was the Dalit Panthers in Maharashtra, and it derived ideological direction from the philosophy of Dr B R Ambedkar.

3. "Bakala" is based on the myth of Bakalamuni, particularly popular among the Madiga (Chamar) community of Karnataka. The myth of Bakalamuni centres around the rigorous tapasya (meditation) supposed to have been undertaken in the aftermath of the Ramayana and Mahabharata wars which destroyed the world altogether. Bakalamuni is so called because he adopted the one legged posture of the Bakala (crane) while meditating. As a result of his meditation, a tree sprouted out of his limbs, and became the origin of a rejuvenated universe.

CAST(E)ING WICKED SPELLS:
GENDERED ERRANCY IN MAHASWETA DEVI'S BAYEN

BRINDA BOSE

We ... enter an area of darkness. This is the domtoli ... The ostracized existence of the domtoli reveals the pulse of the place ... official institutions for the upliftment of harijans exist, but the untouchables are left untouched ... Why independence? Why say we are a free nation? What right have we to do so? ... Our untouchables have made us untouchables too, for we have allowed this curse ... to flourish and stay.

(188-90)

Santhals are numerically the majority tribals in West Bengal. The witch-cult is the first among other customs which are hindering their progress ... In fact, there is no such inhuman, merciless rite among the Santhals as the witch-custom. Every year countless innocent and simple lives are lost, numerous hapless families are driven to destitution, many face barbaric tortures.

(179)

Mahasweta Devi, *Dust on the Road: The Activist Writings*[1]

Mahasweta Devi's "Bayen" weaves the politics of caste, gender and superstition in an intricately patterned fabric that finally threatens to tear under the weight of its multiple social concerns. We realize, of course, that a rent is what the writer seeks: there is no beauty in the interplay of intra-caste frustrations and hostilities, and Mahasweta Devi provides no prettiness for relief. There is, instead, the singular starkness of the power of truth, a literary manifestation of a consciousness raising tour de force.

Activist and writer, Mahasweta Devi has for over two decades found her subject in the economically marginalized and the socially ostracized communities of Bengal and its neighbouring regions. The tribals, who constitute eight per cent, and the scheduled castes, that constitute seventeen per cent of India's population, touch the nadir of India's caste hierarchy. This structure, as Mahasweta Devi's writings reveal, is systematically reinforced by Hindu fundamentalists, not merely by maintaining the divide between the depressed communities and their "higher" counterparts, but more dangerously by constantly creating and fanning antagonisms within them. The exploitation of the so-called scheduled tribes and classes thus continues unchecked. While these communities continue to suffer in their entirety, there are some within them who are singled out for even greater discriminations. Mahasweta Devi, the fiction writer, transforms into moving prose the true stories of misery that Mahasweta Devi the tireless social activist uncovers on her trails.

In "Bayen," Chandidasi Gangadasi – beautiful woman, devoted wife and mother, and proud descendant of a Dom community that had inherited "all the burning ghats of the world" for their own from the ancient king Harishchandra – executed her given task of burying the dead children of the village, and guarding their graves, with passion and commitment until the day she suddenly felt that she just did not have "the heart to do it any more." It was a weakness that she developed when she had a child of her own:

> Because of her own child, she now felt a deep pain for
> every dead child. Her breast ached with milk if she
> stayed too long in the graveyard. She silently blamed
> her father as she dug the graves. He had no right to
> bring her to this work.[2] (34)

But she had no right to choose her calling, just as, apparently, she and her husband Malindar and son Bhagirath had no right to a relatively contented existence, fulfilled in themselves and in their work. When almost overnight, Chandi was transformed into a "bayen" – a witch who could not be killed "because to kill a bayen means death for your children" – and ostracized from the community, even her husband, much as he apparently loved her, was unable to defend and protect his woman from the villagers who commanded her to isolation for the rest of her life – she, "a human being was banished from the human world to the condemned world of the supernatural" (29). Clearly, the demons that plague the rich in their happiness are doubly active in the lives of the downtrodden.

Untouchability, Superstition, Gender

Mahasweta Devi's concerns in this story are multiple, the focus is trained on three aspects of lower caste life, untouchability, superstition and gender. In her own words, her commitment is not to literature, but to social history:

> It is my conviction that a storywriter should be motivated by a sense of history that would help her readers understand their own times. I have never had the capacity nor the urge to create art for art's sake. Since I haven't ever learnt to do anything more useful, I have gone on writing. I have found authentic documentation to be the best medium for protest against injustice and exploitation ... To capture the continuities between past and present held together in the folk imagination, I bring legends, mythical figures and mythical happenings into a contemporary setting, and make an ironic use of these, as I do with ... the legend of Kalu Dom in my Bayen.[3]

"Bayen" explores the interaction of community frustrations and deep-rooted superstition, and its combined effects upon the lowliest of the lower castes and tribes, and their women. It is an exposition on some of the most extreme forms that social jealousy can take, particularly when fuelled by superstition and intra-caste rivalries. According to Samik Bandyopadhyay, translator and critic,

> The metaphoric core of Bayen ... lies deeper than the obvious protest against the inhumanity of superstition ... Mahasweta touches the larger space of the social forces that separate mother and son in a male-dominated system.[4]

Certainly, "Bayen" is a sad commentary on what such societies do to their women, often their best human resource, in the stress and strain of poverty-ridden, mean souled existences. It is a chastening tale, in its unsentimental account of the horror of a perfectly regular existence – if one can deem a gravetender's life to be so – shattered at a whim of an illiterate and stubbornly superstitious community. And it is particularly chastening to us because it never condemns this community – Mahasweta Devi's pen records, reviews, and empathizes with them while she berates us, the literate and the enlightened, for condoning such horrors in our silence.

Mahasweta Devi offers her own explanations for the community practices that she describes in her fiction. In tracing the transformation of Chandi, the beloved and beautiful wife and mother, into Chandibayen, the witch whose evil shadow supposedly preyed on human children, she comments darkly on the powers of a society which can combine forces to effect nearly the impossible:

> Fear grew in Malindar. Didn't he sometimes fear that perhaps Chandi was turning into a witch? ... Perhaps it was true what people were saying? ... The Dom community did not forget her. The Doms were keeping an eye on her, to her complete ignorance. Covertly or otherwise, a society can maintain its vigil if it wants to. There is nothing a society cannot do. (27)

In an article on witch hunting in West Bengal (1987), Mahasweta Devi writes:

> Faith in witch-cults used to exist in tribal society ... I have my own explanation about [it]. The tribals are losing whatever they had due to overwhelming socio-economic changes and all-devouring political pressures ... In such a dismal scenario, it is natural for them to think that the witch-cult is something which truly belongs to them, something of their own. Why should they have to lose everything? That is why they have embraced the cult with a new vigour, to preserve their identity ... At the very sound of the word "witch," the tribals forget all political differences and act in a frenzy, even victimizing one of their own.[5]

Woman, Witch, Scapegoat.

It is in this frenzy, perhaps to maintain its distinctive identity through cultish superstition, that the Dom community of "Bayen" needlessly sacrifices one of their own and one of their best. Of course, there is hardly any novelty in the idea that even today when a society delineates a scapegoat, it is usually a woman. In this story of Mahasweta Devi's, the idea is reiterated, and once again, no obvious explanations found. Superstition, coupled with a disastrous lack of knowledge about life and health practices, results in the destruction of a spirited woman and her small, happy family. In the story's ironic ending, where Chandi sacrifices her miserable existence to save members of the very same community that had victimized her, one gets a sense of the writer's overwhelming despair. A blameless life has been lost, the scapegoat has crafted her own final sacrifice, in her death, however, she is able to snatch back her identity even as she denies her community a chance for their own salvation. One can only hope that in this final irony lies a learning experience for the community at large.

The tribal/lower caste community of "Bayen" is caught in a strange paradox of being a patriarchal system that is nevertheless in the fearful

135

grip of the alleged magical powers of a single, helpless woman. However, it is by conferring such powers upon her – which she desperately desires to reject – that they seek to, and succeed in, marginalizing a woman who threatens to transgress social norms by taking pride in her own position in the community and in her family. In the process, the male dominated community finds security in flexing its social muscle, as well as pleasure in destroying Chandi's fledgling happiness as a fulfilled woman. Therefore, even while the Dom community attributes certain dangerous powers to Chandi, those very same powers render her completely powerless within the community.

Dev Nathan, in "Gender Transformations in Tribes," analyzes spheres of male control in tribal communities:

> The first critical distinction between men and women is in the sphere of ritual. "Social differentiation hinges, in the first instance, on differential access to social knowledge." This social knowledge is not only of production (and warfare) but also of the ritual and magico-ritual spheres.[6]

It is, perhaps, only by deploying such control over its women through the "magico-ritual spheres" that the males of lower caste – and therefore, exploited and actually powerless – communities endeavour to assert some nebulous sense of power for themselves. In the process, they destroy even further the fragile fabric of social interaction and hierarchy within the community, and critically endanger the peace of their own daily lives. When the community condemns Chandi as a "bayen," they condemn themselves to living in constant fear of the very evil powers that they have deemed fit to confer upon her:

> Come out and see, you son of a bitch! You are keeping a bayen for a wife while our children's lives are at stake. Malindar came out. He could see the burial ground under the banyan tree humming with lamps, torches and people who stood milling around in silence. (28)

In the course of his analysis of tribes and castes, Nathan identifies three "states" which are considered the most "polluting" in tribal societies, and therefore to be punished in order to effect the ritual purification of the community – menstruation, birth and death. Chandi, a young woman of childbearing age who is also a new (still nursing) mother, already fulfills two of the three criteria in her normal course of existence. Unfortunately for her, she is a "pollutant" of the third variety as well, by virtue of her work as a gravetender. As such, Chandi is supremely suited to be singled out as the scapegoat of a society that is constantly looking for ways to purify itself of its stigma of untouchability and other casteist afflictions. This notion of purification appears to be recognized even within Chandi's family circle, in shouldering (unwillingly) the burden of evil in her family, Chandi makes it possible for her husband Malindar, who self-confessedly "used to be a hard and unkind man," to transform himself into a more attractive personality:

> It was as if God came and turned the tables, in a single day, on the Dom community. Chandi became a bayen, a heartless childhunter. Malindar grew gentle. He had to. If one of a family turns inhuman and disappears beyond the magic portals of the supernatural, the other has to stay behind and make a man of himself. (20)

It is presumed, of course, that this effect of improvement on Malindar would spread into the larger community in other ways, the "sacrifice" of Chandi to appease evil spirits would pay at least a few of their moral debts and lessen their load of suffering. In order not to forget completely their reckless sacrifice of an unsuspecting and harmless woman, they would continue to pay for it by a sustained fear for the lives of their children. However, it is only in the continued existence of Chandi as "bayen" – in her continued acceptance of a large share of the price for her community's sins – that such a balance may be retained. When Chandi dies on the railway tracks, in her attempt to save lives in an enormous train disaster, the Railway Department announces a medal for her to be awarded posthumously to her closest survivors. The community shows the grace

137

to be momentarily embarrassed, but in her death they are deprived of the convenience of a scapegoat who, they believed, maintained the balance of their community's share of suffering by her obvious pain and sorrow in life. In death – and a heroic death, at that – she exposes not just the evilly selfish nature of the community at large, but leaves them the task of having to pay for an additional sin, that of having persecuted her in life. Ironically, the "witch" who had no intention of haunting them in life was now to return to haunt them in death.

The Language of a Culture - in Translation

For most of Mahasweta Devi's readers, there are many aspects of her fiction that reach them in "translation," even if they are reading them in Bengali, her language of composition. This is because Mahasweta does not usually write about the lives of those who read her – in Bengali or in translation – but about those who are lesser known. To make them and their often miserable lives known and appreciated is this activist writer's particular social agenda, to applaud Mahasweta Devi's considerable literary skills alone would, therefore, be an injustice to authorial intention. But her signature literary skill lies in the terseness and supple power of her prose that invents a remarkable fluidity between colloquial modern Bengali and the particular native/regional dialect relevant to the story's milieu. Besides the power of her plots which she draws from her "grassroots dedication to the deprived,"[7] the impact of her fiction is contained in the uniqueness of this stark prose that effortlessly reproduces the irregular cadences and intonations of native speech. In fact, Mahasweta Devi's inspired storytelling, readable, colloquial Bengali mirrors the difficult regional dialect just as much as the spoken dialect metamorphoses into a more accessible, comprehensible written language, both at the same time.

Any translator of Mahasweta Devi's fiction sets out with a decided handicap, that of the difficulty – if not the impossibility – of translating the speech rhythms of the native dialects she apes so ably, as well as marking their departures from the colloquial Bengali she uses. Her most well known translator – if the most controversial – Gayatri Chakravorty Spivak, arguably achieves this effect most successfully: "Spivak's work in this area is notable because she achieves a jerky, arhythmic, colloquial idiom which matches Mahasweta Devi's non-mainstream subjects and language."[8] Of course, there is hardly any way of reproducing in translation the actual differences of a dialect with its source language. In translating and dramatizing "Bayen," Samik Bandyopadhyay is able to call upon the various possibilities that the stage offers to convey a sense of the uniqueness of Mahasweta Devi's subject and milieu. Bandyopadhyaya manages quite confidently to depart from the original narrative sequence of the story, perhaps taking liberties for drama's sake: his script commences with the Bayen's sad and fitful singing, and a monologue that echoes the despair of her soul, before the arrival of Malindar and Bhagirath on stage. It may seem surprising that this is the scene inspired by Mahasweta's original unsentimental and terse narrative at the beginning of the story; however, Bandyopadhyay's deliberately more emotional audio-visual appeal, intended for a live audience, seems to be an acknowledgement of what his translation cannot quite do to recreate the unique Mahasweta Devi narrative effect. Bandyopadhyay goes on to take other liberties with the staging of the text. One long interpolation is noteworthy, in which Bandyopadhyay stages a fantasy flashback that tells the story of Malindar and Chandidasi's courtship through a drunken song and dance ritual:

> It was then, on Holi day, that I saw her first. (Pause.
> Pleadingly) Why don't you slip out for a while, child?
> Your father and mother will meet now, fall in love, get
> married, and then you'll be born. (Shoves him out.) You
> shouldn't be watching this. (Bhagirath leaves the stage.)
> Let me walk back to twelve years ago. (Walks. As he
> walks, he uses his fingers to rearrange his hair, rearranges
> his dhoti to a more youthful tightness.) Let me dance.[9]

The liberties available to a translator working for a different medium — in Bandyopadhyay's case, the stage — are of course unavailable to Mahua Bhattacharya. Clearly not comfortable with experimentation, Bhattacharya renders a timid translation that sticks faithfully (almost suffocatingly) to the original narrative without being able to capture the vivid originality of Mahasweta Devi's narrative style. Unfortunately, she is largely unable to recreate either the staccato rhythms of Mahasweta's prose, or the extreme terseness of the Doms' speech which would have magnified the effect already created by the unusual narrative voice. Even while her translation remains extremely close to the text, Bhattacharya is inclined to smoothen out the characteristically jerky speech patterns that clearly typify the dialect. Often, this is done most unobstrusively (as in the example below) but in totality, still manages to undermine even a suggestion of Mahasweta Devi's most celebrated effect, the uncanny reproduction of particular linguistic rhythms. In "Bayen," when Chandi first introduces herself to Malindar, the original reads:

> Ekdin ekta phorsha meye, kota chokh, lalche chool,
> eshe dariyechhilo.
> Bolechhilo – "Aami Chandi, omukh Gangaputter biti,
> baap more gelo. Baaper dala ekhon moke din."
> "Baaper kaaj tui korbi?"
> "Korbo."
> "Toke bhoy lage na."
> "Mor bhoydor nei."[10]

Bhattacharya makes the speech flow in fairly regular cadences:

> One day a fair girl with light eyes and reddish hair came instead of him. "I am Chandi," she announced, "daughter of the Gangaputta. My father is dead. Give me his rations instead."
> "Will you do your father's work then?"
> "Yes, I will bury the dead and guard the graves."
> "Aren't you afraid?"
> "I am not." (21)

The rendering of the text into complete, grammatically correct (albeit short) sentences finally detracts from what could have been a startling quality in its basic rhythm. If, as Bhattacharya seems to intend, the original is to be rendered faithfully, I would draw more attention to Mahasweta Devi's crucial departures from regular Bengali speech patterns:

> One day a fair girl, light eyes, reddish hair, came and stood there. Said, "I am Chandi, that Gangaputta's daughter, father has died. Give father's rations to me now."
>
> "You'll do your father's work?"
>
> "I will."
>
> "You are not afraid."
>
> "I have no fears."

I cannot say for certain whether such an alternative could be sustained throughout the translation without deteriorating into a gimmick, but there is no doubt that Bhattacharya's unsubtle regularization of the original's distinctive cadences ultimately blunts the effect of the translation. In Bhattacharya's English version, "Bayen" is a powerful story sometimes adequately, sometimes indifferently, told. In Mahasweta Devi's original Bengali, it is one that is uniquely narrated. The divergence makes all the difference.

Notes

1   Mahasweta Devi, *Dust on the Road: The Activist Writings*, Maitreyi Ghatak ed (Calcutta: Seagull Books, 1997).

2   Mahasweta Devi, "Bayen," *Separate Journeys*, Geeta Dharmarajan ed, trans. Mahua Bhattacharya (New Delhi: Katha, 1998) 24.

3   Mahasweta Devi, Preface to *Mahasweta Debir Shwonirbachito Shreshtha Galpa* (Calcutta: Proma Prakashan, 1985), quoted in Introduction to *Mahasweta Devi: Five Plays*, trans. Samik Bandyopadhyay (Calcutta: Seagull Books, 1997) xii.

4   Mahasweta Devi, Preface to *Mahasweta Debir Shwonirbachito Shreshtha Galpa*, xiii.

5   Mahasweta Devi, "Witch-Hunting in West Bengal: In Whose Interest?," *Dust on the Road: The Activist Writings*, 167-68.

6   Dev Nathan, "Gender Transformations in Tribes," *Tribe to Caste*, Dev Nathan ed (Shimla: IIAS, 1997) 274-75.

7   Ananda Lal, "Word for Word," *The Statesman* Review, 29 June 1998: 6.

8   Ananda Lal, "Word for Word."

9   Mahasweta Devi, "Bayen," *Mahasweta Devi: Five Plays*, trans. Samik Bandyopadhyay, 79.

10 Mahasweta Devi, "Bayen," *Mahasweta Debir Shwonirbachito Shreshtha Galpo*, (Calcutta: Proma Prakashan, 1985) 176.

TRANSLATIONS: A DALIT GIRL LEARNS TO WRITE

UMA CHAKRAVARTI

Urmila Pawar's "Gosh Seshvachi," (trans. "A Childhood Tale") is a fine example of a Dalit woman's writing which reflects Dalit experiences of living. The narrative of "A Childhood Tale" brings to mind Pawar's statement at an oral history workshop that Dalits write about their experiences, translating directly from life. This is another kind of translation – not from one language to another – but from deep subjective experience to an organized narrative which will be received as an example of the literature of social realism. At the same time the realism itself is expressed both in terms of narrative content, and also powerfully through language where the raw social experiences are often welded into the sound of the words Urmila chooses to deploy, thereby heightening the impact of her writing.[1]

"A Childhood Tale" works at two levels – it is at one level a simple story of an adult woman, now herself a mother, coming to terms with her fraught relationship with her mother through the act of writing. At this level the story is about the lives of two Dalit women, a mother and a daughter in a poor Dalit female headed household. From the author's moving recounting of her life at the history workshop, it is evident that the narrative content of "A Childhood Tale" is based on her own early childhood, and the mother as reconstructed in the story, is virtually indistinguishable from Urmila's mother in real life – the one slides into the other. The intertwining of the two narratives and the direct translation from social experience provides the basis for the emotionally charged narration of "A Childhood Tale" by Urmila Pawar as she relives her experiences with her mother. This brings us to a second level at which the narrative works where art mirrors social life and the literary work is unmediated by "artful" writing strategies, except for those of linguistic emphasis. Take for example the following two passages – one from the oral narration and the other from the written account:

> I told you about my mother. She was troubled and in pain. The boy [son] had died, my father had died; she would cry and she would weave baskets in the town.[2]

> Even though she was ill she never gave up weaving.[3]

> Aai was also skinny like father, but tall and fair, with a permanently mournful expression. She wore a tattered nine yard sari that only came up to her knees ... Aai sat in the courtyard weaving baskets – big ones, small ones, wide ones and shallow ones. Even when one woke up in the morning she could be seen in the courtyard weaving a winnowing fan or a sieve. One could see her like that till one went to sleep at night ... If it was father's legs that moved, with Aai, it was her hands ... (47)

The unmediated writing is an important input, and is the means by which the working out of the relationship between the mother and daughter itself is facilitated by Pawar as it enables a reliving of the experience, with all its complexities, even though the particularities of that experience may long be over. And what is striking about Pawar's narrative is that the reader can see that what her mother expressed through crying, Urmila expresses through her writing. Further, even as Urmila's writing in "A Childhood Tale" reads as if it is a completely unmediated translation from lived social reality to the printed word, the child protagonist is a reconstruction of a Dalit woman whose subjectivity has since then been shaped by a range of social experiences. Devastating poverty and the degradation of caste discrimination as an "untouchable" have left an indelible scar on her personality, but her subjectivity has also been shaped by a new political consciousness which has enabled her to make sense of her conflicted emotions as a child. As a woman who has lived through the formation of the Dalit Panther Movement, Urmila is simultaneously an heir to the historical traditions, which she shares with other Dalits of the sixties and seventies, and is herself helping to forge a new literature in a field where an oppressed community can express itself, and where anger and anguish are a valid basis for writing.

Among the elements that go into the formation of a Dalit woman's subjectivity is a new awareness of Dalit history beginning with Jotiba Phule, Savitribai Phule, Tarabai Shinde, and going on to Ambedkar and crucial struggles that he led in the 1930s. These struggles were for the first time over cultural symbols as well as material resources. Ambedkar had drawn Dalit women into the Dalit movement in the 30s in the struggle for water – a crucial resource in the hands of the upper castes from which the lower castes were excluded. Urmila puts it eloquently while describing the Mahad Satyagraha:

> Even water is divided in this society – this is Brahmin water, this is Maratha water, this is for the BCs. Some did not even get any water and had to walk for ten miles with their pots to get water. Just as water was divided so were the gods ...[4]

Urmila's sharp statement also serves as a response to the allegations made by the upper caste critics of Dalit writers who are charged with limiting their writing to caste categories. In Urmila's view, this is inevitable since the uniqueness of Dalit experience, and within that the uniqueness of Dalit women's experience, will necessarily be reflected only within the framework of "caste categories" because their oppression has a specific caste location. Caste itself is "understood" and analyzed very experientially as untouchability informs events memorialized in the consciousness of childhood. The child protagonist in "A Childhood Tale" hates delivering baskets to upper caste households because the whole process is a reminder of the polluting status of the child. She hates the school for the same reason, because there too, one is reminded of caste, and the child cannot escape from her identity as a "polluter."

The lack of access to material resources at the larger social level is ever present also at the level of every individual Dalit household's struggle for survival. Low wages for degrading work imposes severe limits on the concerns of Dalit households. Urmila's writing captures the tragedy of human beings who are reduced to their stomachs. Urmila describes how her mother feeds her children with low grade food while the children long for good food. When Urmila as a young girl wants to make laddus for Diwali, her mother will not allow her to do so because it requires too much sugar and flour – and then because she is unhappy about saying "no" she cries.[5] As a grown up woman, Urmila's understanding about low wages and primal needs makes for a devastating account of households where the members fight over food. The synonym for Mahars according to her is "those who fight over food."[6] The real tragedy is that instead of turning their anger outwards against those who exploit them and reduce them to their primal needs by underpaying them, the family fights with each other over scarce food that they are able to buy.

Urmila's new political consciousness also enables her to recall her mother's lies as part of her strategies of survival. The child protagonist has noticed her mother's systematic recourse to lying while dealing with her customers, as she is unable to keep to her deadlines even as she literally weaves baskets day and night. Also in a very evocative passage in "A Childhood Tale," the mother, who is aware of the child's reluctance to deliver baskets and be subjected to routinized humiliation in the inter-personal relationships between the "upper" castes and the Dalits, uses lies, blandishments and subterfuge to persuade her little daughter to go through another round of humiliation as she goes to a high caste household with the products of her mother's labour.

The struggle for survival – food and other primal aspects of life – and the tensions that it generates is one aspect of Urmila's reconstruction of childhood, the second aspect is what from Jotiba Phule onwards Dalit leadership has seen as the means to end caste based humiliation linked to their low status occupation – education. Education as privileged by Dalits implies two things, for Phule it meant knowledge, the third eye or traittiya ratana, as he termed it which would be the means to unravel the way the social world was organized and legitimated by those currently wielding power. The traittiya ratana, the possession of knowledge by the Dalits would be a weapon armed with which the Dalits contest the ideologies of Brahminism. At a fundamental level education, formal knowledge, was also a means by which the Dalits could hope to exit from the prisonhouse of caste based low status occupations which was the basis of their "untouchability." Education would be the instrument of social mobility, enabling the Dalits to escape the power of the landed elite in the rural areas who had the coercive means by which they could extract labour as well as impose harsh working conditions and low wages on their own exploitative terms. Through education the Dalits could, at least, partly break out of the stranglehold of caste. It was a way of disrupting the traditional varna-varga congruence of the past and of gaining access to a more stable material basis of life. In "A Childhood Tale" Urmila delineates this understanding of the power of education to transform the lived social reality of Dalits through the person of the dying father, himself a schoolmaster, exhorting her mother to "educate the children" which, according to Urmila, was chanted like a "mantra."

But the dreams of the Dalits are not easily translated into reality. Apart from the difficulties of paying for the essential requirements of schooling — a respectable dress or pencils which the poor families must pay for, the school itself is an arena of discrimination. This adds to the natural disinclination to go to school which all children experience, except that because the stakes are so high for the Dalits, the normal parent-child conflict is exacerbated in a Dalit household. This is the underlying theme of "A Childhood Tale" — the reluctance of a little girl to go to school and be subjected to humiliation and the "tyranny" of parental authority where the parent must literally "force" the Dalit child towards freedom, ironically, by coercive means. The child protagonist of this story hates her father and even wishes him dead — again something many children feel — but is weighed down by guilt when the father actually dies. She has the same emotions for

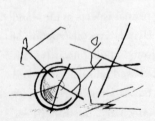

her mother who drives her like a maniac, trying to live upto the dreams of the dying father. Pawar's narrative juxtaposes the adult Dalit consciousness about the value of education with a child's blind rage against parents for the power they exercise over children. The narrative culminates in the illiterate mother taking on the child's high caste teacher for his brutality against the child which seems to be part of everyday humiliation Dalit children are subjected to in the public space of the school. We see what the denouement of "A Childhood Tale" has led us to – an illiterate exploited woman is standing up and taking on established authority, demanding dignity, fairplay and rights for the oppressed. Watching the mother at this moment the child understands who her "enemies," a term she has earlier used for her mother and brother, really are, and who her community of people is. It is the end of childhood and the beginning of a new consciousness – finally the little girl goes to school with a different understanding of her mother, she now wants to go to school to live up to her mother's dreams for a less oppressive future for herself. In writing "A Childhood Tale" Urmila has exorcised many ghosts from her past and created a moving account of a mother-daughter relationship, familiar to all women and yet unique to her specific circumstances.

Notes

1   No translation however competent, as this one certainly is, can do justice to the earthiness of the original Marathi words used by Urmila Pawar in this story. I am indebted to Sudhanva Deshpande who commented on the translation for the purpose of this essay for these observations.

2   Roshan Shahani and C S Lakshmi eds., *Amhihi Ithihas Ghadawala: Urmila Pawar and the Making of History* (Mumbai: Sparrow Archives, 1998) 9.

3   Roshan Shahani and C S Lakshmi eds., *Amhihi Ithihas Ghadawala: Urmila Pawar and the Making of History*, 10.

4   Roshan Shahani and C S Lakshmi eds., *Amhihi Ithihas Ghadawala: Urmila Pawar and the Making of History*, 17.

5   Roshan Shahani and C S Lakshmi eds., *Amhihi Ithihas Ghadawala: Urmila Pawar and the Making of History*, 6.

6   Roshan Shahani and C S Lakshmi eds., *Amhihi Ithihas Ghadawala: Urmila Pawar and the Making of History*, 5.

Caste Overview

Essays by

SISIR KUMAR DAS

TAPAN BASU

UMA CHAKRAVARTI

G ARUNIMA

URMILA PAWAR

THE NARRATIVES OF SUFFERING: CASTE AND THE UNDERPRIVILEGED

Caste as a Theme

With the rise of awareness of social issues concerning caste oppression, the realization of the educated middle class writers about the social privileges enjoyed by them at the expense of the people located within a hierarchical structure fixed for ever, became embarrassing as well as challenging. It was embarrassing because the writers found it extremely difficult to reconcile their pride for Hindu social organizations with the emerging critiques of inequality inherent in the Hindu social structure. It was also challenging because the writers were prompted to take a definite ideological position. Whatever be the objectives of a few social reformers, the majority in the literary community, however, did not adopt any radical posture. Even their reformatory zeal was motivated by a general humanitarianism, rather than by any concrete ideas bringing a real change in the caste hierarchy. Scholars defending the system always argued that the caste system in its original form was not hereditary, but based on psychological foundations, the division of society according to different occupational groups was in fact an exercise towards the recognition of the innate psychological inclinations of men. Some of them agreed that the complete stratification of the society, denying the lower groups any opportunity towards vertical mobility, was unjust and inhuman. And some condemned it severely. But all writings on caste inequality failed to create any significant impact until the movement against the system emerged from the oppressed themselves.

The inequality generated by the caste system is a recurring theme in Indian literature, to which almost all major writers have responded seriously. We cannot think of any writer defending the system, though a very few could actually visualize a caste free society. The movement against caste oppression started by Jotiba Phule, who came from a "low" caste, was an embarrassment to the Brahmins. The criticism of the caste system by Dayananda, a Gujarati Brahmin, or Vivekananda, a Bengali Kayastha, inspired many writers to create a public opinion which became more and more widespread with the passage of time. These leaders exploded the traditional belief with some success, that caste was an integral part of Hindu religion. Gandhi, who once saw the "wonderful power of organization" in the caste system, admitted that "it is harmful both to spiritual and national growth."[1] In 1910, in a powerful poem, Tagore condemned the champions of the caste system with severe indictments.

> My wretched country, those whom you have crushed and
> trampled, deprived of their rights, made them stand and wait
> and never drew them close,
>
> Share you must their indignities and sufferings.
>
> ...
>
> Can you not see Death's messenger at the door
> Stamping his curse on the arrogance of your superiority;
>
> If you still do not beckon them,
> and remain coldly distant
> and still immured in pride,
> then equal must you be in death and ashes of pyre.[2]

(translation mine)

This sentiment has been echoed and re-echoed in different languages throughout this period. The voice that reverberated in poetry and short stories, essays and plays was undoubtedly the voice of a minority, but that became strong enough within a couple of decades. What the minority primarily did was to highlight the suffering of the untouchables and the people belonging to lower castes, which made the readers belonging to the higher castes aware of the inhumanity of this ancient social tradition.

A Madhaviah in *Thillai Govindan* (1908), a novel written in English[3] in an autobiographical form, narrates an incident which can be taken as an illustration of the Indian writer's problematization of the caste system and the insensibility perpetrated by it. Thillai Govindan's grandfather, while returning home after a bath, saw a Shanan (a person belonging to a backward caste) approaching him. This particular Shanan was disliked by the Brahmins because he had converted to Christianity, and he often criticized the customs of the higher caste Hindus. The old man asked the Shanan to step away from the road. The Shanan refused and continued to proceed. Thillai Govindan's grandfather ran into the slushy field to avoid pollution, and asked a Maravan (a man belonging to another backward caste known for its physical strength) working nearby, to teach the Shanan a lesson. Very soon half the village joined him, beat the Shanan, and took him to the village elders who punished him.

This incident, which may not be completely fictional, records the typical attitudes and manners of the higher castes towards the people belonging to the lower castes. The display of Brahminical authority prompted by a well nourished fear of pollution, the denial of basic human right to the lower castes (even when conversion does not effectively change a man's social position), the pitching of one member of lower caste against another in humiliating and assaulting ways are all components of tortured narratives of suffering. The voice of protest, however, is not completely muffled in this novel. The Shanan with injured pride comes to a Christian missionary, who helps him in getting redress at a court of law. The Shanan's protest is more a reflection of the anglicized Indian's faith in British justice, rather than the victim's determination and economic strength to assert his right in a court of law. It may be mentioned here that poets like K P Karuppan and Kumaran Asan found the British regime conferring certain privileges upon the so-called Harijans. They found the British rule protective. The irony of the judicial exercise comes out fully in this novel when the judge punishes the Maravan, and not Thillai Govindan's grandfather for manhandling the Shanan. It is also very significant that the judge who is a Brahmin, executes the law of the country, but protects the interest of his own caste as far as practicable, and remains totally indifferent to the plight of the person victimized by a Brahmin.

One more interesting point that should not escape one's notice is the Hindu attitude towards the "converted" Christians. Despite the fact that Hinduism did not treat the Harijans with dignity, many leaders, including many writers, did not favour their conversion to Christianity. Ramdas of *Malapalli* is not "allured" by "the temptations and glamours" of Christianity, and remains a Hindu. In his *Pather Dabi* and *Bipradas*, Sarat Chandra presents a rather lukewarm attitude towards those who have renounced Hinduism. Shyam Kishor Varma's *Kasi Yatra* (1916) in Hindi fanatically denounces Christianity, and Mannan Dvivedi in his *Ram Lal* (1917) also in Hindi presents an outcast Hindu who desires to marry a Christian, but is frightened of public condemnation. The presentation of a converted Christian in Madhaviah's novel also reveals the Hindu antagonism against Indian Christians in particular.[4] The novel, written long before any properly organized movement of the underprivileged, at least thought of the possibility of protecting their basic human rights through legislation, and not simply by evoking the norms of humanity which was the dominant note in literature.

The voice against social tyranny, however, is not a modern phenomenon, but was heard throughout the medieval period. Pampa, the tenth century Kannada poet, puts the words "Kulam kulamaltu, calam kulam, anmu kulam, abhimanam kulam"(the lineage is not lineage, firmness is lineage, valour is lineage, self-respect is lineage) in the mouth of Karna. Caste system has been criticized from time to time by saints like Basavanna and Kabir, Nanak and Chaitanya, Sarala Das and Sankaradev. Pampa's criticism is not only a Jain critique of the Hindu caste system, but it articulates the milieu's feelings against the idea of birth as the sole determining factor of a man's life. The difference between the medieval

Indian criticism of the caste and that of the late nineteenth or of the early twentieth century lies in the treatment of the human suffering and the understanding of the complexities within the system that makes the downtrodden act against each other.

Impact of Ambedkar

In 1920, Gandhi emphasized that removal of untouchability must be considered a major programme of the Congress. It was the year when B R Ambedkar (1891-1956), the greatest leader and spokesperson of the Harijans, published the Marathi fortnightly *Muk Nayak* (1920). Ambedkar, a brilliant scholar, the first graduate from the untouchable Mahar community[5] and the future maker of the Indian Constitution, started the first mass based movement of the Harijans. It is significant that the protagonist in V S Khandekar's novel *Don Mane* (Two Minds) is an untouchable Mahar who fights against Hindu injustice with determination and conviction. Ambedkar fought for the Harijan's right of entry into the temple, he also secured their right to participate in the public Ganapati festival. Ambedkar brought a new dimension to the freedom movement by challenging Gandhi's right to represent the Harijans. In 1924, he started Bahiskrit Hitakarini Sabha for the moral and material progress of the untouchables, three years later he led a satyagraha to establish the right of the untouchables to draw water from a public tank at Mahad, and he won the case in the Bombay High Court ten years later. Between 1920 and 1932, the year separate electorate for the untouchables was conceded, Ambedkar fought relentlessly to uphold the right of the Harijans through his journalistic as well as political activities. His struggles, along with the anti-Brahmin, but unabashedly pro-British Justice Party (1917), and the Self-Respect Movement (1925) launched by Periyar E V Ramasami Naicker, brought a new awareness, and initiated an extremely significant debate to which all the writers responded, some directly and most of them obliquely.

Periyar burnt the *Ramayana* and the *Manusmrti*, broke the idol of Vinayaka, beat the portrait of Rama with chappals, and declared that "Those who believe in God are fools." These are all expressions of suppressed anger and pain shared by millions of untouchables. In certain areas of the country caste domination assumed the most degrading proportions. There may not be a proportional literary articulation of the people's anger and humiliation, partly because the victims of the caste hierarchy themselves did not participate in the literary activities, and partly because of the ideological differences between the Congress and the parties, and the organizations championing the cause of the lower castes. To give one example of the state of the relationship between castes, the Kallars, the most backward class of the Ramnad district in Madras during the 1930s were prohibited by the Brahmins from wearing gold and silver ornaments, and good clothes. The Harijan women were prohibited from using flowers, and the Brahmins even wanted to prohibit Harijans from cooking their food in metal vessels, wearing shoes or even using umbrellas. [6]

Gandhi and Ambedkar had completely different understanding of the caste system, the authorities of the scriptures and the reforms to redress the indignities subjected to the Harijans by the upper class.[7] They opposed one another, and the latter demanded a separate homeland for the Harijans. When the government announced its plan to grant separate seats to the Harijans in the assembly, Gandhi, then in Yervada Jail, began a fast unto death in protest, from 30 September 1932. Ambedkar, highly sceptical of Gandhi's move, wrote with sarcasm, "There have been Mahatmas in India whose sole object was to remove untouchability and to elevate and absorb the depressed classes, but every one of them has failed in his mission. Mahatmas have come and Mahatmas have gone, but the untouchables have remained as untouchables."[8] The Gandhi-Ambedkar controversy, ending temporarily, with an agreement known as the Poona Pact, the formation of Harijan Sevak Sangh in Poona, the publication of the journal *Harijan* by Gandhi, and the slowly growing confidence of the Harijans, made a strong impact on the Indian creative psyche burdened with a sense of guilt. When Ambedkar was invited by the Viceroy in 1942 to take the Labour Portfolio in the Executive Council, the move was enthusiastically welcomed by the public. And in 1947 when Ambedkar was invited to be the Chairman of the Drafting Committee of the Indian Constitution, Article 17, which abolished untouchability, the conscience of the Indian elite was partly relieved. But the legal prohibition did not

155

ensure the abolition of the caste or the removal of untouchability in practice. Writers played a significant role in combating the tradition bound perceptions and prejudices.

Although the problems of caste and untouchability appeared in Indian literature from time to time, it received serious attention only with the advent of Ambedkar. One of the first novels that concentrated on the problem of the low caste or the Harijans in India is probably the Telugu novel *Himavati* (1913) by T Suryanarayana. It reflects the middle class sympathy and concern for the upliftment of the Harijans. Not only did the contradictions of the middle class and upper caste writers and readers, in respect to their attitude towards the caste system surface from time to time in this novel and in other writings that followed, but the weakness of the groups themselves designated as lower castes was treated in the writings of this period as well. Thus, one notices the Malayalam poet Kuttamath (1880-1943), a member of the prestigious Nair community, composing inspiring verses claiming the rights of all to enter the temples, and Paliath Kunjunni Achan (1880-1942), a poet who writes about toleration and reverence for all religions, sings for the unity of the country, and opposes the caste system. One also finds, as we have mentioned before, the literary representations of the infighting within the Ezhava community in Kerala that divided it into several sub-castes, and of the Mahars in Maharashtra with eighteen sub-castes without inter-dining and inter-marriage, to which Ambedkar belonged.

Venkata Parvatisvara Kavalu wrote the novel *Matrmandiramu* (1919) on the questions of Harijan's entry into the temple, in two parts. Rangadu, a Brahmin by birth – which is kept as a secret – but brought up by a group of thieves, is the protagonist of the narrative. He grows into a social reformer, tries to stop cow slaughter, loves a Harijan girl and wants to enter the temple. He is prevented by the Brahmins, who reveal his caste identity. The hero changes his attitude – he does not marry the girl, though he continues to love her. This is clearly a compromise formula which does not want the elimination of the caste system, but only advocates some concession for the Harijans. Within two years, however, appeared the epoch making Telugu novel *Malapalli* by Unnava Lakshminarayana, a work distinguished by a broad humanism and deep religiosity.

Kumaran Asan

Narayana Guru (1856-1929), wrote in three languages – Tamil, Sanskrit and Malayalam – and inspired the Ezhava community towards a social and moral transfiguration. The agony of the whole community as well as its hope for a new future was articulated through the writings of Kumaran Asan, a disciple of Narayana Guru, whose well organized socio-cultural movement gave additional power to the poetry of Asan. The theme of his poem concerns suffering caused by caste distinctions. In his poem "Simhanadam" (The Lion's Roar) written in 1919, he urges the people to "Speed up where/the caste-demon rears its ugly face." This emotional appeal, coming as it does from a victim of caste hierarchy, is different from the rhetorical flourishes of the Brahmin writers.

In another long poem *Duravastha* (1922), Kumaran Asan foregrounded the human suffering caused by the rigidities of the caste system with such feeling and tenderness, that it created an unprecedented commotion in the literary circles and amongst the social leaders.[9] The theme of *Duravastha* is quite radical. A Nambudiri (Brahmin from Kerala) girl runs away from her home during the Moplah revolt, and takes shelter in the hut of a Pulaya (a lower caste from Kerala). Although such an event is unthinkable in Kerala in ordinary circumstances, Kumaran Asan used the upheaval of the Moplah revolt which created an atmosphere of social change. By visiting the place of a Harijan, the girl, Savitri, loses her caste and realizes that she can never return to her home, and will be regarded as fallen in the eyes of the community. On the other hand, she is moved by the moral qualities of the Harijan youth, by his love and anxiety for her, and is gradually attracted to him and decides to marry him. The poem, as a work of art, is not regarded very highly by the critics; it has been often criticized as too propagandistic. But the poem presents a very serious problem, and its radical nature – a woman of the higher caste marrying a low caste man – was considered extremely offensive to the traditional sensibility. The solution of the whole problem, the problems created by the artificial distinction between man and man, lies,

157

according to Kumaran Asan, in love and compassion. He writes,

> *The same indeed the Hand that cast*
> *the Brahmin and the Harijan*
> *And what a range of glorious deeds*
> *of valour, love and intellect*
> *hast thou thwarted from fruition*
> *O Hindu faith; because of caste!* [10]

"Such prayers, arguments, exhortations and indictments inspired and sustained all those who stood for social reform," writes P K Parmeshwaran Nair. "Though the more orthodox in society frowned upon him, the nobility of his motives and the justice of Kumaran Asan's cause were destined to win in the long run."[11]

Asan's next poem *Chandala Bhikshuki* (1922) brings the question of caste again. Its theme concerns not the contemporary life, but a Buddhist legend. Ananda, the disciple of Buddha, accepts a drink of water from an untouchable girl. She falls in love with the monk and finally becomes a nun. There was public criticism to her entry into the order, though Buddha intervened and the Chandali, the outcast, became a bhikshuki. The basic inhumanity of the caste system is criticized through the persona of Buddha, but Asan's voice is always modest and gentle. He believes that only through love and compassion, which he eulogizes, man will overcome the social hurdles.

> *Heed not the scriptures that violate the truth*
> *Of man and his moral law; nor the words of men*
> *Who stand to gain by interpreting them wrong.*
> *For the ignorant crowd, yesterday's error*
> *Hardens into today's tradition, tomorrow's law.*
> *It is in love that the world takes its birth.*
> *Love nurses it to growth, his fulfilled bliss*
> *Man finds in the bonds of love, life itself is love,*
> *The Moment of death is when compassion dies.* [12]

Kumaran Asan's last, and claimed to be the greatest work *Karuna* (1923), is also based on the Buddhist tale of the courtesan Vasavadatta and the monk Upagupta. This poem, however, has no relation with caste, but is on "karuna" (compassion) which according to the poet, is the only instrument capable of transforming the world divided into narrow sectors. It is quite interesting that Tagore wrote a poem on the same Buddhist tale under the title "Abhisar" (Tryst) in 1900, and about a decade later the theme of *Chandala Bhikshuki* reappeared in his haunting play *Chandalika* which is also a strong repudiation of the caste system.

The period between 1930 and 1947 witnessed a vigorous growth of literature, foregrounding the problems of caste. The contemporary agitation, whether for the right of entry into the temples, or of using the wells reserved exclusively for the Brahmins and other higher castes, gave the initial impulse for several artistic creations. D R Bendre's tragic play in Kannada, *Uddara* (1932), on the Harijan attempt to enter a temple, and Tagore's *Chandalika* have the same social urge. Similarly, the Self-Respect Movement inspired several writers. Kirijadevi, for example, wrote the novel *Mokanarancani Allatu Camukat Torram* (1931) in support of the inter-caste marriage. It tells the story of a girl of the Vellala community marrying a boy of the Nadar community.

Love and Marriage

Traditionally, caste is an endogamous unit, that is, it restricts individuals from marrying someone belonging to any caste other than his own. Matrimonial alliance and inter-dining are the two important units of measurement of the rigidity of the caste organization. Many writers have tried to highlight the inhumanity of the system that segregated one human being from the other through various social relationships, all of which are denied their natural growth. One of the most popular and frequent themes in Indian literature throughout the twentieth century is love frustrated, mainly, if not entirely, due to the rigidities of endogamy. It is a living institution all over India, accepted by all Hindus, and even by the Muslims and Christians, all of whom accept the principle of "arranged marriages." Any exercise of one's own choice in selecting one's partner is interpreted both as a defiance to the patriarchal authority and a threat to endogamy. The defence of love, particularly the adulation of love between members belonging to different castes, was itself a powerful criticism of the caste system, its appeal being more direct and response more instinctive. The theme of Laila Majnu or Romeo and Juliet, and various stories of frustrated love current in different regions of India acquired new significance in the twentieth century. Maraimalai Adigal's Tamil novel *Kokilampal Katitankal* (1921) presents the heroine Kokilampal, a Brahmin girl, in love with a non-Brahmin boy. Adigal, as it may be mentioned, wanted to prove in his prose work *Velalar Nakarikam* (1923), that the caste system was an Aryan custom introduced by the Brahmins in Tamil Nadu. With the precise purpose of the removal of caste distinction, P C Mudaliyar wrote a play *Piramananum Cuttiranum Allatu Pariharan* (1933) in Tamil, on the marriage between a Brahmin boy and a non-Brahmin girl. He describes his play as "a new Tamil social drama." Yogananda Jha's novel *Bhalamanus* (1944) written in Maithili, which became extremely popular, is an example of the people's response to this archetypal theme of frustration of love due to caste prejudice. Asanand Mamtora goes a step forward in his novel *Sair* (1941) which advocates the inter-caste marriage between a Sindhi boy and a Kashmiri girl.

S K Kolhatkar, Mama Varerkar or Vittal Ranji Sharde, all presented humanistic critique of the caste system in their plays and novels, where noble young heroes dedicated themselves to the cause of the Harijans. Kolhatkar's play *Parivartan* (1923) raises the issue of untouchability which is more strongly focussed in Mama Varerkar's play *Sattece Gulam* (1927), inspired by the Gandhian vision. Kolhatkar's novel *Syam Sundar* (1925) records the sacrifice and dedication of an upper caste young man for the upliftment of the untouchable. Vittal Ranji Shonde, a member of the Prarthana Samaj, wrote an extremely erudite essay on untouchability, "Bharatiya asprsyatatice Prasna" (1933). If the power of impact is our criterion, then, however, V S Khandekar's treatment of the theme of untouchability is far more inspiring and profound. His well known novel *Don Mane* (1938) presents an untouchable hero and a high caste heroine, as in *Duravastha* of Asan. The Marathi writers exploited the situation fully, much to the discomfort of the orthodox section. The view of C M Bandivadekar, that literature did not add anything new to the caste discourse in Maharashtra, is not exactly tenable.[13] The appearance of the Harijans or the untouchables in literature as protagonists, is in itself a significant change; it signals the reversals of the literary codes determining the "heroic" qualities. The hero of *Don Mane* is an untouchable, and the hero of *Hirwa Capha* is a Kunbi, also a low caste. The heroines in both the novels are from the upper caste, and both are beautiful. The heroes of *Phat Ki Vakal* (1941) and *Mi Ram Josi* (1941), on the other hand, belong to the higher caste, and their lovers are from the lower, all of them intelligent, educated and accomplished. Khandekar sees the possibility of the vertical mobility within the caste system through education, which alone can lend dignity to the deprived class. Varerkar goes one step forward. His *Tarte Potad* (1940) argues against the narrowness of religious injunctions and caste rigidities, and finds the inter-caste marriage to be the greatest challenge to the caste system. Phadke's *Majha Dharu* also brings the issue to focus, though it is a novel poorly constructed with exciting, but totally unconvincing incidents where the hero is psychologically prepared to marry an untouchable. In the novel *Mahapu* (1943) by Vithal Dattatreya Chindarkar, too, one finds a high caste girl in love with a carpenter boy.

The Marathi examples can be generalized without ignoring the regional peculiarities in respect of caste prejudices and inter-caste attitudes. While love provided the space for the expressions of human emotions with all their intensity, rural constructions and social work provided even a larger space for the interactions among the members of different castes. The hero of *Syam Sundar*, very much like the son of the crooked landlord of the Telugu novel *Malapalli*, lives with the untouchables in a small village and works for their improvement. In V M Joshi's novel *Susileca Dev* (1930), his best according to critical consensus, the protagonist Sushila, a woman from the upper class, dedicates herself to the upliftment of the poor untouchables. In his earlier novel, *Indu Kale Va Sarala Mole* (1925), written in epistolary form, the Gandhian hero Vinayak Rao keeps a Harijan boy in his house, defying social ostracization. The narratives of love between the members of different caste, their struggles and agonies and failures have certainly made greater impact on the reading public. But the narratives of idealism and dedication, on the other hand, presented the social reality with greater objectivity and demonstrated that without a programmme of social change, relationship between individuals cannot

161

be sustained at all. The idealistic hero as social worker is only an inevitable extension of the idealistic hero as the lover.

Malapalli

The Telugu novel *Malapalli* (1922) by Unnava Lakshminarayana deserves special mention, it being a faithful record of the life of a Harijan family and their unending suffering, as well as of the ambivalence of the people towards Gandhism and their attraction towards the revolutionary tactics, and finally towards organized trade union movements. The author studied law in Ireland, practised as an advocate, grew under the influence of the social reformer K Veeresalingam and later derived inspiration from Tilak and Gandhi. During his stay in Ireland he took great interest in the movement led by De Valera, and was also exposed to Bolshevism, which left a profound mark on him. Back home, he responded to Gandhi's call for non-cooperation. As a part of his campaign against untouchability, and for the remarriage of the widows, he founded Sarada Niketan at Guntur. He fought against levying the tax called "pollari" for grazing cows in the forests of Palnadu area. He was jailed for participating in this movement known as the Pullari Satyagraha. Before he wrote this novel, he published a short work on politics under the title *Rajatantramu*, which is an evidence of his great interest in political issues and ideologies. While in jail at Vellore, he started writing this novel on the life of the untouchables, hence the subtitle of the work is "Harijan Cetto."

A narrative of all the major movements of the time, social and political, it ranges in issues as diverse as the conversion of the Hindus by Christian missionaries, unionization of labourers, atrocities of the caste hierarchy, the political ideals of Tilak or Gokhale, the problematics of non-violence and the October revolution. In one sense, the author does not have any consistent political thought. One notices a mixture of political pragmatism and sentimental romanticism, almost Job-like faith in God's action, and also militant protests of the Harijan. But the contradictions of thought and programmes, the co-existence of different and contrasting ideologies can be very well seen as the political reality of contemporary India. The Telugu critics are unanimous in the praise of this work distinguished by its deep humanism and documentation, though many of them do not claim high literary merit for it.

Malapalli narrates the story of Ramadas, the head of the Harijans in Mangalpur village at Guntur, and his family. Ramadas, a deeply religious man, accepts almost everything as God's decree. His younger son Sangadas works in the house of the local landlord Chandrarayya, whose son Ramanaidu, despite his higher caste and wealth, is attracted to Sangadas and becomes his friend. Sangadas grows into a powerful peasant leader and receives support from Ramanaidu. Their friendship, and particularly Sangadas' defiant activities infuriate Chandrarayya, the landlord, to such an extent, that he kills him in a fit of passion. The landlord bribes the police and escapes trial. This action draws Ramanaidu even more close to the peasants, and he dedicates himself completely to the upliftment of the Harijans. Ramadas and his wife come to know of the murder of their son, they do not express any anger, but accept the tragedy with great fortitude. They, however, refuse to accept the money offered by Chandrarayya as compensation. The Harijans raise a modest memorial and establish a school, "Sanga Mandiram," to propagate the ideals of their leaders. But it does not remain a Harijan enterprise only. People belonging to upper castes also join them. The tyrannical landlord evicts Ramadas and his wife from his land and home. Ramdas accepts all with a rare philosophical detachment. But Venkatadas, the eldest son of Ramadas, wants to settle scores with the landlord, and avenge the death of his brother. He creates a secret army of "Santan" (which is reminiscent of Bankimchandra's *Ananda Math*), lives in a dense forest under a new name Takella Jaggayya, and mobilizes the poor and the downtrodden against the rich.

The story narrates in great detail the silent suffering of Ramadas and his wife, their privations and humiliations. Ramadas gets a job in a rich man's house which is looted by the associates of Takella Jaggayya. The police arrests Ramadas and sends him to jail. Ramadas meets his son, Venkata, in jail, where he dies miserably. Ramadas endures the pain with his usual calm.

The last part of the novel is a projection of hope – it describes the release of the prisoners after the attainment of freedom. Ramadas returns to his village. Ramanaidu donates all his property for the cause of the Harijans, and persuades Ramadas to stay in the village to help and guide the work started by the great leader Sangadas. But Ramadas finally leaves for the forest.

Within months of its publication, the Government of Madras represented by C P Ramaswamy Iyer, who was the Law Member then, banned the circulation of the novel, until the passages inciting the labourers against the landlords and those preaching Communism were deleted. A new edition was brought out in 1935 which was prescribed as classroom text in Andhra University. But the book was banned again – the ban was lifted in 1937 after the formation of the Congress Ministry by Rajagopalachari. The ban was put in place, it must be mentioned, not only because of its sympathies for the Bolsheviks, but because of clear indictments against the British rule. The government has often been referred pejoratively as a "she-buffalo," the police as "vulture," the English men as "raksasas" (monsters). The novel also visualizes the end of the British rule. Along with these there were also reasons related to caste politics of the times. Lakshminarayana was a Brahmin. The anti-Brahmin movement in the South coincided with the growth of the nationalist movement, but the non-Brahmin members of the local Justice Party did not always take Lakshminarayana's statements very kindly, and they misconstrued his texts. His depiction of the landlord Chandrarayya, a non-Brahmin, and the elopement of his daughter-in-law were taken as the Brahmin attempt to slander the non-Brahmins, and the novel was seen as an attempt towards the vilification of the Kama Zamindars, who were quite influential in the Justice Party.

When the novel was prescribed as a text by Andhra University, there was a pressure from interested parties to remove it. This was the time when the Communist Party was making use of certain parts of the speeches of Venkatadas in the pamphlets they distributed amongst the workers. His inspiring speech in the courtroom refers to the economic inequality and the exploitation of the poor by the rich.

The novel is also known by the name *Sangha Vijayamu* (The Victory of Sangha) which in the final analysis is the victory of Sangha, the Society or Organization. Some critics, however, detect a note of defeatism in the way the novel is concluded.

Though the author presents the unity forged by the workers as a force to meet the inhumanity of the exploiting class, Unnava ultimately retreats and leaves the triumph of the proletariat uncertain. After all the fret and fury, it is Ramadas who survives, and not the leaders of agitators ... and

Ramadas retires from all strife, reflecting the author's own attitude of resignation.[14]

Idealism and Experience

In the portrayal of the suffering of the downtrodden, one section of the writers, as I have observed earlier, was moved by a broad humanism, but without any real experience. With a few exceptions, most of the writings, poems, novels and plays, presenting idealistic heroes plunging into social service, are made of emotional stuff that quickly disintegrates. T S Satyanath's observations in this respect are worth quoting here.

> The Gandhian approach towards the untouchables in Kannada literature ... is highly idealistic and concentrated on issues like entry to temples, but did not look into the social and economic problems of the untouchables. Kuvempu's *Jalagara* (1928) and M R Srinivasamurthy's *Nagarika* present pictures of a scavenger with robust idealism. They have been depicted more like the Brahmin heroes of the time ... as if they are educated and enlightened ...[15]

Shivaram Karanth's novel *Chomana Dudi* (The Drum of Choma) appears conspicuously fresh and bold in this background. While the rest of the Kannada writers (and this is true of most of the writers in other Indian languages), influenced by Gandhian thought, wrote about social changes without a direct contact with social reality, Karanth, who too responded to Gandhian ideology, was acutely aware of the gap existing between the ideals and the reality. Similarly, the poet Changampuzha Krishna Pillai, one of the most adored figures in Malayalam literature, wrote eloquently and from the depth of his felt experience against inequality and exploitation. In his famous poem *Vazhakkula* (Banana Bunch), he narrates the plight of a poor Harijan who plants a banana plant in front of the hut, his little child weaving dreams around it. The child's dreams are shattered, as the father cuts off the banana bunch, and according to the law of the land, presents it to the landlord. Such narrations, establishing relationship between the plight of the poor and the deprived, and the social convention and economic

165

exploitation, are more poignant and direct because of their concrete specificities. Karanth's ability in concretizing the situation and presenting the men and women in a cultural context, makes the issues so real and living. The most important feature of the thirties is not only the high caste heroes trying to identify themselves with the Harijans, but the emergence of the Harijan hero. This can be found in Adya Rangcharya's Kannada play *Harijanavara* (1934) as well as in Karanth's *Chomana Dudi*, initiating a new trend that soon spread in different literatures.

Choma, the protagonist of the story, belongs to the lowliest of the untouchables, the Mari, who survive by scavenging on the left over food (ucchista) of the upper caste or the dead cattle. The novel is the record of Choma's struggle to get a piece of land on lease and live like any other dignified human being. With great artistic power, Karanth delineates how social and economic factors cause suffering and frustration, and bring about the ultimate ruination of the whole family. Choma works as a labourer in a coffee estate. His life, as narrated by Karanth, is a series of frustrations, and confrontations with deaths. His wife dies, leaving a large family, four sons and one daughter. Despite that painful death, Choma hopes for a better future. He still has the children and two oxen that keep his hope of becoming a respectable tenant alive. And he has the drum, which is the symbol of his hope and joy, as well as his agony. His master Sankappayya sympathizes with him and agrees to give him a piece of land on lease. But Sankappayya's old mother stands in the way. Although the old women of Karanth are generally progressive, this lady represents the tradition with all obstinacy. "Has any one done it before? ... You do not have to become the first one to give a piece of land to an untouchable."

While on the one hand there is a strong social resistance against kind and generous behaviour towards the untouchables, on the other hand, the economic exploitation of the untouchables continues from one generation to another. Choma's children Chaniya and Guruva, were forced to work in the estate because of arrears of loan taken by him. Guruva falls in love with a Christian girl, accepts Christianity, and escapes from the estate, while the other son, Chaniya, dies of fever. It is now the turn of Belli, the daughter of Choma, to serve the estate to clear the dues. She is seduced by the clerk of the estate. Choma flares up in anger and almost kills her. Around this time, his youngest son Nila gets drowned in the river. Because of the fear of pollution, the upper caste Brahmins who could rescue him, did not help. The life of Choma is a grim tragedy without any glory, a slow and agonizing disintegration that kills all hopes and all desires. The beating of the drum has been used as a poignant symbol of the rhythm of life as well as its final extinction. All occasions of the life of Choma is celebrated through the beating of the drum, the only medium expressing the deep and intense passions of the man. The novel started with the beating of the drum and so does it end.

> At once Choma started beating his drum. He closed the door of the hut so that others should not share the joy of his beating of the drum. He had not played the drum like that in his entire life before; he was not to play it like that once again. He played it only for a short while. But it was like the beating of the drum of Shiva at the time of the destruction of the world. The dum-dum of the drum stopped abruptly. Belli felt scared and ran towards the door; the two oxen had also come up to the door step ...[16]

Karanth's Choma remained the only authentic representation of the untouchable for a long time in Kannada literature till the writers from the "untouchable" caste started writing for themselves in the sixties. Among the very few writers who succeeded in creating such a story of deep pathos with the untouchable as the protagonist, are Tarashankar Bandyopadhyay and Thakazi Sivasankara Pillai.

The Story of a Poet

Tarashankar Bandyopadhyay, in his novel *Kabi* (The Poet), presents Netai, a "Dom" (an untouchable community) as the protagonist. The Doms are known for their physical strength, often condemned as criminals, and are supposed to be one of the lowest castes. From the mid-eighteenth century there were groups of poets in Bengal who used to delight the audience by their power of impromptu compositions. There were often contests between two groups on a given theme. It was a popular entertainment in Bengal, and continued in the rural areas till the beginning of the twentieth century. Netai, whose relatives were all hardened criminals, decided to be a "kabi" (a poet). This is a story of the struggle of an outcast towards vertical mobility. The novel begins with the sentence — "A wonder indeed, the son of a criminal has become a poet. Of course, there are precedences, Prahlad was born in the family of a demon and Valmiki was a dacoit. But those are parts of mythical wonders." The poet protagonist knows that, "No one will ever eat and drink things offered by him." The narratorial voice raises the questions, "Why should one be ashamed of being a Dom? How is a Dom inferior to a Brahmin?" But the questions are not answered by the social guardians. There are intense moments in the life of the protagonist who face the hurdles of a caste ridden society, which are further dramatized by his strong determination to achieve his goal. It is the struggle of an individual, of an extremely sensitive and creative person whose life gets enriched through various experiences of love and passion. His frustration and agony make him both pitiable and lovable — he attains his goal, becomes a "poet," transcends the caste barrier, disproves the theory of heredity and rejects the doctrine of "Karma." One of the most romantic and passionate narratives in Bengali, *Kabi*, created by an author deeply rooted in his Brahminical tradition, is a manifestation of the humanistic approach to inequality, its emphasis being on love and affection, friendship and sacrifice, rather than on social tyranny and economic exploitation.

The Protesting Hero

Thakazhi's *Tottiyute Makan* (Scavenger's Son, 1947)[17] which has a saga like quality, is a story of three generations of night soil carriers in their perpetual inhuman existence in a small town in Kerala. Coming as it does in the year of Indian Independence, the novel is also a candid document of an age-old shame and an agenda of future social transformation. The story begins with Isukkumuttu lying in his bed. Isukkumuttu had been working as a scavenger in the Alleppey municipality for thirty years. He has accepted it as his destiny, and even in his death bed expresses his intention, "To hand over his scavenger's tin and shovel before he died. He had told a succession of overseers that, when he was no longer able to work, his son should be taken on in his place." His son Chudalamuttu, however, decides not to be a scavenger, and to live a different life. He, and his wife, Valli, try to save money and dream of having a house of their own. He refuses to join the union as that might frustrate his plans. The authorities exploit him and make use of him in breaking another union. Like the story of Choma of Karanth and Netai of Tarashankar, it is also a story of the desire of moving upwards in the social structure, and also like those, it ends in frustration and humiliation. Chudalmuttu and his wife do not want their son to be a scavenger. They give the child the name Mohanan which no scavenger ever had, and send him to school even at the cost of their ostracization. But their sudden death change the fortunes of the boy who becomes a scavenger again.

But Mohanan is not like his grandfather who willingly accepted his fate. He is not like Chudalamuttu either, who wanted to improve his own life, isolating himself from other scavengers. Mohanan knows that the change can come only through social transformation, and through the power of organized struggle.

> The poor worker who lives starving and deprived in the low huts that are to be seen around us – him we do not fear. What is there he can do to us? Are we afraid of the beggar who comes, supported on a crude stick, and stands at our door calling for alms? Till today has the caste worker who toils in the fields beneath the rain and the hot sun ever stood up against anybody? ... But today we are afraid, not of those individuals, but of the sum total of their emotions. With every day, every minute, it is taking on gigantic proportions.

Is the fear only because of that? Is there not a sense of guilt for the wrongs we have done? [18]

A Ray of Hope

Mulk Raj Anand's first novel *Untouchable* (1935) is yet another powerful novel, exposing the dehumanizing role of caste narrativized through a fine analysis of a day's activity of a sweeper boy, Bakha, explored through small details. The dirt and filth of the public latrines, the odour of the hides and skins of dead carcasses, the most offensive abuses heaped upon the boy by the upper caste, make his life an unending nightmare, with all its horrors and pain. The humiliations the boy starts the day with as his father wakes him, "Get up, ohe you Bakhya ohe son of a pig," begins to intensify and accumulate as the day proceeds:

> Keep to the side of the road, ohe low caste vermin! he suddenly heard some one shouting at him, why don't you call, you swine and announce your approach! Do you know you have touched me and defiled me, cock-eyed son of a bow-legged scorpion! Now I will have to go and take a bath to purify myself ...

> Bakha stood amazed, embarrassed. He was deaf and dumb. His senses were paralyzed. Only fear gripped his soul, fear and humility and servility. He was used to being spoken to roughly. But he had seldom been taken unawares ...

The tensions and conflicts of the forenoon that expose the heartlessness and the inner filth of the caste Hindus are only the natural culmination of the situation in which he finds himself every morning of his life. Bakha meanders through hope and despair in the afternoon, to confident conviction at evening. He feels the joy of regeneration at a public meeting addressed by Gandhi, and hopes for emancipation through mechanized sanitation that flushes out the evils of untouchability from the Indian society. Gandhi gives him a new dignity. At times, during his menial work, he felt "as if burning and destruction were for him (part of his everyday exercise of cleansing) an art of purification. His mother had told him that his work was good." Gandhi, Bakha learns with surprise, tells of a Brahmin boy who does the scavenging in his Ashram. And the poet, tells him "Take a ploughman from the plough, wash off his dirt, and he is fit to rule a kingdom" is an old Indian proverb. The poet brings hope. The caste system must be destroyed. The sweepers will no longer remain untouchables once they change their profession. And machine can be introduced to do the work of man, and there will be "a casteless and classless society" one day. Gandhi moved him in a way he had never experienced before. Gandhi came as a strange God of hope who spoke a language of enigma; he did not give any clear answer, but a queer strength. The poet, on the other hand, with the idea of a machine that will give him freedom, brings a new ray of hope, more concrete and yet distant. "Perhaps I can find the poet on the way and ask him about his machine" is Bakha's last thought as he proceeds homewards.[19]

Pathos, Anger, Irony

Sarat Chandra forcefully brought out the issue of caste in some of his writings, most remarkable of which is the short story "Abhagir Svarga" (The Heaven for the Hapless). This is a story of a woman belonging to the low caste Dule who wanted to have an upper caste funeral on a pyre, so that she could go to heaven. The custom among the Dules was not to cremate, but to bury the dead. The family of Abhagi (literally "hapless") did not have the money to pay for the wood required for a proper funeral, nor was there any one sympathetic to the last wishes of a woman of "low caste." The story is interwoven with compassion and irony. The wish of Abhagi is to attain a spiritual status through the observance of the Brahminical rituals. The Brahminical society treats all such efforts of mobility with great contempt. The final solution – burial of Abhagi on the bank of the river and then lighting a bale of hay as a compromise – heightens the pathos.

Sarat Chandra, however, does not take up caste discrimination as a major theme, although his criticism of the Brahminical order is quite loud and sharp at times. His novel *Bamuner Meye* (The Brahmin's Daughter) published in 1921 presents the issue of untouchability marginally, its main theme being Brahminical orthodoxies and the Brahminical anxiety to maintain its pretended superiority by making fine distinctions within its own caste. There has been sustained caricature of the defendants of Hindu orthodoxies, though there is hardly any strong voice of protest against their meanness and insensibilities. Yet the strongest repudiation of caste (jat) and lineage (kul) comes from one of the elderly women who argues with her daughter-in-law in defence of her granddaughter who is not allowed to marry a man of her choice because he offered shelter to two orphan girls belonging to a low caste.

> Jagaddhatri said in suppressed anger: "They may be orphans, but should these low caste creatures live in the house of a Brahmin? Do scriptures permit this?"

> The mother-in-law replied: "I don't know what the scriptures say, my dear. But I know the intensity of my suffering. I can't talk about that to anyone, but had you suffered this way, you would have realized how God punishes one for humiliating man on the plea of low caste ... you think caste and lineage are very real, but is the existence of two lives unreal? Is that false?"

> Jagaddhatri said with distress: "Then, do you think this world cares only for this falsehood." The mother-in-law smiled sadly and replied, "No, not the world, it is our cursed nation that cares for it."

The criticism against the caste system comes from this old woman who lives in Kashi, renouncing the world, and who realizes the essential falsehood of the caste distinction that breeds meanness, insensibility and false pride. She continues,

> This demarcation between man and man is man-made: this can't be the law of God. God's gateway of union is wide, but man because of his depravity narrows it and creates the barrier stronger; it is man who makes room for filth and sin in God's world.

This is the state of the Brahminical society weakened from within, its hypocrisy and pretentions fully exposed. The pathos of Sarat Chandra is transformed into the anger in Nazrul Islam's alliterative line "jater name bajjati sab jat jaliyat khelche jua" (all this calumny in the name of caste; these frauds and imposters are gambling with life) and fun in Chilakamarti Lakshminarasimhan's *Ganapati* (1920), a humorous and satirical novel on the model of *Don Quixote*, ridiculing the brahmins.

In *Sevasadan*, Premchand raises the question of Dom, whom the "caste Hindus treat ... worse than animals but they woo them for political expediency." Abul-wafa exposes the Hindu Politics of befriending the doms to counter Muslim votes. In fact, Premchand visualizes the India after Independence where politicians, despite their public pronouncements against caste system, would make it the most lethal instrument to wield power. Premchand's contemporary, Venkata Parvatisvara Kavalu's *Matrmandiramu* (1918), tears the mask of Brahminic hypocrisy into pieces and advocates very strongly the admission of Harijans to the temples. It also visualizes in India, the ideal temple, where everybody is welcome.

Premchand's literary treatment of caste and the suffering of the untouchables is intimately connected with his relationship with Gandhi on the one hand, and his own experience of the Indian village reality on the other. The novel *Karmabhumi* (1932) was the first of his major writings to present the problem of the untouchable with a remarkable sense of realism. The hero Amarkant's first reaction to the pitiable condition of the Harijan village is that of shock and fear, and does not betray the slightest traces of hollow idealism or sickening romanticism. A sense of fright rudely awakens the romantic young man to the realization that the greatest stumbling block for the educated upper caste in its understanding of the untouchables, is the lack of actual experience of rural society. Premchand realizes that compassion and sympathy are not enough, and individual protests are too feeble to demolish the fortress of tradition. Organized protests with a clear political and social agenda are the only weapons to fight against the caste system and rural poverty. He was the first to analyze the causes of the economic privations of the Harijans and their social indignities. The slow change in Amarkant brought by his actual experience of Harijan life led him in the direction of political action.

Premchand was engaged with the problem of caste from the very early stage of his literary career. In his story "Sirf Ek Awaz" (1913) there is a Sanyasi, reminiscent of Vivekanand, who criticizes the caste system. Another story, "Sudra" (1925), is about an untouchable girl who becomes a victim of the woman-traffic. The chamarin grasscutter Muliya in the story

"Ghaswali" (1929) rebukes the lecherous landlord in an emotionally charged language, asserting the human right of the untouchable, "Do you think that because Mahavir is a chamar he has no blood in his body, that he feels no shame, that he has no thought of honour." The story brings out another aspect of the Harijan problem of poverty, heightening the vulnerability of the poor. The hypocrisy of the doctrine of "untouchability" is further exposed when the high caste Hindu, without any qualms seduces the Harijan woman to satisfy his carnal desire. Silia, an untouchable girl in "Godan," is seduced by the priest Matadin. The mother of the hapless girl cries out, "You will sleep with her but you won't drink the water touched by her."

Towards the end of 1930 appeared Premchand's memorable story "Sadgati," portraying the plight of Dukhi, a Chamar, and the heartlessness and cruelties of the Brahmin pandit and his wife. Told in a controlled manner, the story generates tremendous power with its understatements and irony, especially with the last act of the Brahmin in the role of the untouchable. The story also indicates the growing anger of the Harijans expressed in their refusal to clear off the dead body of Dukhi, who died at the Brahmin's compound. The Brahmin, in desperation, throws a rope around the dead man's leg and drags the corpse outside the village – the work of the Chamars and the work that gives justification to their being considered "untouchable." The Brahmin returns home, purifies himself, while the dead body of Dukhi lies exposed and feasted upon by vultures and dogs.

Premchand is the greatest artist of the suffering of the untouchables, not only because of his great anxiety for the century long oppression of the Harijans, but for his uncanny sense of realism with which he presents the characters belonging to the oppressed group, free from all sentimentality and pious idealism. "Thakur Ka Kua" (1932) is a perfect example of his great power as a narrator with a rare insight into human behaviour that leaves the reader overawed by the intensity and horror of human suffering. The village well for the untouchables has a dead animal in it, and therefore Gangi, the wife of Jokhu, who is down with high fever, decides to fetch some water from the well reserved for the Thakurs. The untouchables are prohibited from going there, and she knows she will be severely punished if she gets caught. The story moves in a slow pace where every action anticipates fear and punishment, and grows through suspense and breathlessness. Gangi reaches the well, determined to bring some water, uncontaminated and fresh – one's basic need, irrespective of social position. She almost succeeds, but suddenly finds the Thakur's doors about to be opened, and in the fright of her life drops the vessel and runs away. Running out of breath, she reaches home only to find Jokhu drinking the stinking water drawn from the untouchable's well. This story may be contrasted with Rajagopalchari's story "Mukundan Paraiyanana Kathai" (The Story of Mukundan who becomes Paraiya) written around this time. Puvayi, wife of Mari, secretly takes a pail of water from the well prohibited to the outcastes. She gets caught and is beaten severely.

This Maupassant grimness and austerity that marks the story of Gangi finds another outlet in "Dudh ka Dam" (The Price of the Milk) which has a thematic relationship with Bengali stories of Subodh Ghosh's "Parasuram" and Mahasweta Devi's "Stanadayini." This is a story of a sweeper (bhangi) woman who acts as the foster mother of a landlord, neglecting her own son. When she dies, the landlord takes care of her orphan son, but the landlord's son, fed on the bhangi's milk, treats the orphan contemptuously. This is the price of her "mother's" milk. Premchand's power to depict the degeneration and dehumanization brought by poverty, economic and social inequality, is at its height in "Kafan" (1935), one of the best stories he ever wrote. It is the story of Ghishu and his son Madhav, both completely denuded of human compassion and sympathy, and turned into animals for whom self- preservation is the only concern. The labour cries of his wife do not move Madhav, nor do they have any effect on Ghishu. They eat their roasted potatoes, and when they finish eating, they sleep like animals. The wretched woman dies, but her death does not bring any sorrow to them. They go out and beg in order to arrange for the funeral. They collect enough money for the shroud that they sell, and drink in callous joy, hoping that people will help them get yet another shroud. Premchand's continuous engagement with the problems of caste and poverty, religious prejudices and inequality, all of them associated with one another, was prompted by the Gandhian campaign against caste which alienated, points out Geetanjali Pandey,[20] "The orthodox Hindus within the Congress and also the radicals who felt that it was a digression." She rightly observes, "there is a convergence between Premchand's best stories and most impassioned writings on the subject, and the more radical tendencies of the thirties working together with Gandhi's inspiration." In fact, there was a convergence between Indian literature and several socio-political movements launched by Gandhi. The question of untouchability moved the consciousness of the whole people in an extremely significant manner — it disturbed and provoked the literary community. Even a language like Dogri, which had very little literary activity in this period, produces a satirical play, *Achuta*, written by Khajuri in 1935. It is worth mentioning that the tremendous popularity enjoyed by the Hindi film *Acchut Kanya* (1936) in this period, only speaks of the common man's instinctive opposition against untouchability. Devika Rani appeared as a Harijan girl in love with a Brahmin youth portrayed by a relatively unknown actor Ashok Kumar, who grew into a matinee idol later. *The Hindu* wrote in its review that it is a story of "a human sacrifice at the altar of bigotry."[21] It may not be out of place to mention here that the play *Jamadarin* produced by Habib Tanvir — which has raised violent protest from a political party recently — was originally conceived by Sukh Ram and Sita Ram of Chattisgarh around 1936. This is one of the hilarious satires against priest craft and untouchability by the victims of the institution of the caste system.

Protests from Below

While the Gandhian movement gave a moral dimension to the critique of caste, the Marxist doctrines of class war with which the Indian writers were exposed since the late twenties widened their vision. In a literary conference in 1924, Sarat Chandra Chatterji declared that "In this land of hunger and oppression when we shall delve deep into the society and discover the sorrow and anxiety of the common man as in Russian literature, only then the literary exercises of our country will be meaningful." Two years later he wrote *Abhagir Svarga*, which we have already referred to, and *Mahesh* one of the most powerful Bengali stories, that focusses attention on a poor Muslim farmer living in a village ruled by a Brahmin landlord. The Muslim farmer, Gafoor, loves his bull, whom he affectionately calls Mahesh (a name of Siva), but poverty forces him to kill the animal in a fit of anger. Not only is he ostracized by the Hindu landlord for killing the bull, but he is finally forced to leave the village. Sarat Chandra's controlled portrayal of the situation suggestively points out the factors – social and economic – responsible in bringing about changes in the life of the agricultural labourers, many of whom were forced to move out of the village to join factories in the industrial areas. Before leaving his home Gafoor looks up to the starlit black sky and prays, "Allah, punish me as much as you would, but my Mahesh died of thirst. Don't forgive those who have denied him of your gifts, grass and water." This voice of anger reaches a crescendo in Nazrul Islam's volcanic lines,

> They snatch the morsel of food from thirty three crores of mouths. Let their destruction be announced in letters written with my blood.

The writers associated with the Bengali journal *Kallol* (1923), though none of them were Marxists, developed interest in the lives of the underdogs, partly inspired by Russian and Scandinavian literature, and partly in response to the changing middle class values under the impact of political movements. They presented the life of the daily labourers, the workers in the mines, the working women, mostly maid servants, the life in the slums and of the urban poor and lower middle class slowly turning into proletariat. The beggar and the pick pocket, the prostitute, the servant and the daily wage earner became frequent characters in the fiction in particular, and other genres in general. The common man was celebrated with great compassion and feeling, and among the common man the downtrodden and the deprived assumed even greater importance. K C Venkataramani introduced the rural man in his *Murukan – A Tiller* (1927), later translated into Tamil. In his second novel *Kundan, The Patriot* (1932), a Gandhian novel, he presents several characters Nandan, Mukkam, Nallan, Kariyan – all Harijans and agricultural coolies. Pudumaippittan, in his short story "Tunbakeni" written in the thirties, narrates the life of the Tamil labourers, some of them belonging to low caste, who were forced to go to Sri Lanka as coolies. Most of the people were serfs belonging to Palla and Paraiya community. They were brought by "Kankanis" (agents) to the tea garden. The coolies in the tea garden were subjected to barbaric treatment and ruthless exploitation. In addition to that, they were victims of disease and died without treatment. The lives of the women were even worse. They were the objects of sexual lust of the Kankanis as well as of the white officers. Pudumaippittan's story records the suffering and frustration of the coolies as well as their spontaneous uprising, which is effectively controlled.

The theme of exploitation of labourers cutting across caste – though it was the lower caste who were the worst sufferers – received the attention of many socially conscious authors. Anand's *Coolie* (1936) written with a deeper understanding of the nature of exploitation in a colonial situation, stands out as a powerful work. "The dark dingy Sir George Cotton Mill that specializes in low paid woman and child labour," as Dr Satender Singh points out, "is a symbol of their (British) technologcial power and economic dominance."[22] Like *Untouchable*, the protagonist of the *Coolie* is also a boy, in fact an orphan village boy, who has set out in the wide world in search of food and shelter. The locale of Anand's next novel, *Two Leaves and a Bud* (1937), is a tea plantation in Assam, and its hero, a Punjabi peasant Gangu, is an extension of the same narrative of suffering and exploitation and also of protest. By the mid thirties, the life of the agricultural labourers and industrial workers became important themes in Indian literature. Jhinabhai Desai's poem *Arghaja* (1935) as well as Meghani's *Yug Vandana* (1935) – both written in Gujarati – foregrounded the theme of the downtrodden against the background of Gandhian movement and Marxian doctrines. It is quite natural that in Dogri, free from the debates on modernity, Dinu Bhai Pant chose the life of a bonded labourer as the theme for his poem "Mangu di Chabila" (1946).

Indian literature discovered a new potentiality in the life of the low and the lowliest, the deprived and the humiliated. The hero-centric world finally vanished, yielding place to the anti-hero. The Dalit literature, however, was yet to emerge, but the signs had already appeared. The poem *Violence Zad* (The Tree of Violence) by N L Dhasal (b 1949), the founder-leader of the Dalit Panther movement, is only two decades far from the midnight of Indian Independence.

Notes

1 "Harijan," *Selections from Gandhi*, N K Bose ed (Ahmedabad: Navajivan Publishing House,1948) 264-65.

2 "Gitanjali"(translation mine) Verse 108 from *Rabindra Rachanabali 2* (Santiniketan: Government of West Bengal, 1961).

3. Trans. (Madras: Dinamani Kariyalayam, 1944).

4 B D Bhushan's unpublished dissertation on untouchability submitted for the MPhil degree of Delhi University in 1989.

5 Mahar group is one of the major sections of the untouchables, normally believed to be the original inhabitants of Maharashtra.

6 B Kuppuswamy, *Serial Change in India*, (Delhi: Oxford UP, 1987) also J H Huton, *Caste in India* (London: Oxford UP, 1951) 205-06.

7 See G S Lokhande, *Bhimrao Ramji Ambedkar*, (New Delhi: Sterling, 1977) 113-19. For a study of Gandhi-Ambedkar relationship see Eleanor Zelliot, "Gandhi and Ambedkar – A Study in Leadership," J Michael Mahar ed., *The Untouchables in Contemporary India*, (Arizona: The U of Arizona P, 1972) 69-96.

8 Quoted in Kuppuswamy, *Serial Change in India*, 212.

9 P K Parmeswaran Nair, *History of Malaylam Literature,* trans. E M J Venniyoor, (New Delhi:Sahitya Akademi, 1967) 187.

10. P K Parmeswaran Nair, *History of Malaylam Literature*, 188.

11 P K Parmeswaran Nair, *History of Malaylam Literature*.

12 Trans. Krishna Chaitanya. *A History of Malaylam Literature* (Delhi: Orient Longman, 1971) 227.

13 C M Bandivadekar, *Hindi aur Marathi Ke Samajik Upanyaska Tulanatmak Adhyayan*. (Ajmer: Krishna Brothers, 1969) 174.

14 S S Prabhakar Rao, "Malapalli," *Encyclopaedia of Indian Literature*, Vol 3 (1987-89) 2557.

15 T S Satyanath, "The Depiction of the Downtrodden in Kannada Literature" (unpublished), presented at a seminar in Department of Modern Indian Languages, University of Delhi.

16 Trans. Satyanath

17 Trans. R E Asher, (New Delhi: Orient Paperback, n.d.).

18 Trans. R E Asher 139-40.

19 The problems of scavenging in India remained unsolved for a long time after the Independence.

See Bindeshwar Pathak, *Road to Freedom* (Delhi: Motilal Banarasi Das, 1991), a study of scavenging and suggestions for providing technology for its total abolition.

20 Geetanjali Pandey, *Between Two Worlds*, (New Delhi: Manohar Publications, 1989).

21 Quoted in E Barnollow and S Krishnaswamy, *Indian Film* (New Delhi: Oxford UP, 1980) A review of the film appeared in *The Hindu* 25 June 1957.

22 Satender Singh, response to questionnaire 1992.

NARRATIVES OF SUFFERING: DALIT PERSPECTIVES[1]

TAPAN BASU

In his monumental *History of Indian Literature 1911-1956* (1995), Sisir Kumar Das concludes the chapter on "Narratives of Suffering: Caste and the Underprivileged" with the following observation:

> Indian literature discovered a new potentiality in the life of the low and the lowliest, the deprived and the humiliated. The hero-centric world would finally vanish yielding place to the anti-hero. The Dalit literature, however, was yet to emerge but the signs had already appeared. The poem "Violence Zad" (The Tree of Violence) by N L Dhasal (b 1949), the founder leader of the Dalit Panther movement, is only two decades far from the midnight of Indian independence.[2]

In this paper, I shall survey the rise and development of the so-called Dalit Sahitya (Dalit literature), to start with in Maharashtra of the 1960s and the 1970s, and then gradually across the length and breadth of the country through the 1980s and the 1990s. In doing so, I shall also look at the pre-history of this literature in the literature produced by members of the "untouchable" castes in earlier eras as well as the literature produced by upper caste progressives on the "evil of untouchability" before the "untouchable" writers themselves took up their own cause.

One of the consequences in fact, of the efflorescence of Dalit literature from almost all over India has been the extension of the horizons of literature written about caste and caste related issues. Unlike in the late nineteenth and early twentieth centuries when upper caste progressives Rabindranath Tagore (Bangla), Prem Chand (Hindi) and Mulk Raj Anand (English) alone seemed to be writing against untouchability, the emergence in later decades of lower caste authors who have powerfully protested the plight of the "untouchables" has obviously enriched a corpus of literature which includes the sensitive statements by upper caste writers like Mahasweta Devi, Vijay Tendulkar and U R Ananthamurthy and others towards a critique of untouchability precepts and practices. While upper caste criticism of untouchability has undoubtedly helped to harness social opinion against casteism, Dalit writings have instilled a tone of immediacy to the note of intensity informing most upper caste criticism of untouchability.[3] As S P Punalekar has explained,

> Dalit writers themselves are either victims or witness to social inequities and violence. Some have direct or indirect links with social, political and cultural organizations of Dalits. A few among them are staunch social activists and use literature as a vehicle to propagate their views on Dalit identity and the prevailing social consciousness.[4]

Perhaps the overshadowing of lower caste writings by upper caste writings against casteism in early modern India was inevitable, given the caste composition of Indian writers of that period. As Sisir Kumar Das has remarked, "The Brahmins and the Kayasthas (mostly in Bengali, Maithili, Assamese, Oriya and the Hindi speaking areas and in Maharashtra), the Nambudiris and the Nairs (in Kerala), the Kshatriyas (mainly in Orissa and occasionally among Punjabi-Urdu writers), the Reddys and Naidus (in Andhra Pradesh) and the Banias and the Patels, of course with the Brahmins (in Gujarat), dominated the literary scene."[5]

Nevertheless, some writers from the lower castes, exceptions though they were, did raise their voices against caste atrocities. Among the earliest writers in this category was the Telegu poet Joshua Garran (1863-1971), a Christian coming from among the "untouchables." He learned Sanskrit, worked as a school master, and later occupied high public positions as a member of the legislative council of Andhra Pradesh. Another poet, a Malayali, who is not even mentioned in many literary histories, is Mooloor Padmanabha Pannikar, the first major poet in his language to come from a low caste, the Ezhava. Mooloor Pannikar (1869-1931) was a disciple of Narayana Guru (1856-1929), an enlightened social reformer who wrote in three languages, Malayalam, Tamil and Sanskrit, and inspired the exploited Ezhava community towards social regeneration. Narayana Guru was also the mentor of another poet from among the Ezhavas, namely Kumaran Asan, who turned out to be one of the greatest poets of Malayalam for all times. Kumaran Asan articulated the agony of the Ezhavas as a consequence of caste distinctions in society. He also exhorted them, as in his poem "Simhanandam" (The Lion's Roar, 1919), to "speed up where the caste demon rears its ugly face." This note of confrontation in a lower caste writer's negotiation of casteism in society had a different impact from the note of compassion in a upper caste writer's negotiation of casteism in society. Another Malayali poet of considerable merit, K P Karuppan (1884-1957) belonged to a family of fisherfolk. Two more early twentieth century writers from Kerala, hailing from lower castes, who have achieved eminence, are V K Kalath (dates not certain) and Tokoco Vaduthala (dates not certain). Among the pioneering lower caste writers was also Vindan (dates not certain), the Tamil writer, writing in the 1940s and the 1950s, who eventually started his own journal *Manithan* (Man), entirely devoted to the cause of the working class. Unfortunately, however, for many of this early generation of lower caste writers, even though they were mostly located in culturally advanced pockets of the southern states of India where literacy estimates and educational levels were much higher than in the northern states, their achievements were very often downplayed by a conservative establishment in the world of learning and letters.

Literary historians have variously identified the antecedents of all these writers in the Buddha (6th century BC), Chokhamela (14th century AD) and Jotiba Phule (1828-90).[6] Each of these historical figures was, and continues to be in his own way, a source of inspiration for anti-caste agitations and movements all over India.

However, the chief inspirational figure as far as Dalit Sahitya of the modern era is concerned, is that of Babasaheb Ramji Ambedkar (1891-1956), the doyen among Dalit leaders of the twentieth century. It is no coincidence, as Arjun Dangle, founder member of the Maharashtrian Dalit youth organization of the 1970s, the Dalit Panthers, has observed, that the Dalit literary groundswell began in Maharashtra, the birthplace of Dr Ambedkar's Dalit liberation enterprise.[7] Dr Ambedkar's revolutionary ideas stirred towards revolutionary actions all the Dalits of Maharashtra, and gave them a new energy. Dalit literature is nothing but the literary expression of this energy. Little wonder that Dr Ambedkar appears repeatedly, as person and as emblem, if not as a trope of inspiration, in much of Dalit literature.

The term "Dalit literature" can be traced to the first Dalit literary conference in 1958, organized by the Maharashtra Dalit Sahitya Sangha. "Bandhumadav," a Dalit intellectual, in his article in the *Prabuddha Bharat* of 15th February, 1958, explains the necessity of such a conference and its aim.

> Just as the Russian writers helped the revolution by the spreading of Lenin's revolutionary ideology through their works, our writers should spread Dr Ambedkar's philosophy to the villages ... Politics is just one way of attacking opposition. Unless we attack from all sides we cannot defeat those who have inflicted injustice on us for the last thousands of years.

Resolution No 5, passed at the end of the conference, declared that "the literature written by the Dalits and that written by others about the Dalits in Marathi be accepted as a separate entity known as Dalit literature, and realizing its cultural importance, the universities and literary organizations should give it its proper place."

The first conference of Dalit writers did not create much of an impact, either outside the Dalit community, due to social bias against the Dalits, or inside it, due to fractions and frictions within. Dr Ambedkar's death and the subsequent schisms within the Republican Party of India which he initiated, proved to be setbacks for Dalit literary as much as for Dalit political activity. Thus, till the 1960s no Dalit writer of note from the post-Ambedkar generation rose to prominence in Maharashtra or elsewhere.

Dr Ambedkar's own prolific production as a writer was primarily political. From 1920 on, he published newspapers, at times including a poem or a story. But the newspapers were chiefly intended to be a channel of information for the Dalits, their substance spreading somehow among a people whose reading writing members were less than three percent. The newspapers were themselves signifiers of literary success within the Dalit liberation enterprise, and while Ambedkar's flourished, many others quested. It is significant that when in 1962 A S Rampise published a list of newspapers started by depressed caste persons of India, these numbered one hundred and twenty, the great majority of them in Marathi.

The 1960s saw also an efflorescence of the Little Magazine in Maharastra. The publication of the Little Magazines was a transgressive endeavour, their agenda being to struggle against "polite" modes of writing. They formed a forum for expression for social rebels – angry young men who wrote in Marathi about the problems of the working class and other under privileged sections of society.

Not that rebellious literature of this sort was not already being written by upper caste writers. Narayan Surve, for instance, wrote about working class problems, while Anna Bhau Sathe and Shankar Rao Kharat wrote about the predicament of the Dalits.

But the writer who, to use the words of Arjun Dangle, "gave momentum to Dalit literature," was Baburao Bagul.[8] Baburao Bagul used the Little Magazine *Fatka* to publish his poems of social rebellion. He also published, independently, some stories in a collection called *Jevha Mi Jaat Chorli Hoti* (When I Had Concealed My Caste), a collection which took the entire literary world by storm, because of its frankness and ferocity in indicting the caste system of the Hindus. Whereas Anna Bhau Sathe

185

and Shankar Rao Kharat had written about the predicament of the Dalits with pathos, Bagul addressed the same with a passion which set the pattern for the representation of Dalit problems in Dalit literature afterwards.

Such individual contributions to the development of Dalit literature apart, institutional contributions cannot be overlooked. The most important institutional contribution was made by Milind College, the institution of higher education in Aurangabad, founded by Dr Ambedkar. A majority of students in this college were from the rural areas and most of the faculty were Dalits. The non-Dalit faculty too were associated with the Dalit liberation enterprise. The college annual, edited by the Principal M B Chitnis, encouraged exchanges of opinions on cultural and literary issues. Principal M N Wankhede, who had been to the United States of America for higher studies, also returned about the same time to Aurangabad and brought with him the knowledge of Black American literature, its recording of Black American sufferings and its sentiments of revolt against the mainstream. He made a comparative study of the Black Americans and the Indian Dalits.

Inevitably, a Milind Sahitya Parishad was set up by the faculty and students of Milind College and in turn a new journal, *Asmita* (now *Asmitadarsha*), to discuss the direction in which Dalit literature was going. The contributors to this journal included both seasoned writers, non-Dalit as well as Dalit, and novices.

In the later 1960s, some of these writers got together at a conference in Bombay held under the aegis of Maharashtra Bauddha Sahitya Sabha. This meet brought on one platform Dalit writers from all over Maharastra. The first representative collection of poems by Dalits, *Akar*, was published in this conference. *Akar* included poems by Baburao Bagul, Daya Pawar, Arjun Dangle, Yadavrao Gangurde, Chokha Kamble, et cetera, but not all of them wrote from a Dalit perspective about Dalit problems. Yet it comprised, in essence, an expression of an evolving Dalit identity, at least in Maharashtra.

Dalit literature was still a new literary phenomenon. Hence it was not spontaneously accepted as "great literature" by many upper caste critics and even a few lower caste critics. The former usually dismissed this literature as "propagandist" while the latter berated it for its "retrogade" representation of the Dalit community.

In this context, the conferment of a state government award on Baburao Bagul in 1968 for his second collection of stories *Maran Swasta Hot Ahe* (Death is Getting Cheaper) was indeed significant. It was the candour of his depiction of Dalit life in all its deprivations that earned Baburao Bagul the adulation of almost every reviewer cutting across ideological lines.

During this same acrimonious period, another writers' conference was held, this time at Mahad, once again organized by the Maharashtra Bauddha Sahitya Sabha. Mahad had a memorable resonance from the history of the Dalit liberation enterprise. Dr Ambedkar had inaugurated his political career here in 1927 with the Chavadar Tale Satyagraha by making a bonfire of the *Manusmriti*. The conference at Mahad was presided over by Baburao Bagul who was acknowledged generally to be the father figure of Dalit literature, particularly after the publication in serial shape of his controversial novel *Paushya* in the periodical *Amhi* which he himself had launched.

A year or two later, that is, in 1972, there was further re-orientation of Dalit literature with the publication of *Gopitha,* a collection of poems by the young Dalit writer, Namdeo Dhasal. *Gopitha* was written in a language unfamiliar to mainstream writers in Marathi, upper caste as well as lower caste. So was *Athvaninche Pakshi* written by P E Sonkamble. In either case, the authors used the colloquial languages of the lower castes they were representing, rather than the cultivated language of upper caste literature. The "roughness" of idiom in these languages struck a jarring note in the existing symphony of Marathi literature.

Such self-confident self-assertion on the part of Dalit writers was at odds with the deprivations which Dalit masses still had to put up with in both towns and villages. Despite modernization of an ancient economy, the economic condition of the poorer segments of society, which included most Dalits, did not improve. In fact, the upper caste stranglehold on economic resources and rewards was accentuated further with the increasing concentration of capital in the possession of the already powerful and already prosperous social segments. The Dalit poor, or more pertinently, the poor Dalit, was rendered more penurious than ever before.

The existing Dalit organizations such as the Republican Party of India did nothing to combat the injustices in society. The predicament of the Dalits cried out for deeds (political action) rather than words (political rhetoric). The result was that writers such as Namdeo Dhasal, J V Pawar, and Arjun Dangle took the initiative and established the Dalit Panthers in Bombay on the model of the Black Panthers of Oakland, a militant army of youths fighting for Black American liberation in the United States of America. The Dalit Panthers was established on 9th July, 1972. Its agenda was to fight for the liberation of the Indian Dalits through "a complete revolution." As the Dalit Panthers Manifesto of 1973 put it, the Dalit's were not to be satisfied easily now. "We do not want a little place in the Brahman Alley. We want the rule of the whole lane." The Dalit Panthers observed Independence Day that year, which incidentally was the silver jubilee of Indian Independence, as Black Day, and black flag demonstrations were held at different points in Bombay. The most striking thing about the Dalit Panthers movement was that it typified a political upheaval instigated by a literary upheaval. Dalit literature, at least in Maharashtra, had finally come of age.[9] Between 1972 and 1978, under the direct influence of the Dalit Panthers of Maharashtra, writers drawn from the Dalit communities of Gujarat, Karnataka, Andhra Pradesh, Orissa and Tamil Nadu began to write about caste and caste related themes.

Gujarati Dalit literature, though strongly influenced by Marathi Dalit literature, remained for many years, to quote K M Sherrif, its "poor country cousin." The first publication of Gujarati Dalit literature, *Panther* was started by Ramesh Chandra Parmar in 1975. Following this, a number of periodicals devoted to Dalit literature sprang up during the second half of the 1970s *Akrosh, Kalo, Sooraj, Garud, Dalit Bandhu, Naya Marg* and *Disha* were some of the more prominent ones. By the end of the decade, Dalit literature, which had begun as a counter literary trend in Gujarati literature, often matched conventional literature in quality if not in quantity. In the 1980s, several of the notable works in poetry and prose written in Gujarati came from writings by Dalits. The Dalit writers of these works, however, did not necessarily want to be noted by the culture elite of Gujarat. As Neerav Patel, one of these writers, memorably put it in the preface to one of his books, "... I have deliberatately decided not to give a glossary to our *desi* dictionary, at least to tease *them*, to annoy *them*, yes, a childish revenge!" Predictably, official recognition of the merit of these Dalit writers did not come very easily. It is only of late that several Dalit writers such as Joseph Macwan, Mohan Parmar, Harish Manglam, Mangal Rathod and Kisan Sosa have been acknowledged for their writings by the literary establishment of Gujarat.

Dalit literature in Gujarati has successfully experimented with the regional dialects of Gujarat and has drawn extensively from the folk literature of Gujarat. The structure and substance of folk songs and folk tales have been widely adopted by the Dalit writers. This intimate relationship between Gujarati Dalit literature and the folk literature of Gujarat does not come out with clarity in English translations. Traditional poetic forms like "ghazal" and "muktak" have been radically re-moulded by Dalit authors.

Another noteworthy achievement of Gujarati Dalit literature is the creation of a subaltern mythology to counter hegemonic Hindu mythology with its casteist bias. It is the Buddha who takes up the *sudarshan chakra* to destroy evil in the universe. Eklavya and Shambuka become epic heroes. The quest for the Golden Age leads to the ruins of Mohenjadaro and Harrappa and the caves of Bhimbetka.

A major bone of contention among Dalit writers of Gujarat derives from a division of opinion regarding the implications of the term "Dalit" itself. While Harish Manglam, for instance, has categorically stated that Dalit literature is literature about Dalits, Mangal Rathod and others have felt that Dalit literature ought to have a wider range of reference than only literature referring to caste discrimination. Nevertheless, even as the debate about definitions continues, the corpus of Gujarati Dalit literature has been increasing and improving almost day by day without getting bogged down by an unsavoury polemics.[10]

It was around the 1970s again, that the early writings by Dalits emerged in Karnataka. As against the earlier writings by non-Dalits on Dalits which combined commiseration with condescension, Dalits wrote about themselves without unnecessary bathos. D R Nagraj, one of the foremost critics of Kannada literature, has distinguished between two schools of Kannada Dalit literature, which, according to him, reflect two kinds of responses to the oppression of Dalits in society – materialist negotiation of the problem and spiritualist transcendence of the problem. While the latter school exemplified by writers such as Devanoor Mahadeva, K Siddaiah and Govindaiah advised the suffering Dalits to take the path of resignation, the former school exemplified by writers such as Siddalingaiah, Mogalli Ganesh, and A Mallagatti advised the suffering Dalits to take the path of resistance. Among these writers, Siddalingaiah and Devanoor Mahadeva belong to a first generation of Kannada Dalit writers who gained prominence in the wake of the social and political ferment among Dalits, as well as other marginalized social groups within Karnataka in the wake of the lifting of the Indira Gandhi imposed Emergency in India. The rest belong to a post- eighties second generation.

The two schools exhibited two conflicting attitudes towards the cultural self of the Dalits. The materialist negotiation perspective called for repudiation of Hindu Scriptures while the spiritualist transcendence perspective called for the reformulation of Hindu scriptures. Thus, what the materialist negotiation perspective abjured as obscurantist mumbo jumbo, the spiritualist transcendence perspective adapted as oppositional metaphor.

The duality which, in the opinion of Nagaraj, divided the Dalit writers of Karnataka in the 1970s, to a certain extent, prevented Kannada Dalit writings from representing a collective Dalit self. The formation of the Dalit self has further been hindered by fragmentations which have afflicted the Dalit movement in recent years.[11]

The Dalit movements in Andhra Pradesh and Tamil Nadu of the same period, however, did not experience such fractures. But Tamil and Telegu Dalit writers really came into their own a little later, to be precise, in the 1980s and the 1990s – each tradition drawing heavily upon the Dalit Panthers paradigm.

Quite a few of these Dalit writers of the 1970s were first generation educated middle class professionals who had struggled out of lives of hardship and poverty. In Orissa it was the professional class Dalits who, in the 1970s, started the tradition of Dalit writings, with Bichitra Mand Nayak publishing his poetry of anger at caste oppression in 1973. Nayak deliberately invoked a Dalit personality and a Dalit perspective in his poetry.

By the 1980s and the 1990s, even conservative critics from conventional circles such as literary academics of the different literatures and languages recognized the talents of the Dalit writers. Many Dalit writers, hitherto unknown, now came into the limelight. In Orissa these included short story writers Dr Samir Ranjan, a medical specialist, and Prof Ramachandra Sethi, an university teacher, and novelists Kalindi Chandra Behara and Jagannath Mallik.[12]

In Andhra Pradesh, the most promising among young Dalit writers have been the novelists. The Dalit novel which had a sensational impact was *Khaki Bathukulu* (1990) by "Spartacus," pen name of Mohan Rao, a Dalit. The novel deals with the unhappy lives of police constables, who though apparently powerful can be actually powerless, especially if they happen to belong to the powerless, lower castes. The novel focusses upon the humiliating existence of one such police constable who is constantly "shown his place" by his upper caste police officers. Other Telugu Dalit novels of note have been Boya Jangaiah's *Jathara* (1988) and Akkineni Kutumba Rao's *Sorrajjem* (1992).[13]

In Tamil Nadu, Dalit writings took root, as in Andhra Pradesh, in the late 1980s and the early 1990s, but in the guise of news magazines. A spate of magazines, *Kodangi, Kalam, Manusangada, Nirapirihai, Dalit, Kazhakku*, and so on came on the scene. Dalit writings, as Venkat Swaminathan has argued, have enriched the contemporary Tamil literary scene. They have, beginning with the novel *Pirahu* (And Then), published by Poomani in the 1970s, added an earthiness and a worldliness to Tamil literature of the contemporary years. In this respect, special attention needs to be paid to the narratives of Bama, the Dalit woman writer – her first narrative, *Karukku*, an autobiographical account of her life in the convent, *Sangati*, which is a quaint string of accounts of Dalit life told by her grandmother, and *Armachi*, a tale of subversive humour. There are also the tales of the other Dalit authors, Abhimani and Unjai Rajan, based on their own experience and knowledge. And last but not the least, there is the Tamil Dalit writer Imayam, who has disclaimed a pure Dalit identity, and thereby earned the ire of fellow Tamil Dalit writers. His novel *Koveru Kathudaihal* (Mules) reports in realistic details the pathetic plight of a Dalit Christian family whose duty it is to wash the clothes of other Dalits who have become upwardly mobile through education or enterprise, and who then exploit the labour of the poor Dalits of their community. Imayam is thus one of the few Dalit writers to talk about how the class system in modern society sometimes helped to complicate the ancient caste system.[14]

As Raj Gautaman has noted, there is in Tamil Dalit writing a very powerful sense of the self and the community as Dalit, which rejects outright the notion of varna, and which simultaneously resists the attempt to "Sanskritize," or to evaluate marginal Dalit life according to mainstream Hindu values. Bama, perhaps the most innovative of Dalit writers from Tamil Nadu, does this by overturning the artistry and aesthetics of received upper class, upper caste Tamil. She breaks the rules of Tamil grammar and diction throughout, and misconstructs and misrepresents the language, demanding from her readers a different and a difficult pattern of reading. *Karukku*, especially, is distinguished through the use of an informal speech sense which seeks to establish an intimacy between reader and narrator – an intimacy which then implicates the reader in the consciousness of the narrator.[15]

Up north, in the so-called "cow belt" of India, the heartland of Hindutva chauvinism, awareness of Dalit rights has been nebulous even among the Dalits. It is only within the last two decades, against the backdrop of a few affirmative action measuers sponsored by the central government and a virulent anti-Dalit backlash on the part of upper castes, that educated Dalit youth of the North Indian states have started speaking up for themselves as Dalits. "For the first time," as Ram Narayan, scholar on Dalit society at the University of Delhi, says, "a new literature is emerging in North India which aims to speak and interpret [Dalit problems] for itself." It seems that Dalits no longer wish to be spoken for by others, however sympathetic to their cause these others might be. The Dalit Sahitya Research Foundation, set up in 1994, publishes over fifty volumes of Dalit poems and stories every year. A number of books are published at the expense of the writers themselves.

Predictably, there have been a spate of autobiographical publications by Dalit writers, mostly in Hindi. These include Om Parkash Valmiki's *Jhootan*, Jai Prakash Kardam's *Jhappar*, Mohandas Namisrai's *Apne Apne Pinjre* – all attempts on the part of Dalit authors to articulate their anxieties and their aspirations. The last named text is the first known Dalit autobiography in Hindi. Sheoraj Singh Bechain, author of pioneering research on Ambedkar and also the convener of the Dalit Writers' Forum, observes:

> Knowledge has never been democratic in this country. In intellectual life ... the arts or in academics there is no presence of Dalit traditions of learning. This is a loss for the whole country, because we need more traditions of knowledge, not the repetition of the same history.

There is now a concerted endeavour on the part of Dalit scholars of the Hindi heartland to develop and disseminate a Dalit tradition of thought. Many monographs have been recently produced by them, all intended to make the Dalit people aware of their rights and duties – for instance, Suresh Chandra Kushwaha's *Arakshan ke Hatyare,* Buddhshran Hans' *Kash Hum Hindu Na Hote* and Mata Prasad's *Achhut Virangana Nautanki.* The *Achhut Virangana Nautanki* dramatizes the story of a lower caste heroine who struggles severely with Brahminical prejudices, enters a temple and marries a man of her choice without the assistance of any priest. The play is enframed within the form of nautanki. It is the chronicle of a female protagonist who, according to her creator, defies Hindu orthodoxy. Folk forms like kawali, doha, chaubola, daud and lavni are also used in this story. It is worth putting on record that the rise of Dalit literature in North India has followed the success of Dalit organizations such as the DS4, the BAMCEF and the Bahujan Samaj Party in the realm of politics, while in South India, perhaps, the success of Dalits in the realm of politics was prepared for by a cultural revolution by Dalits. Not surprisingly, in the north, Dalit literature has flourished most in states such as Uttar Pradesh, Madhya Pradesh and Bihar in which the political mobilization of the Dalits has been the strongest.[16]

With a sizeable Dalit population, stretching across to the Sikh community as well, Punjab has been more hospitable to Dalit writers than other North Indian states. In the late 1980s and early 1990s the Dalit trend in literature became very strong. A Dalit Sahit Sabha was formed and it held its first Punjabi Dalit Sahit Sammelan in 1994 in Phagwara.

Earlier too, writers like Prem Gorkhi, Kirpal Kazak, Attarjee, Bhura Singh Kaler, Nachhatar and Lal Singh had made their Dalit identity evident through their writings.

Dalit writers of the 1980s and the 1990s, Bhagwant Rasulpuri, Des Raj Kali and Jinder, continued to depict the sorrows of Dalit life, yet the real hero had emerged in the character of Jageer of *Marhi Da Diwa*. This novel by Gurdial Singh had been published as early as the late 1960s, and it proved to be a path breaking Punjabi novel. Later, Gurdial Singh wrote many more novels. In *Anhoe* and *Paisa*, he continued the tradition set by himself in *Marhi Da Diwa*. Jaswant Virdi's novel *Nihchal Nahi Cheet* focusses on the life of Vishwakarma, the deity of working people who hails from among the "untouchables." *Dastan Dalitan Di*, a novel by Ninder Gill which of course was more journalistic than literary makes an elaborate historical study of Dalits in Punjab.

In Punjabi poetry too, the Dalit trend has been an influential trend. Many Punjabi poets come from a Dalit background, though not all of them make Dalit life the theme of their poetry. One such poet is Lal Singh Dil, who though a Punjabi Dalit poet, writes on subjects which are not necessarily only of Dalit interest. Some other Punjabi poets who are more typically Dalit are Gurdas Ram Aalam, the late Manjit Qadar, the late Sant Ram Udasi, Gurmit Kalarmajri, Madan Vira and Dharam Kameana.

The first Dalit autobiography in Punjabi, *Gair Hazir Aadmi* (The Absent Person) written by Prem Gorkhi, was published in 1994. It was designed in the mould of the Marathi Dalit autobiographies published during the earlier decades.[17]

From 1978 to 1986 there had been a spate of Dalit autobiographies in Marathi. These autobiographies emerged in a milieu in which there was increasing acknowledgement of the value of Dalit writing within the literary mainstream. A number of Dalit writers had received literary awards. Dalit literature came to be included within school as well as university syllabi. It was being translated into Indian as well as foreign languages. Most of the Dalit autobiographies were not restricted to life histories of the individual writers. They were life histories of the Dalit community in Maharastra – books by male authors such as Daya Pawar (*Baluta*), P E Sonkamble (*Athvaninche Pakshi*), Laxman Mane (*Upara*) and female authors such as Shantabai Kamble, Kumud Pawade, Mukta Sarvagod and Babytai Kamble.

As evident from my survey of twentieth century Dalit literature from different regions of India, Dalit women writers are still numerically few and far between as compared to Dalit men writers in most regions. But as the example of Bama testifies, this lag is not due to the lack of literary potential in the Dalit women writers. As mentioned before also, Dalit women writers from Maharashtra have already blazed a trail of glory in writing their autobiographies. There are other Dalit women writers such as Jyoti Lanjewar, also from Maharashtra, who have tried to theorize about the writings of Dalit women. As Lanjewar has observed, Dalit women are also Dalits in relation to Dalit men within the Dalit community. They are thus Dalits twice over insofar as they bear the burden of both gender and caste oppression.[18] The Telugu Dalit woman writer Challapalli Swaroopa Rani's lines bear eloquent testimony to the double downtroddenness of Dalit women. Herein lies the distinctive strain of Dalit women's writings as opposed to Dalit men's writing – its attempt to challenge the domination of Dalit women on the basis of caste as much as on the basis of gender.

> When has my life been truly mine,
> In the home male arrogance
> Sets my cheeks stinging,
> While in the street caste arrogance
> Splits the other cheek open.[19]

Yet in this very weakness of Dalit women lies the true strength of Dalit women's writings – their ability to challenge the social structures that dominate Dalit women by going beyond the ideological limitations of the resistance offered either by an exclusive Dalit movement or an exclusive women's movement.

> This complaint of mine is against the orthodox culture
> Which has imprisoned us in a sealed room
> Where the wind treats us as strangers
> Where the monsoon gives us only famines ...

We are rejecting this "unclean" life
And to escape from these cruel curses
Will you give me a bright auspicious moon?
My countrymen to your court
I have brought a complaint,
Will you give me justice? [20]

Notes

1   Much of the information about contemporary Dalit writers of India provided in this article has been garnered from essays in journals and periodicals. In many cases, these essays have omitted to mention the exact dates of the life and works of these writers. Efforts to get these missing details from directories/encyclopaedias on Indian literature have not been successful either. Most Dalit writers, I discovered, still remain virtually unknown and unrecognized as far as the Indian literary establishment is concerned.

2   Sisir Kumar Das, *A History of Indian Literature 1911-1956*, (New Delhi: Sahitya Akademi, 1995).

3   See Barbara R Joshi ed.,"Introduction," *Untouchable! Voices of the Dalit Liberation Movement*, (London: Zed Books, 1986).

4   S P Punalekar, "Dalit Literature and Dalit Identity," *Dalit Identity And Politics*, Ghanshyam Shah ed(New Delhi: Sage Publications, 2001).

5   Sisir Kumar Das, *A History of Indian Literature 1911-1956,* 13.

6   Arjun Dangle, "Dalit Literature: Past, Present and Future," *Poisoned Bread Translation from Modern Dalit Literature*, (Bombay: Orient Longman, 1992) 238.

7   Arjun Dangle, "Dalit Literature: Past, Present and Future," *Poisoned Bread Translation from Modern Dalit Literature*, 243.

8   Information about modern Marathi Dalit Literature has been collected largely from the book edited by Arjun Dangle, cited earlier, as well as from Mulk Raj Anand and Eleanor Zelliot eds., *An Anthology of Dalit Literature*, (New Delhi: Gyan Publishing House, 1992).

9   See *Dalit Panthers Manifesto*, (Bombay: Dalit Panthers, 1973) extracted in Barbara R Joshi ed., *Untouchable! Voices of The Dalit Liberation Movement*, (London: Zed Books, 1986), as well as Gangadhar Pantwani's essay on the development of Dalit culture in the same volume.

10 Information about modern Gujarati Dalit Literature has been collected largely from K M Sherrif, "Gujarati Dalit Literature: An Overview," *Indian Literature* 159, 9-11. *Indian Literature* 159 is a special issue on Gujarati Dalit Literature.

11. Information about modern Kannada Dalit Literature

has been collected largely from D R Nagaraj, *The Flaming Feet: A Study of the Dalit Movement*. (Bangalore: South Forum Press and ICRA, 1993).

12. Information about modern Oriya Dalit Literature has been provided to me by Mr Raj Kumar, lecturer, Department of English, SGTB Khalsa College, a scholar on the subject.

13. Information about modern Telugu Dalit Literature has been collected largely from A Satyanarayana "Dalit Protest Literature in Telugu. A Historical Perspective," *Economic and Political Weekly*, 21 January 1993: 171-75 and B Tirupati Rao, "Telugu Literature Survey," *Indian Literature* 192, 29-35.

14. Information about modern Tamil Dalit Literature has been collected largely from *Indian Literature* 193, a special issue focussing on Tamil Dalit Literature.

15. Raj Gautaman, "Oivaanga Vaiyillai" ("We Don't Need Haloes"), *India Today*, Tamil edition, annual issue, 1995, 95-98. Quoted in the Introduction of Bama's *Karukku*, trans. Lakshmi Holmstrom, (Chennai: Macmillan India, 1992).

16. Information about modern Hindi Dalit Literature has been collected largely from Sagarika Ghosh, "The Eklavya Complex," *Outlook*, 16 November 1998, and from Badri Narayan, *Documenting Dissent: Contesting Fables, Contested Memories and Dalit Political Discourse* (Shimla: IIAS, 2001).

17. Information about modern Punjabi Dalit Literature has been collected largely from *Indian Literature* 185, a special issue focussing on Punjabi Dalit Literature.

18. Jyoti Lanjewar, "Dalit Literature and Dalit Women," *Dalit Women in India:Issues and Perspectives*, P G Jogdand ed (New Delhi: Gyan Publishing House, 1995).

19. Challapalli Swaroopa Rani, "Dalit Women's Writing in Telugu," *Economic and Political Weekly*, 25 April 1998, WS 22.

20. Heera Bansode, Poem quoted by Gangadhar Pantwani in his article "Evolving a New Identity: The Development of a Dalit Culture," *Untouchable! Voices of the Dalit Liberation Movement*, Barbara R Joshi ed (London: Zed Books, 1986).

THROUGH ANOTHER LENS:
MEN, WOMEN AND CASTE

UMA CHAKRAVARTI

At the height of the anti-Mandal agitation in Delhi, spearheaded by "upper"[1] caste students and legitimated by prominent sociologists of Delhi University, women students of south Delhi colleges demonstrated in the streets carrying placards that read "We don't want unemployed husbands!" The irony of this statement was lost on most readers of English language newspapers – all upper caste themselves – who widely shared the ideology of these protesters. Since the anti-Mandal agitation was about the government's decision to implement a quota for the OBCs in the recruitment to the Public Services – that is into the IAS, IFS, IPS and other Central Services, the share of the positions for the "forward" castes or the upper castes would fall proportionately. So while potential aspirants comprising upper caste male students poured out of the hostels of Delhi University and rampaged the streets of the city, women students protested not for themselves but on behalf of their potential husbands. What the placards were saying is that these girls would be deprived of upper caste IAS husbands. What they were also saying is that the OBCs and Dalits in the IAS could never be their potential husbands.

But who had told them that they could not marry the new entrants into the IAS drawn from the "backward" castes? That was not a clause in the ordinance on reservation announced in the official gazette. Nevertheless, here were upper caste women students passing a self-denying ordinance upon themselves, they were proclaiming a self-regulatory code, a consequence of internalizing the ideology of mandatory endogamous marriages, a crucial characteristic of the caste system. Simultaneously, they were displaying their revulsion for the "lower" caste male. This was the underside of all the high minded rhetoric that circulated during the anti-Mandal agitation which was consciously crafted by its ideologues as a resistance to the forcing of caste identities upon a secular-liberal new generation of people by a corrupt state. No one from the leadership of the movement issued a condemnation of such a poster for controverting the stated ideals of the "movement." The contrast between the rhetoric of the anti-Mandal agitation and the actual concerns that drew men and women into the protest were swept under the carpet in the drama and hype of the self-immolations.

Perhaps it is time to recall these issues now and take a good hard look at caste ideologies which have been so naturalized by the upper caste, middle class in India that they do not even recognize the contradictions in their own positions. In that sense the ideology of the caste system, which still governs the lives of people in Hindu society, remains within the textual models which sanction inequalities of status and the attribution of specific privileges to the upper castes despite the constitutional guarantee of social and political equality. Unlike racism, the practitioners of which may experience guilt and conflict because the existential order does not match the ideal order laid out in their constitution,[2] in Hindu society the real behaviour of upper castes vis-a-vis the lower castes harmonizes with the ideals laid out in ancient texts, and therefore creates much less ambivalence. Indeed, it may even provide validation despite its deviance from the constitutional ideal of equality. This, and the continued power of the upper castes over the lower castes, based on their material conditions, are the only reasons why the caste system continues to be so pervasive in India, and not as the middle classes like to argue, the policy of reservation, which in any case is a drop in the ocean. If this essay stirs the conscience of its readership and our own complicity in reproducing the caste system, as the stories will perhaps do at the emotional level, there may be some kind of rationale for such an essay in a collection of short stories – otherwise not.

It might be useful to begin this essay with clarifying our understanding of caste as a specific and unique kind of stratification that is distinct from class, but not completely unrelated to it. The caste system comprises a series of hereditary groups or jatis characterized by hierarchy or gradations according to ritual status. The basis of inequality underlying the caste system in India is the application of evaluative standards in placing particular castes as high or low. These standards are rooted in the dharmashastras, the religio-legal texts of the Hindus. As the system developed, the high and the low were opposed to each other because of their respective associations with notions of pure and impure. The notion of the pure high and the impure low was expressed ideologically in ritual terms. But since work itself was classified as pure and impure, the two were required to be kept separate, the low being in a position of repulsion with respect to the high.[3] This accounts for the elaborate rules that govern contact to ensure the separation between the high and the low. Ideologically, there is great danger from the mixing together of things that must be kept separate to avoid impurity. Each caste is a bounded group and all social relations are represented in terms of bounded groups – eating, physical contact and marriage are highly ritualized and confined to other members of each bounded group.

To this notion of caste, drawn from the Brahminical texts and based on ritual specialization, certain social scientists have added many features which are more useful in understanding the power that the "higher" castes wield over the "lower" castes. First, they have contested the view that suggests that since social inequality is a common condition of all human societies, the historical specificity of the caste system itself can be undermined. This can also lend itself to a position where the relationship between the castes is regarded as one of interdependence and mutual obligations. However, there is a profound inequality between the castes in terms of access to knowledge, productive resources and social status. This is evident even in the early formulations of the caste system in the

Brahminical texts. A prescribed inequality exists even in the naming of persons. According to Manu "The name of a brahmana should have a word for auspicious, of a kshatriya for strength, and the name of a vaishya and shudra should breed disgust."[4] The most striking aspect of Manu's formulations is in the sphere of punishment for breaking the law where the quantum of punishment increases as one goes down the caste hierarchy.[5] Similarly, the privileges and immunities in the context of punishment are concentrated in the person of the Brahmana. The concentration of privileges at the top and disabilities at the bottom cannot be a system of "interdependence," or a mere division of labour, as my students often describe the caste system. Berreman aptly describes the caste system as "institutionalized inequality," which "guaranteed differential access to the valued things of life."[6] In contrast to Dumont's outlining of the opposition between the pure and impure as the most significant principle of the caste system,[7] Berreman provides another set of juxtapositions. "The human meaning of caste for those who live it" he states "is power and vulnerability, privilege and oppression, honour and degradation, plenty and want, reward and deprivation, security and anxiety."[8] Unequal access to material resources and power is an inherent feature of the caste system in terms of lived experience, which the pure-impure dichotomy elides.

Dalit intellectuals like V T Rajashekhar have also stressed the role of violence and coercion in the origin and the functioning of the caste system.[9] Even today, especially in rural India, the caste system hinges on the power to enforce caste-based obligations to the privileged upper castes by the dominant caste of the area. Dominance is based on wealth, i.e., control over land, which also gives the dominant caste access to political power. In a sense, basically there are two kinds of castes – those who hold the land and those who do not.[10] The most numerous castes in a village are the dominant caste and that which provides the greatest part of the labour force, usually the "untouchables." The dominant caste reproduced the royal function of exercising coercion at the village level. Class relationships were closely tied to the caste system, though not necessarily exhausted by them.

Two hierarchies are therefore operative in Indian society – one according to ritual purity with the Brahmin on top and the "untouchables" at the bottom, the other according to the political and economic status with the landlords at the top and the landless labourers at the bottom. The first corresponds to the formal representation of society, the second to the reality.[11] Exploitation occurred, and continues, through the old relationships of servitude or through the existence of compulsory loans and debts which lasted sometimes for generations. These class relationships clearly cannot be fitted into the harmonious pattern of the justifiers of the caste system comprising of interdependence and mutual cooperation that we have alluded to earlier. According to Meillasox,[12] exploitation as expressed through the caste system is a process based on violence. For example, among the rules imposed by the Kallars of Ramnad on the lower castes, whom they dominated, were that adult men and women be condemned to work in the service of the landlord for a pittance, all access to land and education for their children be forbidden and the latter forced to look after livestock. If they did not comply, their homes, goods and granaries were burnt and their livestock looted.[13]

The repressive effect of the caste system, I would stress, is coherently related to the ideological and religious notions associated with Brahminical representations of society. Notions of purity were regarded as the most powerful protection against social contamination, and efforts were made to erect it as the universal hierarchical principle. Such an ideology codified pre-existing relations of domination and the alienation of those subordinated from the means of production "since one must be alienated in order to accept being impure."[14] Further, the pure have to constantly resort to persecution, and when that is not enough, to violence to keep the lower orders in their impurities. In reality, then, impurity was one more weapon in the repressive ideological arsenal (in which monopoly over knowledge was another, as Phule argued[15]), it was used in one direction only, arbitrarily and opportunistically, as a means of discrimination, oppression and exploitation. In sum, according to Meillasox, caste is an ideological screen that hides social reality by scattering social divisions along the whole length of a formal hierarchy, submerging exploitative relations.[16] These aspects of the caste system resonate in the literature of the oppressed as depicted here in "Paddy Harvest" and "Oorakali" as well as in a novel like *Chomana Dudi*.

This brings us to a crucial element in the relationship between caste and class and the relationship between ideology and production relations, the monopoly over knowledge in the hands of the brahmins and the concomitant barring of knowledge to the lowest castes. Shudras and "untouchables" were to be severely punished for violating the ban according to the Brahminical texts. Over the centuries, the monopoly over knowledge that Brahmin men had was not merely evident in the area of ritual or religious knowledge, but also in the field of secular knowledge. This gave them an advantage in that this was used to gain control of social production in new territories being incorporated into a particular social formation. The growing monopolization of knowledge by the Brahmins may have met with some resistance earlier, as Kumkum Roy has shown.[17] But this resistance was confined to the upper varnas, and more specifically to the kshatriyas, the labouring caste of the shudras were outside the pale of such contestations. Occasional examples of those who did not conform to the codes and sought to gain knowledge or skills from which they had been barred such as Shambuka, who practiced austerities normally reserved for Brahmins, or Ekalavya, who acquired skills in archery, a privilege of the kshatriyas, met with severe punishment. If, finally, only the Brahminical view of the caste system has prevailed, and has now become canonical in sociological theories of the caste system, it is not unrelated to the Brahmin's control over knowledge and through that to hegemonic forms of representation. It was only in the nineteenth century when Phule provided alternative and critical analyses of the caste systems in writings such as *Gulamgiri* and *Traitya Ratna*,[18] that this monopoly could be broken. It is because of the traditional exclusion from learning that Dalit intellectuals like Phule and Ambedkar have placed such importance on education as a weapon to be used in the resistance to Brahminism.

The imperatives of separation within the ideology of pure and impure have meant that since each jati is a bounded group, it must be reproduced as a bounded group in order to preserve it as a discrete social unit.

Endogamous marriages have been the primary means by which this separation is achieved. Marriages must conform to the rule of endogamy. There is, therefore, a crucial relationship between caste and gender in the working of the caste system.[19] It has been argued that a fundamental principle of Hindu social organization was to construct a closed structure to preserve land, women and ritual quality within it.[20] These three are structurally linked and it is impossible to maintain all three without stringently controlling female sexuality. Neither land nor ritual quality, that is the purity of caste, can be ensured without closely guarding women who form the pivot of the entire structure. Caste blood is always bilateral, i.e., its ritual quality is received from both parents. Thus, ideally both parents must be of the same caste and this is reiterated in the dharmashastras. However, there can be leakages in the system. The anxiety about polluting the ritual order and the quality of blood through women is best demonstrated in the horror of miscegeny, the mixing of the castes aptly termed as varnasamkara. Varnasamkara is a theoretical explanation for the proliferation of the most polluting and low castes. The most polluting castes are those that are the products of the most reprehensible unions between women of a higher caste and men of a lower caste. The ideologues of the caste system had a particular horror of hypogamy or pratiloma[21] – literally against the grain, and reserved the severest condemnation for it. The dharmashastras recommended severe punishments for violations including death for the lower caste man and mutilation, physical punishment and excommunication for the offending woman.[22] There is, thus, a close connection between class, caste, gender and the state laid down in the religio-legal texts of Brahminic Hinduism. Kaliyuga, the time when the normative structure is upturned, is typically a time when women and the lower castes do not perform their duties, and there is the mixing of castes. As detailed in the Bhagavad Gita, kaliyuga is a time when families are broken, rites are forgotten, women are defiled, and from this corruption comes the mixing of castes.[23] Given this structure, the honour and respectability of upper caste men is protected and preserved by women who, therefore, must be closely guarded and whose sexuality is stringently monitored. Upper caste women are regarded as the gateway – literally points of entrance into the caste system. The lower caste male whose sexuality is a threat to upper caste purity has to be institutionally prevented from having sexual access to the women of the higher castes through an effective system of surveillance and seclusion. The upper caste woman's compliance to this situation is ensured through the production of consent, through the ideology of pativrata[24] and stridharma,[25] and the application of coercion by male kinsmen and/or by the king or state.[26]

An aspect of the existential order of the caste system, in distinction from its normative order, is the variety of practices permitted or tolerated by Hindu society. Nevertheless, there is a larger material and ideological structure within which the diversity of cultural practices is contained and whereby the hierarchical order is maintained.[27] While the upper caste woman's sexuality is stringently controlled and she is primarily regarded as the progenitor of sons, the upper caste male's sexuality is much less controlled. Many castes practise hypergamy where a lower caste woman is married to a higher caste man, enabling the woman's caste to gradually move up in the hierarchy. Nair women practised sambandham unions with Nambudiri men. This was a convenient arrangement for the Nambudiris. Since the Nairs were matrilineal, the children of these unions were incorporated into the mother's household. The Nambudiri fathers were thus absolved of responsibility towards their children by Nair women.

Apart from such marriages, upper caste men have had sexual access to lower caste women – an aspect of the material power they have over the lower castes. Thus, while a lower caste man's alleged, or actual, sexual relationship with a "higher" caste woman causes hysteria, and brings swift and violent retribution upon the lower caste man, and often on both persons,[28] the upper caste man's casual or continuous use of a lower caste woman is naturalized. Fairly early on a "black" woman was regarded as the natural object of desire and pleasure. Apart from using their labour, masters of dasis in early literature used the sexual services of women in servitude. This is a practice that has continued through the centuries. Women of the lower orders were not regarded as grihinis, or family women, as unlike women of the upper castes even their children could be denied to them by their masters.[29] As their sexual availability was part of the material structure of domination by the higher castes, it was something that both men and women of the lower castes were forced to accept. This is the social context of "Oorakali" where no resistance is available to the lower caste man and his young son except in seeking to abort the child of the upper caste man, which his daughter must otherwise bear. It is only with class mobilization in recent years that the rape and sexual abuse of lower caste women is being resisted by the Dalits. The issue of izzat is central to peasant movements under Marxist Leninist leadership[30] in Bihar.

While Dalit mobilization has focussed attention and created the basis of resistance on the issue of rape or the abuse of the lower caste woman's sexuality, the lower caste man who dares to fall in love or enter into a relationship, or elope with and marry a higher caste woman is still subject to the collective power of the upper castes. The last few years have witnessed a spate of brutal killings of such couples. Since women's sexuality is still under patriarchal and caste control and still requires to be formally transferred from father to husband, these killings have the explicit consent of the community, especially that to which the woman belongs.[31] Both men and women of the upper castes uphold the ideology of private justice, or rather retribution, to deal with "errant" couples who violate the norm of endogamy. To some extent this locates for us the anger that the protagonist expresses in "Kulaghati" when his lower caste wife suggests that their daughter, for whom he has been unable to find a bridegroom belonging to his own caste, could perhaps marry the Dalit boy with whom she is friendly.

To sum up this discussion of the caste system and Brahminical patriarchy in India we need to take note of the continued resilience of both, despite the constitutional guarantee of social and political equality to all citizens. The broad congruence between caste and class has continued into contemporary times. Local dominance in rural India combines landholding and caste status with access to state power. These are the factors that account for the social power of the dominant castes which enables them to have a continued hold over the landless labouring poor, largely comprising Dalits. Caste and class links have made it possible for dominant groups to appropriate, in a sense, "the paraphernalia of the state."[32] This is marvellously brought out in "Paddy Harvest," which is a sharp indictment of state agencies and their partisanship for the upper castes. The Constitution has formally ended caste-based discrimination in public spaces, but it has neither broken the hold of the upper castes on material resources, nor their hold over the state machinery. Consequently, the enforcement of the non-discriminatory provisions in public spaces remains a dead letter because the enforcers themselves, in many cases, subscribe to the ideology of caste. At the same time Brahminical patriarchy remains intact because men and women are complicitous in upholding endogamous marriages, even in urban India, as the matrimonial columns of the national newspapers amply bear out. Even the Constitution can do nothing about marriage practices! Women of the upper castes may experience gender-based discrimination, but they also share the material resources and the ideology of the men of their caste. The violence unleashed on the Dalits at Tsunduru is a potent reminder to us about the continuing recourse to violence by the upper castes in suppressing the lower castes. What is also significant is that upper caste women backed their men folk to the hilt in the violence in Tsunduru,[33] providing ample evidence of their complete identification with the ideology of the caste system. At the other end of the hierarchy, Dalit women and men, the dramatis personae of our stories, remain the most vulnerable sections of our society. Their existential reality of caste continues to be a phenomenon of our society, even though some of its contours may have changed.

In this section I will attempt to read the short stories included in this volume within the broad rubric of the issues highlighted earlier. I shall begin with "Oorakali," which captures graphically the elements of domination and subordination in the caste system in terms of economic control and the power to exploit the labour of both men and women, and the sexuality of the lower caste woman. The narrator of this story is a young Dalit male belonging to the oorakali caste, which grazes the cattle belonging to the entire village. Using the informant-narrator mode now being popularized in writing the biographies of the Dalits[34] (who have traditionally not had access to writing, and therefore not had a voice in representing the world), the author positions the narrative in terms of the low caste untouchable pointing to the futility of telling his story, given the reality of the caste hierarchy. Beginning thus, the narrator, who remains unnamed in the narrative, proceeds to build up a kind of an anthropological account – of his family, his caste, their traditional duties and their working day. However, this is not merely a dry, anthropological account from a "neutral" observer standpoint but one wherein an oorakali describes for us his daily humiliation.[35] Subjected everyday to verbal brutality, the oorakali treats the word "outcaste" as synonymous with the incapacity to resist. This is a repeated motif in the narration:

> And what could we do? We are outcastes sami. Could we have dared to talk back? They would have said, "What? Has the oorakali's tongue swollen? That dog lives on food begged from the whole village. His tongue should be pulled out and cut to pieces!" (2)
>
> What could I do but walk away, embarrassed and humiliated. We, who had no right to walk the streets of the village with our slippers on, could not afford to be assertive. (5)
>
> Sami was it blood that ran in my father's body? The abuses had hardened us. Of what use were feelings of self respect to our bodies? If ever the fire of resentment raged in my father, he would douse it with liquor. So why did he live? Why did he keep himself imprisoned in that body of his? (4)
>
> Sami, are our lives even more despised than that of hens? (6) What could these poor dumb animals do about the atrocities of their masters, sami? Their condition was as miserable as ours ... (4)

The telling of the narrative includes many allusions to the miseries of the oorakalis, wherein animals and Dalits share the same conditions of living. But whereas the oorakali is able to provide tender care to the animals, their humanity is not matched by the upper caste masters who "only know how to take" but never to give anything in return.

While the oorakalis eke out their existence in a state of degradation, economic changes hit the village and they lose their traditional livelihood. The servility of the lower castes continue, and is reaffirmed in the new situation with the young oorakali narrator being bonded to the upper caste master's household in return for grain. Performing dangerous jobs for the upper caste master is part of the bondage, and the oorakali household remains as incapable of resistance as before.

The narrative now moves on to its tragic denouement, the destruction of the oorakali family. Along with the economic exploitation and the power to humiliate and degrade the Dalits, upper caste men also have the power to sexually exploit women of the lower castes. In the earlier part of the narrative there is a description of the predatory sexual behaviour of the strong uncastrated bulls with the "virgin" heifers, and we can read this as an allusion to the upper caste Nattar male in relation to low caste women. There are also direct allusions to the narrator's mother having "lain" with the Nattar, and the beloved and beautiful sister of the narrator not being the child of the father, though tenderly cared for by him. As women from the families of bonded labourers must also work for their masters, the sister goes to work in the master's household at Thangatchi. The sister is soon pregnant, the father who has borne all manner of humiliations, including the sexual use of his wife by an upper caste man, now seeks to "assert" himself, for once, by insisting that his daughter must have an abortion. Unfortunately, the daughter dies a tortured death in the course of the abortion. Unable to bear the loss and perhaps the guilt over her death, the father too dies. The oorakali family is ruined. At the other end of the hierarchy the master's family carries on as before, holding on to their land and cattle, only making sure that the priests ward off the evil spirits for them. The young oorakali, the sole survivor of his family, interrogates the entire structure of the caste system. After all the misery and torture, is he to still refer to the upper castes as "sami" and ask them for justice – they who are complicit in the multiple levels of exploitation of the lower castes?

There are a number of significant factors from the point of view of caste and gender in this simple, but powerful story. The most striking aspect of the narrative is that the women of the family, with one exception, do not speak at all. Instead, they are spoken about. The story is about the anguish and the anger of oorakali men as they accept the exploitation of their labour, and even their degraded status, but cannot bear the humiliation of the upper caste's routine (ab)use of "their" women, which emasculates them. While there are a number of occasions when the narrator indicates that the oorakali father cannot resist the oppression unleashed on them by the upper castes, when he finally does attempt to do so, according to his own understanding, it is the daughter who pays the price, not the master. We know nothing about how the daughter feels, not even if she understands what is happening to her. There is a suggestion in the father's recounting of events that both mother and daughter have been seduced rather than ravished. Perhaps the oorakali father is angry that the women are unable to resist the advances of upper caste men. I am somewhat uncomfortable about this suggestion, particularly because this appears to be the only sign of agency allotted to the low caste women in the narrative, a point I shall return to later in this essay. However, it needs to be noted that the narrative is fairly complex and there is a great deal of ambiguity in the representation of the sexual encounters between the oorakali women and their upper caste masters. The father uses both "desire" and "force" as possibilities in explaining the women's ultimate predicament. The father's anger against the upper castes who "will lie with their women" but neither marry, nor accept responsibility for their children is perhaps compounded by his suspicion that his wife may have desired the Nattar. This double anger is deflected on the helpless daughter who has no control over the course of her life. The one line she utters before she dies registers the fear and lack of control in her relationship with the ayyah (master) who fathers her unborn child, but by implication, also in relation to the men of her own family. The counterpart of the doubled anger of lower caste men is the doubled dimension of patriarchal oppression experienced by lower caste women.

There is one final point that strikes me about this narrative – the allusion that it is Thangatchi's entry into the household of the master as a servile labourer that brings her to the attention of the upper caste segment of the village. I cannot help recalling a pragmatic statement in the *Kamasutra*, that celebrated manual on sex, written from the standpoint of the upper caste male. It states that masters can avail of opportunities to seduce bonded women when they bring in the grain to be stored in the houses of the masters,[36] a chilling reminder of how little things may have changed for those at the bottom end of the hierarchy.

The story of the oorakali has a natural link with "Kulaghati," which provides us with an example of an inter-caste marriage located in a changed economic and political environment. The narrative is broken into four parts with the male and female protagonists alternating as the narrators. The male protagonist is an upper caste man who is desperately seeking a groom for his daughter, an intelligent girl studying for her M A. As the narrator records his humiliating experiences, we discover that he has committed the cardinal sin of marrying a woman from one of the Dalit castes, it is for the daughter of this couple that the search is on. The tension in the narrative comes from the fact that the father is looking for a groom from his own caste – a virtual impossibility in high caste society. There is a doubled tension as the Dalit wife of the upper caste protagonist discovers her husband's deep rooted contempt for the lower castes generally and revulsion at the idea of a pratiloma marriage for his daughter, whom he regards as a high caste woman, with a Dalit boy. For the Dalit wife this is a revelation that brutally exposes her husband's ingrained casteist ideology. It also exposes the hypocrisy of the upper caste male who can put on the garb of a liberal, but has been unable to shake off Manu's horror of the lower caste male having sexual access to an upper caste woman. This is a tragic moment for both the protagonists. For the woman, her husband's outraged statement, "Are you in your right mind? Marry my daughter to a Chamar?" is something she has been waiting to hear because it is proof of his (and his castes') double standard of morality. While they can take a woman from the lower castes they cannot give a woman to the lower castes. The Dalit woman realizes that it is not egalitarianism that accounts for the upper caste hero's "willingness" to marry her despite her low caste status, but rather it is a demonstration of his power over the caste woman. Such an action gives the upper castes "a feeling of victory, a victory over the weak" as the Dalit wife aptly puts it. For the man his own sense of outrage is frightening, it brings to the surface subconscious fears, prejudices

211

and contradictions that damn him as a human being. In this charged moment of self-revelation we can capture the hypocrisy of the Indian middle class, which uses the rhetoric of a casteless society and, at the same time, wants only upper caste IAS husbands for their daughters as was evident at the time of the anti-Mandal agitation.[37]

Mahasweta Devi's story "Bayen" introduces a new dimension to the working of the caste system and the multiple manifestations of patriarchies in the different caste groups. "Bayen," which is the term for a witch who is to be outcasted, but not killed like other witches, is set among the doms, a caste traditionally responsible for dealing with the dead. The story is a poignant account of the forms of cruelty and hierarchies that exist even amongst the most marginalized sections of caste society. While the central character of the story is the bayen, a young dom woman named Chandi who has been stigmatized as a witch, and condemned to live at the edge of the village as an outcaste since she spells danger to the rest of her community, it is her young son through whom the narrative unfolds. The world of the doms, their work, their beliefs and their fears is the backdrop for the dramatic shift in the narrative which transforms a fearless dom woman, who has inherited her father's traditional occupation of burying young children, into a fearful, fragmented young mother who begins to find her traditional occupation unbearable. Unable to understand "her deep pain for every dead child" and the resultant overflowing of milk if she stays too long at the graveyard, the community of doms begins to become suspicious of Chandi. At the same time the village is struck by a small pox epidemic and Chandi's niece, who is visiting her house, contracts the disease and dies. Everyone begins to blame Chandi for the death of the little girl, especially because milk spills out of her breasts as Chandi is burying the little girl. In desperation, Chandi tries to quit her work and beseeches her husband to move to the town to escape being branded as a witch, but her own husband begins to fall a prey to the suspicions being voiced by the community. As Mahasweta Devi describes it, the time and the situation is one in which "terrible rage and jealousy could easily take hold of an empty stomach and uncooled head." Chandi is outcasted, banned from all human communication, an action in which her husband colludes as it is he who actually declares her to be a bayen.

Years later her young son meets her, but by then the bayen has internalized her stigmatization and believes that she, who had prayed for every child's life, could actually spell disaster for her own son. In the end she dies in an attempt to save the lives of many people. It is this stray act that finally restores humanity to her, and it is her son's rejection of the bayen stigma and the recuperation of motherhood that makes this possible.

Mahasweta Devi's story is a finely crafted narrative that addresses the difficult issue of the links between lower caste patriarchal practices, lower caste beliefs, poverty, ignorance, disease, death and the inability to control one's destiny, especially when you are amongst the lowest of the low. The lack of an explanatory system for one's wretched existence, in the absence of a political consciousness, can be the ground where primeval fears and existential crises can be deflected upon the most vulnerable amongst a group, in this case a young woman without natal kin. Within a patriarchal structure, beliefs about evil and danger find their targets in deeply gendered ways as the stigma of being a witch falls only upon women. Mahasweta Devi's story, though grim, is not entirely without hope and faith in the humanity of the doms. Although she points to the divergence between principle and practice in "modern" India, in terms of the abolition of untouchability and its continuing presence even in the local school, there is the suggestion that education is a vital resource in order to step out of explanatory systems that find danger amongst the oppressed themselves. Chandi is finally reclaimed by her young son, who has not yet been initiated into patriarchal ideologies, nor fully into dom belief systems, he alone is able to let his humanity come through and reject the self destructive cruelty of dom society. In the last paragraphs of the story, the father who had charged his wife with being a bayen and condemned her to a living death, disappears from the narrative and is replaced by his son who expiates the guilt of both the father and the community doms. The terrible death of the mother is also the moment for the condemnation of dom society and its beliefs which victimize women, even if the oppressors are themselves the oppressed in relation to others.

213

"Paddy Harvest" is a story along a different register. Written by a Dalit, the theme of this story is focussed on the everyday lives and desires of landless Dalits who labour for others, but almost never can fill their stomachs on the wages they receive. The narrative is built around a single day, and single event in which the Dalits will be allowed by the tehsildar to harvest paddy grown illegally by upper caste landowners on common land belonging to the whole village. Except for the fine narrative skills and amazing imagery, all around paddy, and marvellous description of food, the account of this single day reads like a fact finding report on agrarian violence and state repression written by a democratic rights group. The harvesting in the story begins at dawn and proceeds at a frenetic pace. The harvesters, who for a change are working for themselves, need no surveillance because the faster they work the more paddy they will have to take home. Suddenly, there is a disruption, senior bureaucrats and senior police officials arrive in the village and reprimand the tehsildar for overstepping his brief and acting in favour of the untouchables because he is an untouchable himself. The police now invade the houses to recover the grain. The women in particular try to hide, or hold on to, as much of the harvest as they can, but the police are brutal. There is a single act of resistance by a woman which ends in a severe lathi charge against the villagers and the arrest of the resisting woman. The harvest is lost, the untouchables are crushed, but the arrested woman escapes and is almost deified as they wait hopefully for her return.

This story illustrates a number of points made in the first section of this essay on the dominance and social power of upper caste landlords in India. Their dominance enables them to set the terms of exploitation and everyday class relations such, that their lower caste labourers live on less than survival wages.[38] Food, harvest and paddy are virtually reduced to metaphors and the lower castes are reduced to "stealing" in order to survive. The upper castes not only have material resources, but can also expand them illegally and get away with their encroachments through their access to state power. The social power of the upper castes resides in the fact that all the senior bureaucratic and police positions are still the monopoly of the upper castes, and they use the paraphernalia of the state to protect their caste and class interests. Independent India has thus not broken the hold of the upper castes either on material resources or on social power.

In the treatment of its women characters, Mogalli Ganesh's story "Paddy Harvest" also marks a departure from other stories included here. While the narrative is focussed on class and caste based exploitation, its central character, the individual through whom the Dalits express their rejection of the hegemonic power of the upper caste landowners, is a woman named Thopamma who appears to have multiple persona. Other women also feature in the narrative in their capacity as labourers harvesting the paddy and thereafter desperately finding ways to hide the grain. Both upper caste women and Dalit women in this narrative, share the material conditions and world views of the men of their respective castes with the upper caste women being fully complicitous in the illegal acts of their menfolk. What is significant is that neither upper caste women nor lower caste women are essentialized as sexual beings. In contrast to "Oorakali," lower caste women here are represented in terms of their relationship to labour, and through it to economic, rather than sexual exploitation by the upper caste landowners. Sexual exploitation of low caste women by the upper castes, though important in itself, can become a trope, and an especially powerful trope in literature, which can make it appear that inter-caste rape is the single axis along which lower caste women are exploited. It also presents women as victims of upper caste male predatoriness, or as agents in their own seduction, unable to recognize the nature of their exploitation or confront it. It is then left to their men to fully comprehend the full range of caste and class exploitation, as well as determine the nature of their resistance. In "Paddy Harvest," since women are not essentialized merely as sexual beings, their capacity for resistance is not less than that of their men folk. Thopamma does not have to be "protected" by her menfolk, rather, using the very pollution taboos of the upper castes against them, she can ingeniously devise the means of resistance, take its political consequences and find ways to outwit class and state power. Her actions provide us with a hopeful note on which to end this essay.

215

Notes

1   I am forced to use the terms "upper" and "lower" caste even as I am critiquing the ideology of the caste system. In order to distance myself from the values attributed to them I have therefore, put these terms within quotes the first time they appear in this essay.

2   See Anand Chakravarti, "Inequality in Rural India," *Equality and Inequality: Theory and Practice*, Andre Beteille ed, (Delhi: Oxford UP, 1986) 129-81.

3   Celestin Bougle, *Essays on the Caste System*, trans. D F Pocock, (Cambridge: Cambridge UP, 1971) 29.

4   Wendy Doniger and Brian Smith, *The Laws of Manu*, Vol 2, (Delhi: Penguin Books, 1991) 31.

5   Wendy Doniger and Brian Smith, *The Laws of Manu*. Vol 8. 267.

6   Gerald D Berreman, "The Brahminical View of Caste," *Social Stratification*, Dipankar Gupta ed, (Delhi: Oxford UP, 1991) 84-92.

7   Louis Dumont, *Homo Hierarchicus*, (London: Paladin, 1972) 81, n3.

8   Gerald D Berreman, "The Brahminical View of Caste," 88.

9   V T Rajashekhar, *Dialogue of the Bhoodevatas* (Bangalore: Dalit Sahitya Akademi, 1993) 1.

10   Claude Meillasox, "Are There Castes in India?" *Economy and Society*, 2. 1 Feb. 1973: 89-111.

11   Claude Meillasox "Are There Castes in India?" 101.

12   Claude Meillasox "Are There Castes in India?" 101.

13   J H Hutton, *Caste in India* (Cambridge: Cambridge UP, 1946) 179.

14   Claude Meillasox, "Are There Castes in India?" 107.

15   Rosalind O'Hanlon, *Caste, Conflict and Ideology: Mahatma Jotirao Phule and Low Caste Protest in Nineteenth Century Maharashtra*, (Cambridge: Cambridge UP, 1985) 129.

16   Claude Meillasox, "Are There Castes in India?"110.

17   Kumkum Roy, "Some Problems in Constructing Varna Identities in Early North India," *From Tribe to Caste*, ed. Dev Nathan, (Shimla: IIAS, 1997) 176-193.

18   Rosalind O'Hanlon, *Caste, Conflict and Ideology: Mahatma Jotirao Phule and Low Caste Protest in Nineteenth Century Maharashtra*, 129.

19   Uma Chakravarti, "Conceptualising Brahminical Patriarchy in Early India: Gender, Caste, Class and the State," *Economic and Political Weekly*, 27.14. 3 April 1993: 579-485.

20   Nur Yalman, "On the Purity of Women in the Castes of Ceylon and Malabar," *Journal of the Royal Anthropological Institute of Great Britain and Ireland*, 93,1962: 25-28.

21   Pratiloma literally means contrary to natural course or order; contrary to caste hierarchy, as when mother is of higher caste than father for example, Kshatriya father, Brahmin mother; born in the inverse order of classes. See an English-Sanskrit Dictionary compiled by Monier Monier Williams, (New Delhi: Motilal Banarsidas,1999).

22   Uma Chakravarti, "Conceptualising Brahminical Patriarchy in Early India: Gender, Caste, Class and the State,": 579.

23 Uma Chakravarti, "Conceptualising Brahminical Patriarchy in Early India: Gender, Caste, Class and the State,": 580.

24 Pativrata literally means loyalty or fidelity to husband; devoted or virtuous wife. See an English-Sanskrit Dictionary compiled by Monier Monier Williams, (New Delhi: Motilal Banarsidas,1999).

25 Stridharma is the rights and duties of a woman. See *Stridharma Padhati*, trans. Julia Leslie, (Harmondsworth: Penguin Books, 1995).

26 Uma Chakravarti, "Conceptualising Brahminical Patriarchy in Early India: Gender, Caste, Class and the State,": 579-85.

27 Uma Chakravarti, "Gender, Caste and Labour: The Ideological and Material Structure of Widowhood," *Economic and Political Weekly*,30.36, 9 Sept.1995: 2248-2256.

28 Prem Chowdhry, "Gender and Violence in North India: Enforcing Cultural Codes," *Economic and Political Weekly*, 32.19, 10-17 May 1997: 1019-1028.

29 Uma Chakravarti, "Of Dasas and Karmakaras: Servitude in Ancient India," *Chains of Servitude: Bondage and Slavery in India*, eds. Utsa Patnaik and Manjari Dingwaney, (Delhi: Sangam Books, 1985) 63.

30 People's Union for Democratic Rights (PUDR) team, *Bitter Harvest*, (Delhi: PUDR, 1994) 30.

31 Prem Chowdhry, "Gender and Violence in North India: Enforcing Cultural Codes,": 1019-1020.

32 People's Union for Democratic Rights, *Bitter Harvest*. 13-17; Rashme Sehgal, "They Don't Dare Abuse Us Anymore," *Times of India*, 4 Oct 1998.

33 Vasanth Kannabhiran and Kalpana Kannabhiran, "Caste and Gender: Understanding Dynamics of Power and Violence," *Economic and Political Weekly*, 27.37, 14 Sept. 1991: 2130-2133.

34 James Freeman, *Untouchable: An Indian Life History*, (London: George Allen and Unwin, 1979); Josiane Racine and Jean Racine, *Viramma: Life of an Untouchable*, (London: Verso, 1997).

35 Dr B R Ambedkar provides a striking formulation of the caste system where human beings are placed in an ascending scale of reverence and a descending scale of contempt, capturing for us the nature of social oppression which goes far beyond mere economic exploitation. (B R Ambedkar, "Who Were the Shudras," cited in Olivier Herrenschmidt, "Ambedkar and the Hindu Social Order," paper presented at a conference on Ambedkar and Buddhism, Pune University, 5-7 Oct., 1998).

36 *Kamasutra*, V.5.5.

37 There are a number of other significant aspects of this story. Some of which resonate with the arguments circulating during the anti-Mandal agitation that reveal the upper castes extreme fear of the potential for upward mobility becoming available to the lower castes through the policies of reservations. Among the interesting statements in this story is that money (class) cannot substitute for "purity of blood."

This is a running theme with many references to Hitler thrown in. The story reflects social processes whereby lower castes are using both recruitment into the bureaucracy and independent economic opportunities such as contract work to move upward in the social scale. This explains some of the hysteria we witnessed at the time of the anti-Mandal agitation. What the upper caste male appears to fear most is the loss of his hitherto undisputed status in Indian society and the fact that through upward mobility Dalit men could have access to "his" women – a veritable Kalyug scenario.

38   Anand Chakravarti, *Social Power and Everyday Class Relations*, forthcoming.

SOME ISSUES IN AN ANALYSIS OF CASTE AND GENDER IN MODERN INDIA

G ARUNIMA

To say that both women and lower castes are oppressed would be a mere commonplace in the context of India. Nevertheless, there is little evidence from either history or contemporary Indian politics to show that there have been attempts to find a common ground between patriarchy and caste oppression. In contemporary India, neither feminist politics nor the Dalit movements have been able to address adequately the issue of Dalit women's oppression. Gail Omvedt comments, uncompromisingly, that despite the feminist recognition of women's oppression as both "specific" and "simultaneous" – that is, as Dalit, peasant or tribal, and as women – the mainly middle class nature of the women's movement meant that women from poorer or rural backgrounds were never really represented within it.[1] While it may be true that the power of Dalit polemic, as in the songs and slogans created by the young men involved with the Dalit Panther Movement may have been more attractive to lower caste women,[2] they are still marginal to lower caste politics. As R S Khare has forcefully argued, Dalit women fear not only personal and social dishonour, but even the right to minimum physical safety. While within the home or "private" sphere Dalit women may suffer from verbal and physical abuse at the hands of their fathers and husbands, outside in the "public" realm, forced, unpaid and often indentured labour conditions are compounded by sexual harassment, and a real risk to physical life.[3] Many are increasingly aware that "their interests are either pushed aside or lost within 'serious male power politics.'"[4]

I would suggest that reasons for the specificities of caste and gender oppression can be understood by examining the changing social history of colonial India in the 19th and early 20th centuries. Two main trends emerge from within the available body of literature on caste and gender. While the bulk of the historiography regarding women focusses on upper caste groups of two regions – Bengal and Maharashtra,[5] there is an increasing number of anthropological writings that deal directly with issues of caste and gender in the context of lower caste women in different parts of India.[6] Apart from the fact that often historical records preserve the testimonies of powerful groups, in an attempt to understand caste and gender hierarchies, an examination of both these sets of literature help us to highlight certain issues. From the historical material it is clear that in the 19th century, while the "women's question" was cast in a general, emancipatory manner, the debates on caste reform that eventually led to the formation of caste associations all over India were premised on a more exclusive notion of identity. A variety of different attributes, including marriage customs, dietary practices and ritual status contributed to the creation of caste identity. While "sanskritization" need not have been the manner in which different, especially lower caste groups chose to reform their past practices, for most of them homogenizing caste norms was central to the reform enterprise. Therefore, ironing out differences amongst sub-castes became an integral part of caste reform, a process in which acknowledging gender difference was often seen as divisive (I have discussed this later in the context of caste reform in Kerala).

Nevertheless, as part of the "social reform" debates, the "women's question" was raised repeatedly in the 19th century. Both in Bengal and Maharashtra issues like child marriage, sati and widow remarriage dominated the public discourse, which was constituted by colonial and both liberal and conservative Hindu male opinion. By the mid 19th century, education for women was also added to the list of reformist demands. However, all of these really were concerns that touched only upper caste Hindu households. Lata Mani has argued that the 19th century debates in Bengal on sati were actually a battle between the colonial government, the younger male reformers and Brahmin pandits to define the "authentic" grounds of tradition. Increasingly, a strong section of feminist opinion, in the wake of Mani's argument, believes that the 19th century debates were mainly about defining "tradition" and not about women or their plight.[7] While Mani's insight provided a much needed corrective to the celebratory manner of studying the issue of social reform, it still does not account for the fact that there were dramatic transformations in the lives of upper caste women in the past two centuries.

With the shift in feminist focus from an analysis of male discourses to women's writings, it is clear that the struggles of many of the women from upper caste households were very real, and provided an impetus for actual social transformation. Acts like reading or writing that today most middle class Indian women treat as their rights, were hard won battles for these early pioneers.[8] And even though a large part of women's education in the 19th century focussed on creating a "companionate" wife for the new Indian (mostly Bengali) man, schooled in liberal ways, some still slipped through the net. The lives of Pandita Ramabai[9] and Tarabai Shinde[10] are good examples of rebellious Brahmin widows who refused to be content with leading a life of misery and destitution. Education for both these women was not merely a means to an end, 19th century society provided no avenues for "upward social mobility" to educated women. While Tarabai wrote a scathing critique of Brahminical Hinduism, Ramabai rejected Hindu society itself, and converted to Christianity. What, perhaps, was most unpalatable to Hindu society about both these women was that they rejected the confines of domestic respectability, a value in women that had even been extolled by nationalists as the "essence" of India's difference with the West.[11]

What is equally clear is that the family and household, indeed kinship itself, was becoming a site of contestation, and an examination of politics within the "private" sphere is essential for understanding both caste and gender oppression. Partha Chatterjee, based on his analysis of Bengali bhadralok politics, has argued for a separation between "outer" and "inner" – the former a freer, public sphere where individual freedom was permissible, and the latter an inviolable private (domestic) space where unanimity was desirable and normative.[12] While interacting with the colonial state was unavoidable in the outer sphere, the inner was meant to be kept out of reach of state intervention. For the nationalists, revamping Indian traditions was to be an internal matter, untouched by colonial intervention. And the primary site of "tradition" and "Indianness" was the home and the family. Persuasive as this argument might seem, it does appear to have a limited validity, even in the Bengali context.[13] In other parts of India in the same period (the late 19th and early 20th centuries) many upper and lower caste groups were rejecting "tradition," a process in which they urgently invited the involvement of the colonial state.

Kerala, in the early 20th century, witnessed many such caste reform movements. Here I shall examine in brief the politics of caste reform amongst the upper castes of the Nambudiri Brahmins and the Nairs in Malabar. Central to these movements were debates about family, household and kinship. Kinship systems in Kerala were notably different from most other parts of the Indian subcontinent, and this was something that had invited tremendous interest and curiosity on the part of colonial officials from the early 19th century onwards. While the Nairs followed matrilineal inheritance, the Nambudiris, like other Brahmins, were a patrilineal community. They were also the largest landholding groups in Malabar. The early colonial officials, involved in the process of administering law and justice in Kerala, were alarmed at the prospect of dealing with Nair matrilineal customs, which did not fit in easily with their ideas of Hindu law. Not only were family structures, property rights and inheritance rules different amongst the Nairs, they also appeared to have different norms regarding marriage and sexuality.

Like other matrilineal societies, amongst the Nairs too, a family or household was constituted by people who could trace their kinship in the female line. Unlike patrilineal households, the husband-wife, neo-local unit did not form the focal point of the kinship system. Sambandham, or sexual unions, need not have been life-long, and many Nair women and men had more than one sexual relationship in their life, moreover, this did not enjoin conjugal co-residence. Therefore, the primary affinity of both women and men was to their own natal households where they continued to live, even after marriage. Matters were complicated by the practice of sambandham unions between Nair women of the bigger landholding households (taravads) and Nambudiri men. Significantly, these cross-caste sexual unions were common only amongst the wealthier sections of both castes. Sub-caste differences were very marked amongst both the Nairs and the Nambudiri Brahmins, and for the poorer or ritually inferior sub-castes, issues of property rights or marriage did not cause as much anxiety as those above them in the social hierarchy.

The caste reform movements amongst both the Nairs and the Nambudiris focussed on attacking their family and marriage systems. Interestingly enough, what began as a critique of the family within the wealthier sections of the Nair community, soon fed into the rhetoric of caste movements. The caste associations necessarily glossed over differences between sub-castes in matters of wealth, status and privilege. Therefore, what had been issues concerning a minority of elites, soon took on the status of "caste" issues. And in the process of distancing themselves from the discredited traditions of the older elite, they were recasting these problems as those confronting the "community." Central to the critique of extant family practices was the issue of marriage and property. From the late 19th century, Nair male reformers had been agitating about the "immorality" of their marriage customs. For five long years from 1891-96, a small section of the Nair elite and the colonial officials debated the need for a marriage law for the community. In this process, a variety of opinions were put forth, but none accounted for what Nair women felt about the issue. They were variously attacked as being promiscuous, adulterous and lacking in morals. Polyandry was held up as the bane of the Nair community, and the frequent divorces and unstable unions its consequence. While the power of the male reformer's rhetoric lay in the moral outcry against women's sexuality, their critique was grounded in a more material complaint. With increasing educational and employment opportunities, larger number of Nair men were beginning to move away from their traditional agrarian pursuits and move into urban locales and professions. Alongside, they wished for a share of their family property to augment their new lifestyle. It is noteworthy that, from the 1880s onwards, both women and younger men had engaged in legal battles against the household heads for a share of the family property. However, the new critique of matriliny and the joint family by Nair men that developed in Malabar in the late 19th century denounced the system on grounds of its being "retrogressive" and "immoral." In other words, it was women's rights inherent within matriliny that were a cause of tremendous discontent. They urged for patriliny and progress, thereby distancing them from a tradition that normatively gave women equal rights as men.

The Nair reformers of the 20th century identified three main problems with the community. One was the persistence of sub-caste differences which created inequality within the community. Coupled with this was the "unnatural" practice of matriliny that allowed no one the right to their father's property. And finally there was the issue of endogamy — sambandhams of Nair women with Nambudiri men were to be outlawed at all cost.[14] The critique of matriliny by the Nair caste associations was clearly more sophisticated than its earlier incarnations in the late 19th century debate on marriage. Now there was a more focussed attack on the power of the taravad within the "public" realm of land relations, and the structural inequity within it in relation to the younger kin, in the "private" realm of the family. The link between both these sets of issues allowed for a broader network of support. For a large section of the middle level tenant groups the attack on landlordism added strength to their ongoing demands for greater fixity of tenure. Equally, the rather vague and general terms of the caste reform rhetoric allowed larger number of people to identify with the issue. To be a Nair no longer implied belonging to a wealthy taravad, even poor peasants could now share in this sense of "community" identity.

Therefore, issues of endogamy (marrying within the community) and marriage reform were discussed endlessly in this period. Polyandry and divorce pointed to the decadence of the marital institution in Malabar, and the only way to rectify the situation was by transforming matrilineal households into patrilineal nuclear families. The call for reform was directed towards Nair men, who were "to rouse [their] manhood and organize."[15] As part of the process of ridding themselves of their customary practices, some Nairs began depending on Brahmin texts like the *Manusmriti* to create an ideal of womanhood and femininity, and addressed themselves to men who were to create the new community by selecting their partners well:

> [men] should not marry a talkative, sick, bald, or a hirsute woman ... she should have no handicap ... she should be graceful and walk like a swan ... any family where husband and wife live happily and contentedly, there will be prosperity.[16]

Not only was the idea of transforming matrilineal practices into a patrilineal system entrenching differences on grounds of gender and a skewed access to property, but it was also premised on the creation of a new familial ideology based on conjugal love. For this to be possible there was the need to create a new ideal type of womanhood and female virtue that would gently and without demur, accommodate itself to the changing times. The script for such womanhood often read in terms like, "A perfect wife is the way to perfect happiness ... good behaviour, wealth and status make a woman an asset to the family ..."[17]

Significantly, the Nair reformers berated the colonial state for impeding the community from making any progress. All that was needed was to change laws to accommodate interests of people who showed the desire to move from a matrilineal to a patrilineal system.[18] Thus wrote the reformer:

> The only way [to achieve] a patrilineal system is individual partitioning and the apportioning of shares. With this it can be said that a new path for progress has been discovered in Kerala.[19]

Not only did the rhetoric of caste reform gloss over the differences in social experience of the lower sub-castes, but it was also premised on clearly demarcated gender roles within the caste. Besides, in this venture they were looking towards the state for decisive legislative interventions in the "private" sphere for making the necessary social transformation.

The Nambudiri reform movement follows a similar trajectory. Like all Hindu castes, the Nambudiris too were divided into several sub-castes, with distinctions in material and ritual power. Within their own vocabulary this was indicated by the differentiation between the higher (aadhyan) and the lower (aasyan) Nambudiris. The main demands of the Yogakshemam and the Unni Nambudiri (as the younger male reformers were known) movements, active in the 1910s, 20s and 30s, were endogamous marriage, the partition of family property, and the provision of Western education for Nambudiris. Once again, the creation of a "community" of caste interests focussed on the problems facing the elite groups. Nevertheless, these were steadily projected as those facing the entire community. Most of the poorer, aasyan, Nambudiris received no formal education, and very little ritual training too. This meant that most of them performed menial chores like cooking or other household work in the families of the wealthier Nambudiris or the royal families. Therefore, the caste movement highlighted their right to a share in the community wealth controlled mainly by the devaswams or religious institutions, by extending education to them. Moreover, a large part of the rhetoric of caste reform focussed on creating a distinct identity of the Nambudiri that was defined in opposition to the Nair. The growing threat of tenancy legislations provided a material context for this desire, because a significant section of the south Malabar tenantry was composed of Nairs. Besides, a growing number of Nairs were entering professional careers like the law and administration, thereby threatening the power of the Nambudiris whose primary strength derived from their position within the agricultural community.

The Nambudiri reformers, like their Nair counterparts, demanded the partition of properties of the patrilineal household and its replacement by nuclear families. According to Nambudiri kinship norms, only the eldest son could marry within the community (up to four wives) and only he could manage the family property. As all other members (younger sons and unmarried daughters) could merely reside in the family home and be maintained at a subsistence level, none of them could expect a share in the family property. In the case of extremely wealthy families, more than one son would receive a schooling, and sometimes even Vedic tutelage. However, the strict rules of primogeniture entailed that even among the richer households wealth would not be shared equitably amongst all members. Besides, not all Nambudiris were large landowners or could aspire to prominence within the community. The rhetoric of family reform was couched in a highly charged and emotive language:

> ... the degenerate state of the Nambudiri community is worse than any other in the world ... exogamous marriages [sambandhams with Nair women] on the one hand, and life long dependence of the younger people on the other ... the sorrowful state of unmarried women, and bickering and strife within families ... it is impossible to find any family where married life is happy.[20]

The only way to stabilize the future of the community was for the younger men to marry within the community. The argument was that an increase in the numerical strength of the Nambudiris would improve their material status. In constantly constructing the identity of the Nambudiri caste in opposition to the Nairs, the reformers both exploited the growing resentment against the matrilineal community on other fronts (like tenancy relations), and bolstered their own sense of community. Moreover, the argument in support of endogamous marriages was not restricted only to improving the population figures of the Nambudiris. It was also used as a device for transforming the existing rules of management and division of property – a concern that was frequently voiced:

> ... without each man receiving his rightful share from the taravad income to enable him to lead a separate life, it is impossible to popularize endogamous marriage or to stall the process of decay facing Nambudiri society.[21]

While notions of privilege centred on age and wealth were undergoing criticism, albeit in restricted ways, the question of gender difference within the community was being dealt with differently by women, younger male reformers, and the older orthodoxy. In the first two decades of the 20th century, the Nambudiri antarjanams (as the women of the community were called, literally meaning the ones who lived inside) in response to the reformist challenge, began to organize around issues particularly affecting them. These ranged from restrictive forms of clothing and lifestyle, like the enforced wearing of white clothes, and carrying palm leaf umbrellas (marakoda) to cover their faces while going out. Even indoors they were expected to remain within the female section of the house, and were not permitted to leave the house unless accompanied by a female servant. Apart from this, women demanded the right to education, to inherit a share of the family property, and to marry within the community.[22]

The political activity of the antarjanams met most often with utter denunciation, in other instances, their issues were appropriated by the Unni Nambudiris. While the orthodoxy portrayed women's organizations as manifestations of immaturity and ignorance, the older reformers too were threatened by the presence of women within the movement. They argued that any political activity undertaken by men would naturally ensure the interests of women, the younger men, while supportive of some of the issues raised by women, like those concerning education or marriage, eventually managed to subsume these within the framework of their protest. This blunted the edge of the issues raised by the women and became a mere part of the movement for forging a common caste identity. Predictably, endogamous marriage became the focal point of the entire movement, and this dovetailed nicely with the idea of partitioning the "joint family" and recreating the community on the basis of "natural" (nuclear) family ideology. The ideal community would comprise several "natural" families, each constituted by a man, woman and their children. Such "natural" ties were to imbue the community with a greater sense of unity and cohesiveness which were impossible earlier, as caste norms had been divisive and did not allow a true sense of community. All through this period, caste and community sentiments were being used to foster internal reform and reorganization.[23]

Both the Nair and the Nambudiri reform movements succeeded in enabling the passing of significant family legislations in Malabar. In the

1930s, a spate of "family regulations" that allowed the division and partition of joint family property were enacted by the colonial government. In the case of the Nairs, this marked a critical step in the process of the eventual abolition of matriliny. Moreover, it highlights the clear departure from past practices that were integral to the creation of new caste identities. In this process, a variety of different strategies were employed – from glossing over internal differences within the caste to necessarily defining its boundaries as distinct and "exclusive" from other castes. While such boundedness provided a new interiority to the reborn caste, it did not fiercely protect this "inner" space from state intervention. This was because the politics of the "interior" was not merely a matter of effect, it reflected concrete material interests that transcended the differences of the "home" and the "world."

Feminist theory over the past two decades has developed increasingly nuanced critiques of the division between the "public" and the "private." The feminist anthropological analysis of caste in India also highlights the connections between the different realms of patriarchal oppression, labour relations and ritual hierarchy. By focussing on women's experience, they have developed a critique of commonly accepted theories of caste that are premised on Brahminical male-centred values.[24] Karin Kapadia, in her study of the Pallar women in Tamil Nadu shows how they are discriminated as women, as "untouchables" and as landless agricultural women, thereby illustrating how gender, caste and class operate in identity formation. On comparing the lives of Pallar women with women of other non-Brahmin castes, she argues that in a developing rural economy, there is an inverse relationship between the status of women and the possibility for upward mobility for the caste itself. This is largely a consequence of women being withdrawn from wage-work. So while in one case there is domestic equality between men and women, it is unmitigated by the relentless burden of poverty in the other. The price for social status is a devaluing of women labour.

Kalpana Ram's work on the Mukkuvar women of the fishing community in Tamil Nadu makes a similar argument, except that she shows that as Catholic converts, the Mukkuvar community occupies a semi-autonomous position in relation to caste Hindu society. She argues that while agricultural society reinforces caste hierarchy, the social experience of the fishing community does not share these values entirely. Their geographical location, on the fringes of mainland society, becomes a "metaphor" not only for "[their] social and economic marginality ... but for the possibilities of an independent cultural identity which this marginality provides."[25] She demonstrates that gender, sexuality, labour roles, and ritual status are constantly inflected by an interaction between caste Hindu norms, the Mukkuvars and the Catholic church. This she amplifies through her discussion of labour and religion. Notions of wage labour, in the case of women, can be understood only by taking into account "uneconomic" factors, like the location of the employment, the age or marital status of the woman, which would be redundant in the case of a man. Similarly, she shows how the discourse of popular Catholicism "both contains and limits women, but also constructs them as powerful, particularly in the domestic domain."[26] Her argument reveals how in the case of women's ritual status, sexuality and labour power are intertwined, and constantly feed off one another.

Therefore, while the caste system in India is far from an immutable given, it can be seen from the experience of the 20th century that caste identity and solidarity has been very much on the increase. Both in the case of the upper and lower castes, the homogenizing tendency of caste politics habitually glossed over gender difference. Besides, as caste politics has always been dominated by male leaders, the issue of gender is either subsumed within its general rhetoric, or simply set aside as trivial and frivolous. Unless the new social movements in India contend seriously with patriarchal oppression, the rhetoric of human rights and democratic values will have no palpable meaning for half the Indian population.

Bibliographical Note

The body of currently available literature on issues of gender and caste in the Indian context is vast and complex. Here I shall mention only a few of these to be seen as a representative sample of the issues being debated at present.

Gail Omvedt, *Reinventing Revolutions: New Social Movements and the Socialist Tradition in India*, (New York: East Gate, 1993). A comprehensive survey of contemporary politics since Independence that explores the links between the social movements of different marginal groups like women, tribals and peasant groups. It also offers a critique of these from the perspective of someone engaged in the politics of this period.

Geraldine Forbes, *Women in Modern India*, The New Cambridge History of India, Vol IV 2, (Cambridge: Cambridge UP, 1996). It includes a broad overview of some of the key questions in women history, and has a comprehensive bibliographical essay at the end.

Uma Chakravarti, *Rewriting History: the Life and Times of Pandita Ramabai*, (New Delhi: Kali for Women, 1998). The book examines the questions of caste, class and patriarchal oppression in the context of 19th century Maharashtra. The third section on the life of Pandita Ramabai provides a fascinating insight into the lives and struggles of upper caste Brahmin women, and how to understand women's resistance in the 19th century.

Rosalind O' Hanlon, *A Comparison between Men and Women: Tarabai Shinde and the Critique of Gender Relations in Colonial India*, (Madras: Oxford UP, 1994). This is a translation of Tarabai Shinde's polemical essays, "Stripurushatulana," a trenchant attack on patriarchy in Maharashtrian society, written in Marathi and published in 1882. The lengthy introduction sets questions of gender and patriarchy at the centre of an attempt to rewrite the social and political history of colonial India.

Susan S Wadley, *Struggling with Destiny in Karimpur*, 1925-1984, (Berkeley: U of California P, 1994) presents the contrasts in the perspectives of rich and poor, men and women and high and low caste by using a rich body of cultural materials like songs, stories and personal testimonies.

Karin Kapadia, *Siva and Sisters: Gender, Caste and Class in Rural South India*, (North Carolina: Westview Press, 1995) examines the lives of five castes in Aruloor in Tamil Nadu to explore the relationship between economic power, symbolic means of production and gender relations. She puts gender at the heart of her analysis and argues for a distinct non-Brahmin, "untouchable," consciousness that is not overdetermined by ideas of Brahminic hegemony.

Kalpana Ram, *Mukkuvar Women: Gender, Hegemony and Capitalist Transformation in a South Indian Fishing Community*, (London: Allen and Unwin, 1991). By exploring the lives of women of the fishing community

231

in coastal Tamil Nadu, a predominantly Catholic people, Kalpana Ram questions the literature on caste and Hinduism in India that includes all social groups within its categories. In her study she draws out the often ambiguous, though complex, relationship between caste, religion, class and gender.

Notes

1   Gail Omvedt, *Reinventing Revolution: New Social Movements and the Socialist Tradition in India*, (New York: East Gate, 1993) 78-9.

2   Gail Omvedt, *Reinventing Revolution: New Social Movements and the Socialist Tradition in India*, 79.

3   R S Khare, "Elusive Social Justice, Distant Human Rights: Untouchable Women's Struggles and Dilemmas in Changing India," *Changing Concepts of Rights and Justice in South Asia*, Michael R Anderson and Sumit Guha eds, (Delhi: Oxford UP, 1998) 198-219.

4   R S Khare, "Elusive Social Justice, Distant Human Rights: Untouchable Women's Struggles and Dilemmas in Changing India," 201.

5   See, for instance Uma Chakravarti, *Rewriting History: the Life and Times of Pandita Ramabai*, (New Delhi: Kali, 1998); Rosalind O' Hanlon, *A Comparison Between Men and Women: Tarabai Shinde and the Critique of Gender Relations in Colonial India*, (Madras: Oxford UP, 1994) amongst others.

6   Kalpana Ram, *Mukkuvar Women: Gender, Hegemony and Capitalist Transformation in a South Indian Community*, (London: Allen and Unwin, 1991); Karin Kapadia, *Siva and her Sisters: Gender, Caste, and Class in Rural South India*, (North Carolina: Westview Press, 1995); Susan S Wadley, *Struggling with Destiny in Karimpur 1925-1984*, (Berkeley: U of California P, 1994) are amongst some of the important works on this issue.

7   Lata Mani, "Contentious traditions: the debate on sati in colonial India," *Recasting Women: Essays in Colonial History*, K Sangari and S Vaid eds, (New Delhi: Kali for Women 1989).

8   Tanika Sarkar, "A Book of Her Own. A Life of her Own: Autobiography of a Nineteenth Century Woman," *History Workshop Journal*, 36, Autumn 1993.

9   Chakravarti, *Rewriting History: the Life and Times of Pandita Ramabai*.

10 O' Hanlon, *A Comparison Between Men and Women: Tarabai Shinde and the Critique of Gender Relations in Colonial India*.

11 O' Hanlon, *A Comparison Between Men and Women: Tarabai Shinde and the Critique of Gender Relations in Colonial India*, 17.

12 Partha Chatterjee, *The Nation and its Fragments: Colonial and Postcolonial Histories*, (Princeton: Princeton, 1993) 12.

13 Figures like Rassundari Debi were making a real break with tradition, and were not fitting into the the then desirable categories of the domesticated woman or the companionate wife. See Tanika Sarkar, "A Book of Her Own. A Life of her Own: Autobiography of a Nineteenth Century Woman," *History Workshop Journal*, 36, Autumn, 1993: 35-65, for a sophisticated reading of the first autobiography written by an Indian woman.

14 K P Kunjunni Menon, "The need for a Nair samajam", *Mathrubhumi*, 14 July 1923; "Aims of the Palghat Nair Association," *Mathrubhumi*, 11 September 1923.

15 K C Nair, *Mathrubhumi*, 8 July 1924.

16 "Marital bliss," *Mathrubhumi*, 10 November 1923.

17. "Marital bliss," *Mathrubhumi*.

18 "Matriliny and the individual division of property," *Mathrubhumi*, 19 April 1924.

19 "Matriliny and the individual division of property," *Mathrubhumi*.

20 "Appeal of the Yuvajanasangham," *Mathrubhumi*, 18 December 1923.

21 Kaplingattu Shankaran Nambudiri, "Nambudiri Family Regulation," *Unni Nambudiri*, 7.7, 1926: 392-403.

22 Kanipayyur Shankaran Nambudiripad, "Strisamajam," *Unni Nambudiri*, 8,6, 1926: 347-57.

23 Kaplingattu Shankaran Nambudiri, "Nambudiri Family Regulation."

24 See for instance, Kapadia, *Siva and her Sisters* and Ram, *Mukkuvar Women*.

25 Ram, *Mukkuvar Women*, xiii.

26 Ram, *Mukkuvar Women*, xvi.

THE DALIT WOMAN SPEAKS UP: AMHIHI ITHIHAS GHADAWALA

INTERVIEW WITH URMILA PAWAR

Urmila Pawar and The Making of History
[Excerpts from a Dialogue with Urmila Pawar at the Oral History Workshop – January 18, 1998 – organized by Sound and Picture Archives for Research on Women (SPARROW)]

Urmila Pawar is a Marathi writer, whose stories are based on Dalit experiences of living, working and existing. Many of her stories are derived from the pain, agony and difficulties of living as a woman and as a Dalit. The frank and direct manner of her storytelling and the earthy language she uses in her stories has made her a controversial writer in Marathi.

Urmila Pawar was born in Pansawle village in Ratnagiri district, and later her family shifted to Ratnagiri. Urmila was the youngest among seven children. Her father, who was a school teacher, died when Urmila was in the third standard. Her mother who was uneducated, brought up her children by weaving baskets and selling them. After passing her Matric in 1964, Urmila joined the Public Works Department. She came to Mumbai in 1976. She got married in 1966 and has two daughters.

On Childhood and Growing Up

Urmila: I come from the Dalit community. My mother was illiterate. I come from a village in Konkan. Though my father had studied up to the sixth standard, everybody in the village would think he had studied a lot. In those days it was possible to get a job after the sixth standard. So he was a teacher. As Brahmins would not come to solemnize weddings in our community, he would also solemnize marriages in our community. My father's forefathers had been solemnizing marriages. The people in our community would get married in our house, and we would get some money and rice. We could, therefore, carry on with our lives.

There were those belonging to Marathas, Brahmins and other castes, living around us. These people would ask mother to weave baskets [for them] and since I was the youngest, she would always ask me to go to such and such person's house to deliver the baskets. I would go but they would make me stand outside their house. Then they would sprinkle water over the basket. They would drop the money from above into my hands. I would feel really hurt. So I would tell my mother that I would not go. As I've written [in my story], I would bunk school. Because I did not go to school, the teacher would also beat me. He would also practise caste discrimination and make me sit in the last row.

I had an older sister.

My father told my sister that she should get a job. She had left school in the fourth or fifth standard. She would wander here and there and [look for odd jobs]. Then she got a job as an ayah in a mental hospital. There even the madam was casteist. So my sister would keep saying that she did not want this job. "They don't let me touch, they don't eat the food that I cook," [she would complain]. So my father said, "Look here, you have to bear it. They are mad. Why do you listen to mad people?" Then with time she learnt to adjust and she kept her job. Her husband also got a job as a teacher.

One good thing was that our father had brought us to a town. We benefited from that. We could see and learn the rituals, traditions and customs, ways of behaviour, ways of eating, how we should keep our clothes clean [and all that] from the Brahmin and Maratha children in our class. And we began to behave like them. We did not have [that kind] of food at home. We did not have the recipes [for that food]. We ate roti and machli because we were from Konkan and the machli that we ate was also of bad quality. We did not know of big fish like halwa and pomfret. We went to their house and learnt how to make laddoos and other things for Diwali. If I tried to make these at home, my mother would scold me because it would need a lot of oil, a lot of flour. So she would not let me do it. And because she was unhappy, she would cry.

The common practice was not to prepare good food but eat second grade food if there was no male member in the house. Even now in some families, if a male is not present for meals and there are only women, they would not bother about what they cooked. So in those years at home, we did not care about what we ate. We would soak amsul (cocum) in water and make a curry, or cook seashells. There is water in the shells. We would make curry out of that, or then, there's dry fish. We would use the worst fish to make curry. If we ate that, there was a high chance of getting an upset stomach. It did happen. But even then the poor women would eat that ...

A Brahmin family used to live in front of our house. There was a road in between and beyond that was their house. They would make pickles. Brahmins make pickles, you know. What would you find in our house ... only dry fish. The minute you entered [the house] it would stink a lot. When my mother would not feel like eating, she would give me one or two paise and say, "Go and get some pickle." So I would go to get pickle. Their pickles would be kept in jars and [the mouths of the jars] would be tied [with cloth]. There would be a big ritual of opening it every time. I would go and say, "I want pickles. Is there anyone at home? I want pickles." As if I had come to steal or beg. "I want pickle for two paise," [I would announce]. Someone would peep and see many times. After some time someone would peep again, and then she would come. After a lot of time, she would take out the pickles, then take the money. The ritual would go on. My brother would say, "You are mad, stupid, foolish. What you should do is go from the backyard saying, Where are the pickles? Go and take some yourself. Dip your hand in it. Then she would give you all of it. The entire jar would be yours." We would have fun in this manner.

On Marriage

Urmila: My father had told my mother that the children should study and they should have jobs. The other wish my father had was that even his daughters should have jobs. He wanted them to be capable [enough] to take up a job. When I took up a job, my education had to be stopped. I got a job, and I also got married. I felt that I should enroll myself in a college and study ahead. After I had three children, I enrolled myself in a college. I studied up to M A But I think I failed [as a mother].

My elder sister was married when my father was alive. The other sister was very dark, very thin and her teeth were also protruding. So, getting her married was a big problem.My brother got a job in Bombay. He thought that she could not be married because of her teeth and that her teeth should be extracted. He got her to Bombay, and actually got her teeth extracted and dentures fixed. It was good. After her teeth were extracted, she was married. Her house was in BIT chawls and she was also working. Her work started at seven in the morning at the Air Force Office. Her father-in-law and mother-in-law were illiterate. So they would feel, she goes to office, sits in a chair, then why does she get tired? She rests in the chair and comes [home]. So they would leave all the [household] work for her, utensils [to wash] and all that. How can she get tired, they felt. They troubled her. Her husband had passed his B A. Even then he would beat her. When she was carrying, he would order her to get up quickly and then kick her [if she didn't]. Dalit men fight for humanity, but what is humanity even they do not know, because they do not have humanity towards their wives. That is why I gave you this example.

On Her Experiences of Discrimination and Affirmative Action in Bombay City

Student: How does caste system work in a city like Bombay?

Urmila: Bombay is a cosmopolitan city. It does not work that way here. When the question of reservation arises, then they tease us [saying],

237

"These people are going ahead, they have left us behind, they have taken away what belongs to us." Actually when I present the case for reservations, I think what I am doing is right. Till India became independent, all the reservations were for the upper caste only. All the posts were reserved only for them. Go anywhere, and they had hundred per cent reservation. But when our constitution was adopted, it said that the backward castes should be given a chance to move ahead. If there were no reservations, I would not have been able to study. Girls, who are of my age in our village, or even younger than me, they take dry wood to the market to sell. They don't have food to eat, no clothes or other things.

Now among the sweepers there seems to be hundred per cent Dalit reservation. Which Brahmin do you find there? Are there any Brahmins there? Why don't they go there and ask for reservation? "Please let me sweep as well, I will also clean the toilets. Why should I not do that?" ... Dr Ambedkar said that if you feed two horses, one healthy and hungry, and the other one weak and hungry, if you put grass in front of them, who will eat more, the healthy horse or the weak one? So let them both first become equals and then race them against each other.

On Writing and Its Connection to Her Life, and the Life of Her Community

Lata: I will ask Urmilaji about when she started writing and her experience of writing. Her writing is closely linked to her own life. And this lifestyle [of her community] is not known to many. Will you tell us more about why you thought people should know about this through your stories? What was the inspiration?

Urmila: I have been writing since 1975. Actually, the community I belong to, the family I was born into, they did not know much about education. My father was a teacher. But he passed away when I was young. Therefore, I could not benefit from his company for long and my mother was totally illiterate. The people around me were totally illiterate. So the knack of writing did not come to me from my forefathers, or from anyone in my family, who was writing and whom I could see or listen to.

There was a widow in our village who got pregnant. Everyone

wondered, how can a widow get pregnant? So they decided to call a meeting and ask her about it. Actually, she knew the name [of the man who was responsible] but he was also among those who were questioning her. So she could not say anything and was punished. She had to bend and all the women would go behind her and kick her. Two women caught hold of her, made her bend, and kicked her till she bled. Her foetus was aborted. The women came and told my mother about what had happened. The women were telling my mother as if they had performed some act of bravery. I was listening to this conversation. And that is when I felt, how can these people do this? They took justice in their own hands and beat this woman till she bled. So then some time later, this incident which had remained with me came out as a story, as *Nyay*.

Lata: The experiences of being born into a Dalit family or Bahujan Samaj does not figure much in literature, [but] it is emerging now. Hari Narayan Apte began to write about these things. With time the Marathi Nava Katha (New Story) emerged. The new story had ideals about the human mind. Freud's ideas were taken up by Gangadhar Gadgil, Arvind Gokhale and Madgulkar. These were the writers who started writing at the level of human consciousness. But their writing reflected the joys and sorrows of only the upper strata of society. They had not tried to reach the backward sections of society – the Dalits. Later, their work began to gradually reflect these issues. But it was in the form of sympathy – that these unfortunate people are backward, depressed, we should look at their situation as well. But when Dr Ambedkar led the Dalits, he clearly said that the Dalits do not need any sympathy or pity. We don't want you to feel sorry for us. The Dalits are going to claim their rights as individuals born on the Indian soil. This language of justice and rights had not yet come to literature, to short story writing, or to poetry.

When Ambedkar led the movement for the upliftment of Dalits, he started publishing periodicals like *Mukhanayak, Janata* and *Prabuddha Bharat*. These magazines then began to reflect the language of the Dalits. The writers who began to write for these magazines, then began to write about Dalit rights – we have these rights, we need to secure them, et cetera. Writing this way gradually became a trend. When the entire community surged forward, there was uneasiness, and they became aware of their self-respect. Why do you think the upper castes have rights? We are also human beings. We should also have rights. This began to mirror in their writing. The Dalit literature talked about Dalitatva, its backwardness, its pain and misery.

On Gender Discrimination among Dalits and its Representation in her writings

Urmila: How are my stories different. Whether I am different or not I don't know, but I have thought about Dalit men who do injustice to their women. So Dalit writers sometimes ask me why I don't write like the way they do. "You should not write like this. You are giving them [the upper caste] a weapon to use against us," is the complaint made by several critics. I said, "Why call it a weapon? When you use it against us, is that justified? You can no longer use it against us women." Sometimes they organize a programme and call me to deliver a speech. When they ask me my story, I in turn ask them: "Where is your wife? Bring her along, then I will also come." Even my husband asks: "Why have you come to call my wife, where is your wife? You have to bring along your wife." These people want their wives to stay at home, cook their food, look after the children and manage everything while they wander around town, work, come home and eat, relax, and invite women to come on the stage and talk.

In the book I recently wrote—*Amhihi Ithihas Ghadawala* (We Also Made History), I have mentioned that Babasaheb Ambedkar started the Dalit movement and just as men participated in the movement, so did women.

I got together with my friend Meenakshi Moon. When we started our research, people ridiculed us. They said, "There were no women in the Ambedkar movement. What are you looking for?" I replied, "How can that be? There is Shantabai Dani, then Dadasaheb Gaikwad's wife, Geetabai Gaikwad." They responded by pointing out that there were no more than four or five women. We then thought of going to Nagpur. Babasaheb Ambedkar was actually born in Konkan. The Dalits there had no education, no money – they were very poor. And a movement needs money to progress. He, therefore, made Nagpur his working place, and he furthered the movement there.

We went about searching ... Some women did talk to us and were very articulate. One of them said, "My husband used to beat me up. When the workers from the movement would come to call me, he would tell me that my husbands had come. Go and have fun with them, he would say."

Whenever Ambedkar conducted one of his programmes, the women would cook and he would say, "Don't waste too much of your time in cooking food." If they made sweets for him, he would say, "I will eat with everyone. I don't want any different food." He would ask the workers to bring their wives along but they would not listen to him.

Daya Pawar's *Baluta* introduced autobiographical writing in Dalit literature. After that came Lakshman Mane's *Upra* (The Outsider), then Lakshman Gaikwad's *Uchlya* (The Wastrel), and many other people started writing in this mode. There was a Sahitya Sammelan in Mumbai organized by Mumbai Marathi Granth Sangrahalaya. Sarojini Vaidya was the Chairperson. And I have read in today's papers that she attacked Dalit writers and Dalit literature. According to her, they are writing only about caste, and are limiting literature to caste categories. Literature cannot progress in this manner, literature will also begin to have a caste, and this is not good, she feels. I do not agree with this at all. I believe that Indian society is scattered into many castes. For example, I can tell you that the Mahar caste has fifty sub-castes. So one caste has fifty sub-castes and similarly – thousands.

Every caste has its own culture, eating and living habits. And every culture has its own experiences; and these experiences are again related to society – so let it happen, let a literature have castes, you cannot restrict in this way. It can be criticized later but to say that it should not arrive even before it has, is not correct.

Language is an important part of social life. It is not that only codified language is the privileged language. Society is divided into languages and castes, and every section has different experiences and these should be welcomed.

SELECT ANNOTATED BIBLIOGRAPHY

1   Early modern accounts of the caste system in India from outside of the domain of Hindu theological writings and British governmental readings, though probably influenced by either or by both, included those by Herbert Risley, *The People of India* (Calcutta: Thacker, Spink and Co, 1908). Arthur de Gobineau, *The Inequality of the Human Races,* trans. by Adrian Collins (New York: H Fortig, 1915), L S O' Malley, *Indian Caste Customs* (Cambridge: Cambridge UP, 1932), J H Hutton, *Caste in India: Its Nature, Function and Origin* (Cambridge: Cambridge UP, 1946). Two important sociological studies of the Indian caste system were by Max Weber, *The Religion of India: The Sociology of Hinduism and Buddhism* (Glenoe, Illinois: Free Press, 1958) and by Bernard Cohn, *India: The Social Anthropology of a Civilization* (Englewood Cliffs, N J: Prentice Hall, 1971).

The trend of looking at the caste system from inside its own parameters continued in the classic work by Louis Dumont, *Homo Hierarchus: The Caste System and its Implications,* trans. by Mark Sainisbury (Chicago: U of Chicago P, 1970).

Dumont's work however initiated a most important debate on the character of the caste system with critiques such as those by Joan Mencher, "The Caste System Upside-Down or the Not-So Mysterious East", *Current Anthropology* 15 (1974) and by Gerald Berreman, *Caste and Other Inequities* (Meerut: Folklore Institute, 1979) contesting that there was consensual acceptance of the caste system among the various castes in Indian society.

A discordant note was struck, of course, by Michael Moffat, *An Untouchable Community in South India: Structure and Consensus* (Princeton N J: Princeton UP, 1979), who argued that the lower castes were invariably and inevitably hegemonized by upper caste conventions and consciousness concerning the caste system.

The appropriation-versus-alienation issue has been recast by recent scholarship such as, for instance, by Sekhar Bandyopadhyay, *Caste, Identity and Protest in Colonial India: The Namasudras of Bengal 1872-1947* (Richmond: Curzon Press, 1997) and by Sumit Sarkar, "Identities and Histories: Some Lower Caste Narratives from Early Twentieth Century Bengal" in *Beyond Nationalist Frames: Relocating Postmodernism, Hindutva, History* (New Delhi: Permanent Black, 2002) which has stressed the need to situate historically the ideological inclination of different caste communities at different moments of place and time. These scholars, therefore, repudiate the existence of any "essential" caste entities.

An effort to engage with caste without lapsing into essentialisms by keeping both its ideational as well as its material axis in view, has been undertaken in Marxist analyses of the operations of the caste system such as those by Claude Meillasox, "Are There Castes in India ?" *Economy and Society* Vol II No 1, February 1973 and by Maurice Godelier, "Infrastructures, Societies and History," *Current Anthropology* Vol xix No 4, February 1978, and much later by Gail Omvedt, "Towards a Historical Materialist Analysis of the Origins and Development of Caste" in her book *Dalits and the Democratic Revolution: Dr Ambedkar and the Dalit Movement in Contemporary India."* (New Delhi: Sage, 1994).

2   The intimate relationship between caste and class in India which has been the focus of Marxist analysts, has been analyzed also in investigations of G S Ghurye, *Caste and Class in India* (Bombay: Popular Book Depot, 1957), Andre Betille, *Caste, Class and Power* (Berkeley: U of California P, 1965) Anil Bhatt, *Caste, Class and Politics: An Empirical Profile of Social Stratification in India* (New Delhi: Manohar, 1975), Martin Klass, *Caste: The Emergence of a South Asian Social System* (Philadelphia: Institute for the Study of Human Affairs, 1980) and K L Sharma ed, *Caste and Class in India* (Pune: Training for Development Scholarship Society, 1994).

3   The caste-race analogy, though frequently drawn, does not really apply within the Indian ambience, though cross-cultural comparisons have yielded fruitful results. Notable among such comparitive enterprises are those by Anthony de Reuck and Julie Knight, eds. *Caste and Race: Comparative Approaches.* (London: J A Churchill Ltd, 1968) and Sidney B Verba, B Ahmad and Anil Bhatt, *Caste, Race and Politics* (Berkeley: Sage Publications, 1971).

4   The intricate relationship between caste and gender in India has been investigated in Vasant Kannabhiran and Kalpana Kannabhiran, "Caste and Gender: Understanding Dynamics of Power and Violence," *Economic and Political Weekly* Vol 27, No 37, (September 14, 1991), Uma Chakravarti, "Conceptualising Brahmanical Patriarchy in Early India: Gender, Caste, Class and the State", *Economic and Political Weekly* Vol 29 No 14, (April 3, 1993)and Kiran Kapadia, *Siva and her Sisters: Gender, Caste and Class in Rural South India* (Boulder, Colorado: Worldview Press, 1995).

5   Caste consciousness among Hindus has proved to be an impediment in the contemporary project to construct and consolidate a Hindu communal identity. Hindu communal organizations have tried and are trying their best to negotiate and to negate caste consciousness within their constituency. Caste identities have located themselves differently at different times and at different places vis-a-vis contemporary Hindutva. The complicated, if not convoluted, inter-relationship between caste

and communalism has been researched upon by Sukumar Muralidharan, "Mandal, Mandir and Masjid: 'Hindu' Communalism and the Crisis of the State, *"Social Scientist"* Vol 18, No 19, Rajni Kothari, "Caste, Communalism and the Democratic Process," and Ghanshyam Shah, "The BJP and the Backward Classes in Gujarat", in Praful Bidwai, Harbans Mukhia and Achin Vanaik, eds., *Religion, Religiosity and Communalism* (New Delhi: Manohar, 1996) and Achin Vanaik, *Communalism Contested: Religion, Modernity and Secularisation* (New Delhi: Sage, 1997).

6   Among the vast corpus of literature that has been published on anti-caste and Dalit movements in India, some are compulsory reading. Early modern anti-caste, non-Brahmin movements are focussed upon in Eugene F Irschic, *Politics and Social Conflict in South India: The Non-Brahman Movement and Tamil Separatism 1916-29*(Berkeley: U of California P, 1969) Rosalind O'Hanlon, *Caste, Conflict and Ideology: Mahatma Jotirao Phule and Low Caste Protest in Nineteenth Century India* (Cambridge: Cambridge UP, 1985) and G P Deshpande ed., *Selected Writings of Jotirao Phule* (New Delhi: LeftWord Books, 2002).

Apart from these books on early modern movements against Brahminism and casteism, there are general historics/readings of such movements in the twentieth century. These include the books Jagjivan Ram *Caste Challenge in India* (New Delhi: Vision Books, 1980), D R Nagraj, *The Flaming Feet: A Study of the Dalit Movement in India* (Bangalore: South Forum Press,1993), Oliver Mendelsohn and Upendra Baxi, eds., *The Rights of Subordinated People* (New Delhi: Oxford UP, 1994), Gail Omvedt, *Dalits and the Democratic Revolution: Dr. Ambedkar and the Dalit Movement in Colonial India* (New Delhi: Sage, 1994), Gail Omvedt, *Dalit Visions* (Hyderabad: Orient Longman, 1995), Oliver Mendelsohn and Maria Vicziany, *The Untouchables: Subordination, Poverty and the State in Modern India* (Cambridge: Cambridge UP, 1998), Susan Bayly, *Caste, Society and Politics in India: From the Eighteenth Century to the Modern Age* (Cambridge: Cambridge UP, 1999), Special Issue on "Dalits", *Seminar* 47 (1999) and Ghanshyam Shah, *Dalit Identity and Politics* (New Delhi: Sage, 2001).

A study of the links between the modern Dalit movement in India and other movements of other subaltern sections of Indian society in the contemporary era has been undertaken by Gail Omvedt, *Re-inventing Revolution: India's New Social Movements* (New York: M E Sharpe, 1993).

A few period specific and region specific studies of Dalit movements provide interesting insights into modes of Dalit resistance, for instance, those by C A Bayly, *Rulers, Townsmen and Bazaars: North Indian Society in the Age of British Expansion 1770-1870* (Cambridge: Cambridge UP, 1983), Francine R Frankel, "Caste, Land and Dominance in Bihar: Breakdown of the Brahmanical Social Order" in Francine R Frankel and M S A Rao, eds., *Dominance and State Power in Modern India: Decline of a Social Order,* Vol I (New Delhi: Oxford UP, 1989), Sudha Pai, "Emergence of New Social Forces in UP", *Mainstream* 32(5) (18 December, 1993), K Srinivasulu, "Centrality of Caste: Understanding UP Elections", *Economic and Political Weekly* 29 (12) (March 1994) and Gail Omvedt, "Kanshi Ram and the Bahujan Samaj Party", Sharad Patil, "Caste and Class in Maharashtra", Rajendra Vora and Suhas Palshikar, "Caste, Class and Ideology in Maharashtra" and Gopal Guru, "Caste, Class and Politics in the Tanneries of Kolhapur" in K L Sharma, ed., *Caste and Class in India* (Jaipur and New Delhi: Rawat Publications, 1994).

Specific works on B R Ambedkar and the Ambedkar phase of the Dalit movement which must be looked at are by Dhananjay Keer, *Dr. Ambedkar: Life and Mission* (Bombay: Popular Prakashan, 1971), W N Kuber, *Dr. Ambedkar: A Critical Study* (New Delhi: People's Publishing House, 1973), W N Kuber, *Ambedkar* (New Delhi: Ministry of Information and Broadcasting, 1978), D C Ahir, *The Legacy of Dr. Ambedkar* (Delhi: B R Publishers, 1990), K N Kadam ed, *B.R. Ambedkar and the Significance of his Movement. A Chronology* (Bombay: Popular Prakashan, 1991), Thomas Mathew, *Ambedkar: Reform or Revolution?* (New Delhi: Segment Books, 1991), M S Gore, *The Social Context of an Ideology, Ambedkar's Social and Political Thought* (New Delhi: Sage, 1993) and Arun Shourie, *Worshipping False Gods:*

Ambedkar and the Facts Which Have Been Erased (New Delhi: ASA Publishing, 1997).

7   Must read works on literature emanating out of the experience of casteism in Indian society include at least three well known anthologies of Dalit expression brought together respectively by Barbara Joshi ed., *Untouchable Voices of the Dalit Liberation Movement* (London: Zed Books, 1986), Mulk Raj Anand and Eleanor Zelliot, eds., *An Anthology of Dalit Literature* (New Delhi: Gyan Publishers, 1992) and Arjun Dargle, *Poisoned Bread: Translations from Modern Marathi Dalit Literature* (Hyderabad: Orient Longman, 1992), each of them with useful introductions. *Indian Literature,* the journal of the Sahitya Akademi has, from time to time, brought out special issues focussing upon Dalit wiritings of different periods and regions. Many of these are cited in the endnotes to the essay on "Narratives of Suffering: Dalit Perspectives" in this volume.

BIOGRAPHICAL NOTES

G Arunima teaches at the Department of History, Lady Shri Ram College for Women, New Delhi, but is currently on leave to fulfill an UGC research fellowship at the Institute for Contemporary Studies, Nehru Memorial Museum and Library, New Delhi. G Arunima's earlier work has been on family, law and kinship in Kerala and she has published several articles based on this work. Her current work is on a cultural history of Kerala, looking at issues of aesthetics and modernity.

Arupa Patangia Kalita teaches English Literature at Tangla College, Assam. She writes features in Asomiya journals as well as short stories and novels, and has, in a very short span of time, made her mark in the literary world. Her works are primarily known for their strong feminist statements and the bold, sensitive portrayal of women. She has won a number of prestigious awards like the Sarlesh Chandra Dasgupta Sahitya Setu Award and the Bharatiya Bhasha Parishad Award for her novel, *Ayananta*. She also edits (with her husband) a little magazine called *Damal* (the bridge).

Brinda Bose teaches at the Department of English, Hindu College, Delhi and researches in post colonial, gender and cultural studies. She has co-edited *Interventions: Feminist Dialogues in Third World Women's Literature and Film* (Garland, 1997) and is the editor of *Translating Desire* (Katha, 2002) and *Amitav Ghosh: Critical Essays* (Pencraft, 2002).

Geeta Sahai was born in Allahabad. She has written a number of English and Hindi short stories for the magazines *Sarika, Vama and Rashtrasahara* She has written a book of poems, adapted the Bhagvad Gita for children and also translated Mridula Garg's Hindi novel into English.

Gita Krishnankutty has been actively involved in translating short stories, novels and anthologies from Malayalam into English. She has a doctorate in English Literature from the University of Mysore.

Hephzibah Israel teaches at the Department of English, Lady Shri Ram College for Women, New Delhi. She is currently on study leave, completing her doctoral dissertation on Tamil translations of the Bible from the School of Oriental and African Studies in the University of London. She is the recipient of the Katha Translation Award for the year 1995-1996 and 2000.

Irathina Karikalan was born in a village called Marungur in Tamil Nadu. With some companions he pioneered a literary movement, Kaalam, which publishes a literary, art and cultural magazine *Kaalamputhithu* and is a member of the magazine's editorial board. He has published two collections of poetry, *Puhaippada Manithargal* and *Appothirundha Edaivelliyil*. His essays, short stories and a short novel have been published in literary magazines. He writes mainly about marginalized classes in the language spoken by them.

Keerti Ramachandra is a fiction editor, multilingual translator and teacher. With a Masters in literature and an MPhil in linguistics she has been teaching in schools and colleges in India and abroad. She is currently teaching a course in Creative Non-Fiction and Structures in English at Xavier Institute of Communication. She can translate from Kannada, Marathi and Hindi and has been actively associated with Katha as a fiction editor.

Krishna Barua was brought up in Tezpur and Shillong. She obtained her MPhil degree from the University of Delhi and is working on her doctoral degree at present. Literature, women's issues and the problems of the less advantaged are topics which interest her deeply.

Mahasweta Devi, an activist-writer who has carved a niche for herself, was awarded the Sahitya Akademi Award in 1979 and the Jnanpith in 1997. She has explored in great detail the overlapping of written and spoken Bangla, and in her stories one often finds colloquial Bangla sliding into the more formal written Bangla, with a sprinkling of English words. Mahasweta Devi also edits the journal *Bartika* which features contributions from the tribal communities she works with. Her "Bayen" has been adapted for the stage.

Mahua Bhattacharya is a lecturer at Calcutta University and a translator.

Mogalli Ganesh holds an MA in Economics from the University of Mysore, from where he also obtained an MA in Folklore. He is at present a research scholar in the same university, working on his doctorate in Folklore. His first collection of short stories, *Buguri* (1992), has been warmly received by critics. "Battha" was published in this collection.

Narain Singh was born in Dhanbad and graduated from St. John's College, Agra. He published his first story in 1968 in *Saraswati* Allahabad. Since then he has published one novel *Alpsankhyak* and two collections of short stories, *Teesra Aadmi* and *Woh Mara Nahin Hai*. He has been awarded the Krishna Pratap Memorial Award twice. His short stories have been translated and published in Urdu as well.

Raghavendra Rao K has completed his doctorate in Political Economy from Toronto University. He has taught Political Science at Guwahati, Karnataka and Mangalore Universities. He has worked extensively on translation of both poetry and fiction from Kannada into English, including the novels *Parva* and *Vamsavriksha* by Bhyrappa. In addition to his publications on political theory, he has published *The Road Taken,* a collection of his poems in English. He

251

has edited, with P Lal, *Modern Indo-Anglian Poetry;* and with Kanavi, *Modern Kannada Poetry.*

Ramanunni K P, has six books to his credit. His works have been translated and published in many other Indian languages. He has received a number of awards, the most recent being the Katha Award for creative fiction and the Padmarajan Award for his story *Jaadi Chodikkuka.* He is a member of the Kerala Sahitya Akademi. He is also the convenor of the editorial board of a magazine called *Sahityalokam.*

Rupalee Verma teaches History in Delhi University. Her specialization in the field of language, literature and History of Southeast Asia is from Laiden University, Netherlands. She has published works on colonial education in Indonesia and Malaysia. Her interest lies in using history and literature of the colonized societies as a means to understanding colonial mentalities. She translates from Dutch and has a keen interest in children's literature written in various languages.

H S Shivaprakash recently appointed as Associate Professor in the School of Arts and Aesthetics in the Jawaharlal Nehru University, New Delhi, is also an Honorary Fellow of Writing at the School of Letters in the University of Iowa. He is a Kannada playwright with innumerable plays on issues of social concern. Some of these include *Mahachaitra, Shakespeare's Swapnanowke, Tipu Sultan, Madhavi* and *The Bride* (2000), the last two, among others, having been translated into English. He is also a critic of Kannada literature, and has served as editor of *Indian Literature,* the journal of the Sahitya Akademi.

Sisir Kumar Das, formerly Tagore Professor of Bengali at the Department of Modern Indian Languages, University of Delhi, is the recepient of the Tagore Memorial Prize (twice), as well as the Nehru Prize of the Federal Republic of Germany for his monograph *Western Sailors, Eastern Seas.* He has also authored two volumes in a projected multivolume *History of Indian Literature* (Sahitya Akademi, 1991 and 1995). He is a lover of Greek theatre and has translated Aristotle's *Poetics* and Euripides' *The Trojan Woman* and other Greek plays into English. He is a playwright himself, and has authored several plays in Bengali including *Bagh* and *Sinduk.*

B I O G R A P H I C A L   N O T E S :

Tapan Basu teaches at the Department of English, Hindu College, Delhi. He has specialized in the study of the literature of the United States and has done focussed work on African-American writers. He is also interested in the exploration of identity politics, identity formations and identity fragmentations in contemporary Indian culture and society. He is the co-author of *Khaki Shorts, Saffron Flags: A critique of the Hindu Right* (New Delhi: Orient Longman, 1993).

Uma Chakravarti formerly a teacher at the Department of History, Miranda House College for Women, Delhi, is engaged in working with the democratic rights movement and the women's rights movement in different parts of India on a variety of issues. She writes history from a people's, specifically a feminist, point of view. Her publications include *Social Dimensions of Early Buddhism* and *The Life and Times of Pandita Ramabai.*

Urmila Pawar is a Marathi writer whose short stories are based on the Dalit experiences of life and labour in a casteist society. A Dalit herself, she records the anguish of being a woman and a Dalit in her short stories, the most powerful among which are included in two collections, *Sanav Bote* and *Chauthi Bhinta,* both of which have won many awards.

Vanajam Ravindran retired as Reader from the Faculty of English of Lady Shri Ram College for Women, University of Delhi. An occasional writer of articles and reviews, she has contributed to journals like *In-between* and the *Indian Review of Books.* Her translations from Malayalam have been published in *Indian Literature, Katha Prize Stories 5, The Wordsmiths* and *Basheer fictions.* For the last book, she has also interviewed M T Vasudevan Nair. Dr Ravindran won the Katha Award for Translation in 1995. She lives in Kozhikode.

Vasudevan Nair M T is acknowledged as one of the outstanding living writers of India. His publications include short stories, novels, a play, and other books which consist of critical writings, stories for children and travelogues. He has received all the prestigious awards for fiction in Malayalam, among them, the Katha Award for creative Fiction and the Kerala Sahitya Academy Award for his novel, *Nalukeltu,* for his play *Gopuranadayil,* and again in 1981 for his short story collection, *Swargam*

Thurakkunna Samayam. He won the Central Sahitya Akademi Award for *Kaalam,* and the President's Gold Medal for the film *Nirmalyam,* written, produced and directed by him. He joined the Malayalam journal, *Mathrubhoomi*, and is presently its editor. He lives in Calicut.

USER'S GUIDE TO NOTES
BIBLIOGRAPHIC REFERENCES AND ABBREVIATIONS

Here are a few points about the style that has been followed in documenting sources in notes and bibliographies.

Documenting volume and issue number in journals.
Volume number precedes issue number. For example, Volume 8, issue 7 is documented as, 8.7.

Note on the use of abbreviations.
University presses are documented as UP. Thus Oxford University Press is Oxford UP. University of California Press is U of California P. n.d for "not dated."

IAS, IFS, IPS, OBC, for Indian Administrative Officer, Indian Foreign Service, Indian Police Service and Other Backward Castes, respectively.

INDEX

261

A NOTE ON SPARROW

As children we have all heard the story of a little sparrow that poked into garbage and found one grain of rice to eat. SPARROW is small like that bird and is also looking for grains of a different kind – grains of facts and information about women's lives, history and language hidden in the crevices of history.

SPARROW is a Trust with persons committed and devoted to the use of oral history and pictorial material for research on women in order to expand the scope of research by including unexplored areas of experience and expression. SPARROW is not just a documentation or consultation centre, but believes in being an active agent in bringing women together for discussion and work and being an agent of conscientisation. A group of educationists, writers and artists appreciate and support the work of SPARROW in many ways.

In the coming years SPARROW will be involved in setting up the first Women's Archives. Apart from collecting, conserving and preserving archival material, SPARROW will take up other activities like oral history recordings, audio-visual projects, workshops with students and teachers, publications and microfilming to generate its own material. Organizing film festivals and photographic exhibitions will also form the extended activities of SPARROW in the future.

About Katha

Katha, a registered nonprofit organization set up in September 1989, works in the areas of education, publishing and community development and endeavours to spread the joy of reading, knowing and living amongst adults and children. Our main objective is **to enhance the pleasures of reading for children and adults,** for experienced readers as well as for those who are just beginning to read. Our attempt is also to stimulate an interest in lifelong learning that will help the child grow into a confident, self-reliant, responsible and responsive adult, as also to help break down gender, cultural and social stereotypes, encourage and foster excellence, applaud quality literature and translations in and between the various Indian languages and work towards community revitalization and economic resurgence. The two wings of Katha are **Katha Vilasam** and **Kalpavriksham.**

KATHA VILASAM, the Story Research and Resource Centre, was set up to foster and applaud quality Indian literature and take these to a wider audience through quality translations and related activities like **Katha Books, Academic Publishing**, the **Katha Awards** for fiction, translation and editing, **Kathakaar** – the Centre for Children's Literature, **Katha Barani** – the Translation Resource Centre, the **Katha Translation Exchange Programme, Translation Contests. Kanchi** – the Katha National Institute of Translation promotes translation through **Katha Academic Centres** in various Indian universities, **Faculty Enhancement Programmes** through Workshops, seminars and discussions, **Sishya** – Katha Clubs in colleges, **Storytellers Unlimited** – the art and craft of storytelling and **KathaRasa** – performances, art fusion and other events at the Katha Centre.

KALPAVRIKSHAM, the Centre for Sustainable Learning, was set up to foster quality education that is relevant and fun for children from nonliterate families, and to promote community revitalization and economic resurgence work. These goals crystallized in the development of the following areas of activities. **Katha Khazana** which includes **Katha Student Support Centre, Katha Public School, Katha School of Entrepreneurship, KITES** – the Katha Information Technology and eCommerce School, **Iccha Ghar** – **The Intel Computer Clubhouse @ Katha, Hamara Gaon** and **The Mandals** – Maa, Bapu, Balika, Balak and Danadini, **Tamasha Roadshow** – a mobile school for street children, **Shakti Khazana** was set up for skills upgradation and income generation activities comprising the Khazana Coop. **Kalpana Vilasam** is the cell for regular research and development of teaching/ learning materials, curricula, syllabi, content comprising **Teacher Training, TaQeEd** – **The Teachers Alliance for Quality eEducation. Tamasha's World!** comprises **Tamasha! the Children's magazine,** *Dhammakdhum! www.tamasha.org* **and ANU** – **Animals, Nature and YOU!**

BE A FRIEND OF KATHA!

If you feel strongly about Indian literature, you belong with us! KathaNet, an invaluable network of our friends, is the mainstay of all our translation related activities. We are happy to invite you to join this ever widening circle of translation activists. Katha, with limited financial resources, is propped up by the unqualified enthusiasm and the indispensable support of nearly 5000 dedicated women and men.

We are constantly on the lookout for people who can spare the time to find stories for us, and to translate them. Katha has been able to access mainly the literature of the major Indian languages. Our efforts to locate resource people who could make the lesser known literatures available to us have not yielded satisfactory results. We are specially eager to find Friends who could introduce us to Bhojpuri, Dogri, Kashmiri, Maithili, Manipuri, Nepali, Rajasthani and Sindhi fiction. And to oral and tribal literature.

Do write to us with details about yourself, your language skills, the ways in which you can help us, and any material that you already have and feel might be publishable under a Katha programme. All this would be a labour of love, of course! But we do offer a discount of 20% on all our publications to Friends of Katha.

Write to us at —
Katha
A-3 Sarvodaya Enclave
Sri Aurobindo Marg   Call us at: 652 4350, 652 4511
New Delhi   110 017   or E-mail us at: info@katha.org

TRANSLATING PARTITION

This Volume of Stories and essays present the literary and historiographic representations of the Partition of the Indian subcontinent in 1947. The essays analyze critically the events that led up to the Partition, the representation of the Partition in Indian newspapers prior to 1947, and treatment of violence and trauma in Partition literature. The stories and essays explore the Partition and its consequence from the perspective of people's history. The stories of displacement, loss, violence, trauma, uprooting, and rebuilding of individuals and communities ... The question, "Why must we write this history today?" is posed as an important one.

"A commendable volume that attempts to provide a new dimension to the travails of Partition".
– Inder Malhotra *Hindustan Times*, Sunday June 24, 2001

Stories by
Manto, Bhisham Sahni, Surendra Prakash
Attia Hossain, Joginder Paul, Kamleshwar
Essays, Criticism
EDITED BY
TARUN K SAINT & RAVIKANT

KATHA'S ACADEMIC SERIES

Essays
Excellently researched ...
innovatively produced

TRANSLATING DESIRE

The Politics
of Gender
and Culture
in India

Translating Desire brings together explosive new academic writing on the politics of sexuality and the production of the cultural text in contemporary India. The volume, comprising eleven essays and one short story, explores the various nuances of desire – its formulation in theory, its depiction in literature and its reflection in the various genres of popular culture. The essayists deal with often controversial, and certainly oft debated subjects like *Fire*, *Bandit Queen*, the Indian Novel in English and popular women's magazines. *Translating Desire* is a comprehensive collection suited to the study of both the dedicated academician and the lay reader interested in cultural praxis.

Essays by

Anjana Sharma Brenda Longfellow Brinda Bose
Dolores Chew Karen Gabriel Nilanjana Gupta
Nivedita Menon PK Vijayan Ratna Kapur Ruth Vanita
Srimati Basu Udaya Kumar

Ed
BRINDA BOSE